HOSPITALITY EMPLOYEE MANAGEMENT AND SUPERVISION

HOSPITALITY EMPLOYEE MANAGEMENT AND SUPERVISION

CONCEPTS AND PRACTICAL APPLICATIONS

Kerry L. Sommerville

John Wiley & Sons, Inc.

Library of Congress Cataloging-in-Publication Data:

Sommerville, Kerry L., 1957–
 Hospitality employee management and supervision: concepts and practical applications / by Kerry L.
Sommerville.
   p. cm.
 Includes index.
 ISBN-13: 978-0-471-74522-8 (pbk.)
 1. Hospitality industry—Personnel management. I. Title.
 TX911.3.P4S66 2007
 647.94068'3—dc22

                                                                                                    2006013299

Printed in the United States of America

10 9 8 7 6 5 4 3 2 1

CONTENTS

CHAPTER **4**

**COMMON LAW, NEGLIGENT HIRING,
AND EMPLOYEE RIGHTS** **65**

CHAPTER **5**

WORKING WITH UNIONS **81**

**UNIT 2   THE EMPLOYEE
SELECTION PROCESS   97**

CHAPTER **6**

**JOB DESCRIPTIONS AND JOB
SPECIFICATIONS** **99**

PREFACE

HOSPITALITY BUSINESSES, BOTH LARGE AND SMALL, struggle valiantly today to recruit, hire, train, and retain quality and motivated employees. Those operations that do these things well often achieve enormous success, while those that do not or will not invest appropriate levels of time, money, and attention to their human resources efforts frequently fail.

In approximately 15 years of teaching at the university level, more than 7000 students have passed through my classroom. A vast majority of these students have shared their *Tales from the Field*. Some of their *tales* were inspiring, but many made me cringe. It is because of my students' *tales* that I became convinced that the time had come to write a hands-on, practical human resources guide for managers and supervisors in the hospitality industry.

While this book covers the fundamental concepts and principles of management and supervision that have stood the test of time, my goal in writing *Hospitality Employee Management and Supervision: Concepts and Practical Applications* is to present a more contemporary, hands-on approach to this material that both two- and four-year college students will find engaging and valuable as they begin their preparation for successful management careers in the hospitality industry.

This book provides comprehensive coverage of the key concepts in a concise and reader friendly manner. It is organized into the following four parts with themes relevant to today's hospitality industry:

Unit 1: The Legal Landscape. Provides a thorough description of how today's legal landscape impacts all employee-related decisions, ranging from hiring to training, compensation, promotion, and termination.

Unit 2: The Employee Selection Process. Provides a discussion of all the resources available to help managers recruit the right applicants for the right jobs and all that must be considered when hiring a competent workforce.

Unit 3: Orientation and Training. Provides important information about effective new-employee orientation and training and discusses standards of performance as well as aspects of ongoing professional development and their impact on employee morale.

Unit 4: Communication and Motivation. Provides techniques for effective communication in the workplace. Also discusses newer, more modern approaches to evaluating employee performance, as well as various theories of motivation and styles of leadership and their effectiveness.

I have also included the following features within each chapter to enhance the students' learning experience:

- **Quotations** from various practitioners in the hospitality industry that help to highlight the focus of each chapter.
- **Chapter Objectives** correspond to the organization of the chapter and highlight the key concepts and ideas to help students succeed in learning the material.
- **HRM in Action Sections** highlight real-world HRM experiences that relate to the content presented in each chapter. These vignettes help to set the stage and provide a focus for the chapter.
- *Tales from the Field* provide accounts from hospitality employees describing the various challenges they face in the industry. These anecdotes provide real-world examples of the concepts presented in each chapter of the text and help students to see how what they've learned in the classroom is applied in real-world situations.
- *Ethical Dilemmas* provide scenarios relating to the hospitality industry where ethics comes into play and relates the ethical aspects to the *10 Ethical Principles for Hospitality Managers* adapted from Josephson Institute of Ethics Core Ethical Principles. They have served as the basis of ethics research coming out of Isbell Hospitality Ethics for the past 15 years. A chapter-by-chapter analysis of short ethical dilemmas emphasizes the importance of adhering to the Ethical Principles for Hospitality Managers during the on-the-job decision-making process. Adherence to these principles will result in the best consequences for all parties involved.[1]
- **End of Chapter Summary** is a bulleted list of the key concepts related to each of the learning objectives presented at the beginning of each chapter.
- **Practice Quiz and Chapter Review Questions** help to reinforce student comprehension of the key concepts covered in each chapter.

---

[1] Christine Jaszay and Paul Dunk, *Ethical Decision Making in the Hospitality Industry* (Upper Saddle River, NJ: Pearson—Prentice Hall, 2006)

- *Hands-on HRM* are included at the end of each chapter and provide mini cases with discussion questions based on real-world situations to enhance student understanding.

- **Key Terms** are bold within the chapter and then listed at the end of each chapter with their definitions. An online glossary of key terms is also available for viewing and download.

There is also a set of resources for instructors:

Instructor's Manual with Test Questions includes lecture outlines, answer keys to review quizzes and *Hands-on HRM* mini-case studies; suggested active learning techniques to enhance student retention of key concepts, additional in-depth chapter review questions; and a test bank containing a variety of true/false, multiple-choice, and essay questions broken down by chapter, unit, and final exam.

Companion Web site includes electronic files for the Instructor's Manual with Test Questions and PowerPoint slides containing lecture outlines for every chapter.

Nearly three-fourths of this book is dedicated to helping students learn and practice the skills that they will need in order to locate, hire, and train quality-hospitality industry employees. When managers and supervisors devote the necessary attention to these matters initially, when developing their workforce on the front end and the "churn and burn" of high-employee turnover—which plagues the hospitality industry—decreases, managers can then focus their energy on what they were hired to do in the first place: Manage!

Some graduates will be blessed with hospitality industry jobs in organizations that staff a professional human resources department, but many graduates who take positions in smaller operations will be the human resources department, and it is these budding supervisors, managers, and future entrepreneurs who I had most in my mind as I wrote this book.

I believe that there has never been a more rewarding or challenging time to be a hospitality industry manager. The reward comes from knowing that effective, efficient managers can and are making a real difference in our industry. The challenges arise from issues associated with staffing hospitality operations, which present a constantly shifting kaleidoscope of competitive pressures and opportunities.

No matter how your specific major fits into the world of hospitality, the content of this course has all the ingredients to be the best course you'll take during your academic career because what you learn in class today, you can apply to your future career in hospitality. So dig in, get involved, and as you tackle the subject matter, remember that your teachers and I wish you great success in this industry that we love so dearly.

ACKNOWLEDGMENTS

One of the most pleasant parts of writing a book is thanking those who have contributed to its evolution.

My first debt of gratitude must go to the great folks at Wiley for believing in this project and seeing it off the ground: Melissa Oliver, acquisitions editor, who breathed life into the project and helped me fine-tune my idea in its early stages, and Cindy Rhoads, developmental editor, whose unflagging patience, constant good humor, and astounding capacity for creative work has made this book possible.

I am also grateful to the dedicated reviewers whose feedback and commentary helped me immensely: Ingrid O'Connell, Schenectady County Community College; Robert M. Kok, Johnson & Wales University; Ray R. Colvin, Western Culinary Institute; and Dan Crafts, Missouri State University. In many ways, this book is as much yours as it is mine, and I hope to meet you all someday so that I may thank you in person.

To my employer, Sullivan University, and, especially, its founder and chancellor, A. R. Sullivan, thank you for believing in me and for providing the wonderful facilities and resources that have allowed me to grow.

I especially wish to thank my immediate coworkers whose continual support, love, and constant encouragement helped to make this project a reality: Albert Schmid, who made me believe in myself and who illuminated my path like only *someone who has been there and done that could;* Dawn McGiffen and Anne Sandhu, both tough critics and beloved confidants; and Eddie Maamry, mein lieber Herr, whose *joie de vivre* inspires us all to be our best everyday. I also want to thank those colleagues who have been so supportive throughout my career: Chef Walter "Spud" Rhea, Chef Tom Hickey, Chef Derek Spendlove, and Chef Kimberly Jones.

To my many students both past and present, and, especially, to those who shared their "Tales from the Field," thank you for your trust and respect; your true identities will remain forever locked away.

And, finally, to Bert, my dear and loving family, and my closest friends—both old and new—thank you for understanding the many long months of neglect and for standing by me. You guys rock!

Kerry Sommerville
Louisville, Kentucky

U N I T

1

THE LEGAL
LANDSCAPE

CHAPTER 1

INTRODUCTION TO HIRING AND SUPERVISING EMPLOYEES

In my experience, one of the most successful elements to running a successful restaurant is your management skills: How well you hire, train, and motivate your staff.[1]

Bob Kinkead, chef/owner, Kinkead's, Washington, D.C.

CHAPTER OBJECTIVES

After completing this chapter, you will be able to

- Identify key factors that have contributed to the labor shortage and its effect on the hospitality industry workforce.

- Define the term *labor market*.

- Define the term *demographics* and explain how changes in demographics affect the workforce.

- Provide examples of how industry-related organizations such as the National Restaurant Association and the American Hotel & Lodging Association can be of assistance to lodging and food service operators.

- Define customer motivations, needs, and expectations (MNEs) and explain their impact on lodging and food service operations.

- Identify the importance of employee training, motivation, and leadership in order to meet customer MNEs.

HRM IN ACTION Today's business climate is extremely turbulent. This is particularly so in the hospitality industry, in which issues of labor **supply and demand** have many managers scratching their heads, wondering where they are going to get enough qualified staff to support their operations. One Louisville, Kentucky, barbecue restaurant recently posted a sign on its front door advising customers that because of its inability to hire adequate restaurant staff and delivery personnel, the restaurant was forced to cut its hours of operation. It is indeed a sad state of affairs when an industrywide labor shortage forces a restaurant operation to cut its hours, even though it has a product and a service for which potential customers are willing to pay money.

Seasoned hospitality veterans will be the first to tell you that locating and hiring quality employees is perhaps the most challenging aspect of managing a modern restaurant or lodging business today. This has not always been the case. Approximately 20 years ago, most operations would simply place an ad in the "help wanted" section of the local newspaper when it became necessary to hire new or replacement workers. A manager could usually expect to receive more than a dozen applications and résumés for each position advertised. After the applications were quickly scanned and sorted, the most qualified applicants would be called in for an interview, and the top applicant often received a job offer on the spot. Unfortunately, when positions are posted today, this is not the case. There is increased competition among various operations within the hospitality industry to hire the most qualified individuals to fill their positions.

OVERVIEW OF WHAT'S TO COME

This book takes a practical, hands-on approach to locating, hiring, training, and retaining quality employees for hospitality businesses both large and small. In Unit One, "The Legal Landscape," we examine important legislation that impacts the recruiting and management activities of all hospitality businesses. Unit Two, "The Employee Selection Process," begins with the creation of the job description and the employee handbook. Advertising and recruiting methods are examined in this section, as well as applications, interviews, and background checks. Orientation to the workplace and new-hire training are the next logical steps once the job applicant becomes an employee of the organization. Unit Three, "Orientation and Training," focuses on these important activities. The fourth and final unit, "Communication and Motivation," details the importance of creating a positive work climate through such activities as conducting performance appraisals, providing effective communication and feedback, applying employee discipline, and sustaining employee motivation through quality leadership.

TALES FROM THE FIELD

I work in a small hotel banquet department and we never seem to have enough help. Our manager is constantly looking for new people to bring on board, but no one sticks around for long, and they rarely know what they're doing when they *are* there. The stress is terrible because everyone else has to work tons of overtime just to take care of all of the functions, and sometimes the clients get upset because things are not handled properly. It's gotten so bad that now they're [management] offering the rest of us cash bonuses if we recommend someone who ends up getting hired and actually stays for 90 days.

Angie, 26, Memphis, Tennessee

INCREASED COMPETITION

Competition for qualified employees is intense, and as the demand for labor continues to outpace the supply of interested and qualified applicants, the future appears to be somewhat grim for those managers and operators forced to deal with the revolving door associated with constantly hiring and training new employees to replace those who have left the operation. The good news for today's hospitality students is that you are in the driver's seat with respect to finding that perfect job! The bad news is that if your new job responsibilities require you to occasionally hire employees, you are going to experience firsthand the challenges associated with adequately staffing a small restaurant or lodging operation.

Important industry trade groups such as the Educational Foundation of the National Restaurant Association (www.nraef.org) and the Educational Institute of the American Hotel & Lodging Association (www.ei-ahla.org) provide a wealth of resources for managers and operators seeking to enhance the quality of their recruitment strategies. These organizations have made it their personal mission to raise awareness of the industry and to elevate the stature of the careers available to motivated hospitality industry employees. The Educational Institute of the American Hotel & Lodging Association has compiled a list of more than 218 possible jobs in the lodging industry alone. Figure 1.1 illustrates potential career paths available to hospitality industry employees.

LODGING INDUSTRY POSITIONS, PROPERTY AND CORPORATE LEVEL COMPILED BY AH&LA INFORMATION CENTER

What can you do when you decide on a career in hospitality? Here are 218 possible jobs for you. Just pick an area that interests you and build a career ladder in your field. The opportunities are endless.

Accounting and Financial Management

Accounting Supervisor
Accounts Payable Clerk
Accounts Payable Supervisor
Accounts Receivable Clerk
Accounts Receivable Supervisor
Assistant Controller
Corporate Controller
Credit Manager
Director of Finance and Administration
Director, Purchasing Department
Hotel Controller
Night Auditor
Payroll Accountant
Payroll Assistant
Payroll Supervisor
Payroll Clerk
Purchasing Manager
Vice President/Chief Financial Officer

Rooms Division/Facilities

Assistant Houseperson
Assistant Parking Facilities Manager
Assistant Reservations Manager
Automobile Valet
Bell Captain
Bell Staff
Cashier
Chauffeur
Concierge
Customer Service Representative
Electrician
Elevator Operator
Engineering Supervisor
Executive Housekeeper
Front Office Cashier
Front Office Manager
Groundskeeper
Guest Service Manager
Hotel Assistant Housekeeping Director
Hotel Front Desk Agent
Hotel Front Office Manager
Hotel General Cashier
Hotel Reservations Operator
Hotel Switchboard Operator
Inspector
Landscapers
Laundry Attendant
Laundry Manager
Linen and Uniform Attendant
Linen Distribution Attendant
Linen Room Supervisor
Lobby Attendant
Mail Information Clerks

Night Clerk
Night Manager
Night Supervisor
Package Room Personnel
Parking Facilities Attendant
Parking Facilities Manager
Receptionist
Reservations Clerk
Reservations Manager
Room Attendant
Rooms Division Manager
Seamstress
Security Director
Security Guard
Security Technician
Security/ Loss Prevention Manager
Supply Clerks
Storeroom Person
Translator
Valet Parking Attendant
Vice President, Operations

Food and Beverage

Assistant Baker
Assistant Banquet Chef
Assistant Banquet Manager
Assistant Beverage Director
Assistant Broiler/Grill Cook
Assistant Executive Steward
Assistant Food/Beverage Director
Assistant Fry Cook
Assistant Pantry Person
Assistant Pastry Chef
Assistant Restaurant Manager
Assistant Service Cook
Assistant Soup/Vegetable Cook
Baker
Banquet Assistant Cook
Banquet Bartender
Banquet Beverage Server
Banquet Beverage Runner
Banquet Busperson
Banquet Captain
Banquet Chef
Banquet Cook
Banquet Houseperson
Banquet Runner
Banquet Server
Banquet Steward
Bartenders
Beverage Manager
Beverage Runner
Broiler Cook
Busperson

Figure 1.1   Potential career paths available to hospitality industry employees. *(Courtesy of the American Hotel & Lodging Association's Educational Institute.)*

Cashier
Catering Director
Catering Manager
Counter Person
Counter Server
Counter Supervisor
Dietary Aide
Dietitian
Dining Manager
Dining Room Manager
Director, Dietary Department
Dishwasher
Executive Chef
Executive Steward
Food and Beverage Controller
Food and Beverage Director
Fry/Sauté Cook
Head Broiler/Grill Cook
Head Cashier
Head Dishwasher
Head Fry Cook
Head Houseperson, Banquets
Head Pantry Person
Head Room Service Cook
Head Soup/Vegetable Cook
Head Steward
Hotel Food and Beverage Controller
Kitchen Attendant
Kitchen Manager
Kitchen Supervisor
Lounge/Bar Manager
Maitre d'
Night Steward
Pastry Cook
Pantry Preparation Person
Pastry Chef
Pastry Cook
Receiving Clerk
Restaurant Manager
Room Service Attendant
Room Service Busperson
Room Service Manager
Service Bartender
Serving Line Attendant
Sommelier
Soup and Sauce Cook
Sous Chef
Steward
Steward's Runner
Vice President, Food and Beverage
Waiter/Waitress

Human Resources

Manager, Equal Employment Opportunity
Personnel Assistant
Personnel/Human Resources Manager
Personnel Specialist
Quality Assurance Manager
Training Manager
Vice President, Human Resources

Sales and Marketing

Assistant Vice President of Sales and Marketing
Catering Sales Representative
Clerical Staff
Communications Manager
Conference Coordinator
Convention Services Manager
Convention Services Coordinator
Director of Communications
Director of Convention Sales
Director, Public Relations
Director, Sales and Marketing
Editor
Graphics Manager
Group Sales Manager
Group Sales Representative
Market Researcher
Meeting/Conference Planner
National Sales Manager
Promotion/Public Relations Specialist
Regional Director of Sales and Marketing
Research/Statistical Manager
Sales Manager
Vice President Sales and Marketing

Information Technology

Manager, Information Technology
Programmer/Analyst
System Programmer
Systems Analyst

Leadership

Assistant General Manager
Association Manager
Division President
Innkeeper Manager, Bed and Breakfast
Hotel General Manager
Owner/Operator
President/CEO
Vice President, Administration
Vice President, Business Development
Vice President, Franchising
Vice President, Hotel Development

Activities

Assistant Golf Professional
Assistant Tennis Professional
Caddie
Entertainer
Golf Professional
Golf Shop Salesperson
Lifeguard
Recreation Specialist
Ski Instructor
Social Activities Manager
Spa Director
Swimming Instructor
Swimming Pool Manager
Tennis Professional
Tour Escort

THE CHANGING LABOR MARKET

Individuals looking for work (supply) and the jobs available in a given area (demand) make up the **labor market**. When demand for workers is high and the supply of qualified workers is low, properly staffing a hospitality operation becomes very challenging for management. The key word here is *challenging,* NOT impossible, as we will learn in later chapters.

Other factors have an important impact on the labor market as well. When you need to fill jobs, you look for individuals with certain knowledge levels, skills, abilities, and attitudes. So, the location of your operation will certainly influence factors such as educational levels, average age of population, personality types, unemployment rates, and so forth. In addition, keep in mind you are competing with other restaurants, hotels, bars, caterers, and even hospitals, banks, nursing homes, and large retail organizations such as Wal-Mart for the same prospective employees, so the recruiting strategies of your competitors as well as their ability to perhaps offer higher wages and/or better **fringe benefits** will have a lot to do with your hiring success. Remember, too, that many hospitality graduates find themselves managing or even owning small operations without the means or the budget to employ a full-blown, professionally staffed **human resources** department to handle the day-to-day hiring of employees. In fact, as the owner, manager, or supervisor at a smaller operation, you *are* the human resources department.

HOSPITALITY INDUSTRY JOBS

While much progress has been made over the years to improve the image of hospitality industry careers, many prospective employees still do not see hotel and restaurant jobs as a viable career choice. This is likely due to an abundance of low-wage, entry-level, part-time jobs. Many of these **back-of-house** jobs require hard work either standing in a hot kitchen or hotel laundry area, cleaning floors and scrubbing toilets, or loading and unloading dishes and pots and pans into a steaming, noisy dishwasher. Where's the glamour in that?

More often than not, **front-of-house** positions, too, seem less glamorous when coupled with the demands of carrying heavy trays of food or constantly dealing with demanding guests and clientele. It is no surprise that the duller and more demanding jobs are more difficult to fill, but the good news is that there are people with no experience and no skills who are willing to take these jobs and who, with proper incentives and training, often become valuable, long-term employees.

A NOTE ABOUT ETHICS

The hospitality industry has become so competitive that if customers and employees are dissatisfied, they will go elsewhere. We want to be able to trust the people we do business with, but life has become more difficult and expensive, and ethical shortcuts have become the norm. The following *10 Ethical Principles for Hospitality Managers* were adopted from Josephson Institute of Ethics' "Core Ethical Principles." They have served as the basis of ethics research coming out of Isbell Hospitality Ethics for the past 15 years. A chapter-by-chapter analysis of a short ethical dilemma underscores the importance of adhering to the Ethical Principles for Hospitality Managers during the decision-making process. Adherence to these principles will result in the best consequences for all parties involved.[2]

1. *Honesty.* Hospitality managers are honest and truthful. They do not mislead or deceive others by misrepresentations.

2. *Integrity.* Hospitality managers demonstrate the courage of their convictions by doing what they know is right even when there is pressure to do otherwise.

3. *Trustworthiness.* Hospitality managers are trustworthy and candid in supplying information and in correcting misapprehensions of fact. They do not create justifications for escaping their promises and commitments.

4. *Loyalty.* Hospitality managers demonstrate loyalty to their companies in devotion to duty and loyalty to colleagues by friendship in adversity. They avoid conflicts of interest; do not use or disclose confidential information; and, should they accept other employment, they respect the proprietary information of their former employer.

5. *Fairness.* Hospitality managers are fair and equitable in all dealings; they neither arbitrarily abuse power nor take undue advantage of another's mistakes or difficulties. They treat all individuals with equality, with tolerance and acceptance of diversity, and with an open mind.

6. *Concern and respect for others.* Hospitality managers are concerned, respectful, compassionate, and kind. They are sensitive to the personal concerns of their colleagues and live the Golden Rule. They respect the rights and interests of all those who have a stake in their decisions.

7. *Commitment to excellence.* Hospitality managers pursue excellence in performing their duties and are willing to put more into their job than they can get out of it.

8. *Leadership.* Hospitality managers are conscious of the responsibility and opportunities of their position of leadership. They realize that the best way to instill ethical principles and ethical awareness in their organizations is by example. They walk their talk!

ethical dilemma

Mark is a banquet sales manager in a medium-sized hotel. He is nervous because a very important client, Mrs. McWilliams, is waiting in his office to go over the folios and charges that were incurred at her daughter's wedding reception that the hotel hosted last month. She is anxious to settle the account, but Mark has procrastinated for days and he still does not have the promised charges and folios organized in such a manner that he can present them to the client. He plans to tell the client that the computer system has been down for two days and that is why the paperwork is still incomplete. He asks his assistant, Christine, to accompany him into his office and to "back up his story." Christine is still somewhat new. She enjoys her job at the hotel very much, so she is reluctant to disobey Mark's request. If you were Christine, what would you do? Which of the *10 Ethical Principles for Hospitality Managers* is being violated? Can Christine avoid this ethical dilemma and still remain in her job? How will her decision affect her relationship with her boss, Mark?

9. *Reputation and morale.* Hospitality managers seek to protect and build the company's reputation and the morale of its employees by engaging in conduct that builds respect. They also take whatever actions are necessary to correct or prevent inappropriate conduct of others.

10. *Accountability.* Hospitality managers are personally accountable for the ethical quality of their decisions, as well as those of their subordinates.

WORKFORCE DEMOGRAPHICS WILL CHANGE

Demographic changes will also pose new challenges. **Demographics** are statistics that include such things as a target group's age, race, sex, income, and educational levels. According to the U.S. Bureau of Labor Statistics, the composition of the labor force is expected to change as general population demographics change. For example, in 2010, the **baby boom generation** will be ages 45 to 64, and this age group will account for a 5 percent larger share of the labor force than it does currently. And even though the 16- to 24-year-old age group is expected to now grow more rapidly than the overall labor force for the first time in 25 years, the median age of the labor force will continue to rise (from 39.3 in 2000 to 40.6 in 2010). Table 1.1 illustrates these changes.

Projected Labor Force Changes by Age					
Group	Level (in thousands)		Percent Change	Percent of Total	
	2000	2010	2000–2010	2000	2010
Total	140,863	157,721	12.0	100.0	100.0
16 to 24 years	22,715	26,081	14.8	16.1	16.5
25 to 54 years	99,974	104,994	5.0	71.0	66.6
55 to 64 years	13,974	21,204	51.7	9.9	13.4
65 and older	4,200	5,442	29.6	3.0	3.5

Table 1.1   The Composition of the Labor Force Is Expected to Change as General Population Demographics Change. (*Source: Bureau of Labor Statistics, Office of Occupational Statistics and Employment Projections 2003–2008 Strategic Plan.*)

Because of high net immigration and higher-than-average birth rates, the Asian and Other and Hispanic labor force groups are projected to increase faster than other groups. The Asian and Other group is expected to grow 44 percent (2000 to 2010) and thereby increase its share of the labor force from 5 to 6 percent. The Hispanic labor force will grow by 36 percent, increasing its share from 11 percent to 13 percent of the total workforce. The Black labor force is expected to grow by 21 percent, more than twice as fast as the White labor force (9 percent). Table 1.2 illustrates these projections.

Projected Labor Force Changes by Race and Ethnicity					
Group	Level (in thousands)		Percent Change	Percent of Total	
	2000	2010	2000–2010	2000	2010
Total	140,863	157,721	12.0	100.0	100.0
White	117,574	128,043	8.9	83.5	81.2
Black	16,603	20,041	20.7	11.8	12.7
Asian and Other	6,687	9,636	44.1	4.7	6.1
Hispanic Origin	15,368	20,947	36.3	10.9	13.3
Non-Hispanic	125,495	136,774	9.0	89.1	86.7

Table 1.2   The Asian and Other and Hispanic labor force groups are projected to increase faster than other groups. (*Source: Bureau of Labor Statistics, Office of Occupational Statistics and Employment Projections 2003–2008 Strategic Plan*).

According to the Bureau of Labor Statistics, other indirect changes will emerge as a result of the country's changing demographics. The likelihood of working side by side with people who are different—in culture, gender, age, and many other ways—will increase, as well as the challenges that hospitality industry managers will face in attracting and retaining a quality workforce with so much competition out there.

NONTRADITIONAL WORKERS

With fewer *traditional* workers to fill the growing demand for hospitality industry employees, many organizations have made a concerted effort to recruit what is often referred to as a *nontraditional employee*. Figure 1.2 lists some typical characteristics of a nontraditional worker.

Nontraditional workers in the hospitality industry might include the following:
• Retirees hoping to supplement retirement income with part-time, flexible hours
• Recent immigrants who may or may not speak English
• Disabled individuals
• Displaced homemakers
• Career changers

Figure 1.2   Labor sources for nontraditional hospitality industry workers.

INCREASED DEMAND

In almost every community, large and small, one needs only to go out to dinner on a busy Friday or Saturday night to witness firsthand the explosive growth of our nation's restaurant industry. If you are unfortunate enough to show up without a reservation, the wait can be in excess of an hour or more in some communities.

Household incomes have risen dramatically in the past decade, which is good news for the restaurant industry. When people have more money to spend, they are more likely to dine out and spend it in restaurants. For many people, the restaurant table is beginning to replace the dinner table at home. Consider these mind-boggling statistics from the National Restaurant Association's 2005 Restaurant Industry Forecast:

<table>
<tr><td>**Photo 1.1**</td><td>Waiting in line to place an order at a fast-food restaurant is commonplace due to the explosive growth in the nation's restaurant industry.</td></tr>
</table>

- Restaurant industry sales reached a record $453.5 billion in 2004—an increase of 5.5 percent from 2003.
- Restaurants will provide more than 70 billion meal and snack occasions in 2005.
- The typical adult purchased a meal or snack from a restaurant 5.3 times a week, on average, in 2004.
- By the year 2015, restaurant industry employment will reach 14.0 million.
- Roughly 900,000 locations offer food service nationwide—up a strong 83 percent from 1972.[3]

In this same report, more than half of quick-service restaurant operators and roughly two out of five table service restaurant operators stated that the availability of labor is having a negative impact on their ability to do business and meet customer expectations. Operators are adopting a range of responses to the challenge. For example, more than half of quick-service operators and nearly one-third of table service restaurant operators report that they plan to devote a bigger share of their budgets to training. The overall expansion of the industry creates many job openings for both entry-level and supervisory positions.

Photo 1.2   Many restaurants and the majority of lodging operations rely heavily on the travel and tourism industry.

INDUSTRY REMAINS STRONG

Many restaurants and most lodging properties rely heavily on tourism (see Photo 1.2). Higher-end full-service restaurants estimate that up to 30 percent of their sales are driven by travelers and visitors.[4] When people do have expendable income, they often choose to dine out. They may be dining out for special occasions such as birthdays or anniversaries, or they may simply be enjoying the company of friends and families. Customers who visit lodging and food service establishments today are very different from those of 50 years ago. At that time, dining out was a luxury; now, it's commonplace. Today's consumer is extremely savvy when it comes to food, service, restaurant or hotel ambience, and travel in general. When many of today's baby boomers were growing up in the late 1950s and 1960s, going out to eat with the family was a rare, special treat, often reserved for Sunday dinner. Young people today may have eaten more restaurant meals in their lifetime than they have eaten in their homes! This familiarity with the restaurant and food service industry has created a generation of diners who have sophisticated tastes with respect to the quality of food and service they expect to receive when dining out. Some experts attribute this to cable TV shows such as those found on the Food Network and the explosion in the popularity of celebrity TV chefs, such as Emeril Lagasse.

Whatever the reason, the bar has been raised considerably, so it is more important than ever that managers and supervisors in the hospitality industry are able to attract the right applicant for the right job; provide that new employee with valuable, ongoing training; and then offer the kind of work environment in which the new employee can self-motivate and become a valuable member of the team.

MOTIVATIONS, NEEDS, AND EXPECTATIONS

Guests and customers visit various hospitality operations today with very distinct **motivations, needs, and expectations (MNEs)**. Your ability to not only meet but actually exceed your guests' MNEs will play a large role in determining your operation's success or failure. The most successful hospitality enterprises understand this concept quite well, and those operations also understand that the very best way to meet and exceed customer MNEs is to have a well-trained, dynamic, and motivated staff. Quality management and leadership is also of the utmost importance; once you have made that all-important hiring decision, the truly hard work has not yet even begun—that is, the training you must provide and management practices that you must consistently adhere to in order to provide the kind of work environment in which your employees can self-motivate and provide high-quality products and services to your valued guests.

There are probably as many reasons for dining out as there are locations to do so. Of course, when we're hungry, we eat, but surprisingly, the simple need for one to put food in one's belly is not a primary motivator for dining out in many cases. Consider the scenarios in Figure 1.3 and think about the food service choices available to you in your hometown.

With each scenario, we get a pretty clear picture of the MNEs for each of the diners. Those hospitality businesses that understand their customers' MNEs and that regularly meet and exceed them are well on their way to success. Review the scenarios again, and think about all of the things that could go wrong—things that would cause each restaurant to fail miserably in meeting its customers' MNEs. Keep in mind that travelers who require overnight lodging come armed with their own special set of MNEs. These concepts can just as easily be applied to any segment of the large and diverse hospitality industry.

TRAINING AND MOTIVATION

Clearly, what motivates us to seek a dining experience as well as what we need and expect to get out of that experience is not always a simple matter. Producing quality products and providing top-notch service requires motivated, well-

- Your parents are coming to town to help you celebrate your twenty-first birthday, and they have promised to take you out for a special dinner and night on the town. What restaurant might you recommend?

- You are a busy sales rep in a downtown office and have invited a client to lunch. You need to impress this client, but you understand that neither one of you can spare more than 60 to 90 minutes for lunch. What restaurant will you choose?

- You are on your way home from work and are in a rush to get there so that you can relieve the babysitter. You have nothing nutritious at home to prepare, so you decide to grab some take out for you and your family for dinner. What restaurant choices do you have?

- You are driving 400 miles on the interstate to visit an old college chum. It's lunchtime and you are hungry, but you do not want to waste valuable driving time by sitting down in a restaurant and ordering off the menu. What are your choices?

- You are in college and you are on a tight budget. It's Thursday night and you and your friends want to go out for beer and pizza. What are your choices?

- You and your brothers and sisters along with your spouses and children have decided to take your mother out to eat for Mother's Day. There are more than 14 of you, and many of the children are under the age of 10. What are your choices?

- You and your spouse decide to celebrate your tenth anniversary in style by going out to dinner at an exclusive restaurant. What are your dining choices?

- You've been invited to a covered-dish picnic and you agreed to bring a salad and a dessert. Unfortunately, you have been too busy to shop for food and prepare it. What are your choices?

Figure 1.3   Restaurant customers' MNEs will determine their choice of food service establishment in each of the scenarios presented here.

trained employees. Hospitality managers who understand this concept and who work hard to match the right applicant with the right job and train the applicant thoroughly are normally very successful. Those who fail to put forth the effort are usually rewarded with a failing business.

Because **turnover rates** in the industry are high and employees seem to come and go, it is far too easy for the supervisor or the manager to start believing that training new employees is not worth the effort. This kind of thinking is a certain recipe for disaster. Professional hospitality industry managers and supervisors are obligated to train their workers, help them become productive, and make them key ambassadors of the establishment. This process will cut down on expensive turnover, and as we will learn in later chapters, hiring the right person for the right job initially is probably the most effective step managers can take when it comes to creating a motivated, dynamic workplace.

■ SUMMARY

- ■ The hospitality industry has experienced tremendous growth in the past few decades.
- ■ Recruiting, hiring, training, and retaining quality workers is one of management's greatest challenges.
- ■ Enhanced customer MNEs require that management hire and retain employees of a high caliber in order to deliver the quality products and services that today's guests demand.
- ■ Managers must work hard to match the right applicant to the right position, and managers must provide quality training and leadership in order to provide the kind of work environment where employees feel a sense of self-worth.

PRACTICE QUIZ

1. Most hotel and restaurant managers operate in an environment where the number of interested and available job seekers far exceeds the number of positions to be filled.

   A. True   B. False

2. Today's hotel and restaurant customers are not as industry-savvy as customers in past decades.

   A. True   B. False

3. The Educational Institute of the American Hotel & Lodging Association provides resources to assist struggling owners and managers in improving their lodging operations.

   A. True   B. False

4. Training has no real impact on overall customer service and customer satisfaction.

   A. True   B. False

5. By the year 2010, the white labor force is expected to grow less than the Asian and Hispanic workforce.

   A. True   B. False

6. The baby boom generation was born between the years of

   A. 1900 to 1932

   B. 1933 to 1945

   C. 1946 to 1964

   D. 1965 to 1981

7. Nontraditional hospitality industry workers include the following:
   A. Displaced homemakers
   B. Recent immigrants
   C. Retirees
   D. All of the above

8. The National Restaurant Association estimates that by the year 2015, restaurant industry employment will reach
   A. 14 million
   B. 11 million
   C. 9 million
   D. None of the above

9. In order to provide quality products and services to customers and guests, employees must
   A. Be paid higher than average industry wages
   B. Have formal hospitality industry education
   C. Be self-motivated and well trained
   D. Have a variety of fringe benefits from which to choose

10. Employee turnover can have a negative impact on which of the following:
   A. Employee morale
   B. Hotel or restaurant product quality
   C. Hotel or restaurant service quality
   D. All of the above

REVIEW QUESTIONS

1. Visit the Web sites of both the National Restaurant Association's Educational Foundation (www.nraef.org) and the Educational Institute of the American Hotel & Lodging Association (www.ei-ahla.org) and find examples of how each association raises awareness of career opportunities in the hospitality industry. Be prepared to share your findings with the rest of the class.

2. Describe an ethical dilemma that you have either encountered or witnessed in either your work experience or in your personal life. Were any of the *10 Ethical Principles for Hospitality Managers* in danger of being violated? What decisions were finally made and what were the outcomes for all parties involved? Share your experiences with the rest of the class.

3. Choose two or three of the dining scenarios presented in Figure 1.3 and make a list of the diners' MNEs for each. Explain how the diners' MNEs would influence this choice of restaurant.

4. Interview the manager or owner of a small, local hospitality business in your area. Determine from your interview the manager's key challenges in

hiring and retaining quality workers. Does the establishment you visited do anything out of the ordinary to attract and retain workers? Be prepared to present your findings to the rest of the class.

5. Visit a local hospitality business in your area and observe whether the establishment has employees who may be classified as "nontraditional workers." You may also choose to use your own personal work experiences to complete this assignment. What challenges, if any, does the establishment face with regard to hiring nontraditional workers?

HANDS-ON HRM ▶

Thelma Johnson is a single mother raising two teenaged children on her own. Mrs. Johnson calls a locally owned Italian take-out restaurant and places an order for carryout two or three Friday evenings per month before she leaves work. She almost always orders the same thing: a large bucket of spaghetti and meatballs, three tossed salads, and an extra order of garlic breadsticks. She appreciates the convenience of not having to cook after a long week at work, and her kids love Italian food.

On this particular Friday night, when Mrs. Johnson gets home, she realizes that the restaurant has forgotten the extra order of garlic breadsticks, even though she paid for them. She immediately telephones the restaurant and speaks to a counterperson named Mary. She explains the situation, and Mary responds, "No problem. Just remind us of this the next time you come in, and we'll throw in a free order of breadsticks."

A few weeks later, Mrs. Johnson places another carryout order, and when she arrives at the restaurant, she goes inside to pay and pick up the order. She tells the man at the counter about the missing breadsticks from two weeks ago, and she asks for her complimentary breadsticks. The man identifies himself as the owner of the restaurant and says to her, "We have no such policy here, and we do not give away free breadsticks." Thelma Johnson is beside herself, collects her order, and leaves the restaurant, vowing under her breath never to return again.

QUESTIONS ▶

1. How could procedures at this restaurant be changed to prevent such occurrences from happening in the future? Be specific and explain your reasoning.

2. How would the restaurant ultimately have benefited if the owner handled things differently? Please explain your response in detail.

3. The restaurant's cost for one order of garlic breadsticks is $0.32. What are the real costs to this restaurant as a result of the owner's reaction to Mrs. Johnson? Please explain how you define the "real costs."

4. If you were Mrs. Johnson, would you tell others about your experience at this restaurant? Why or why not?

Supply and demand In a specific labor market, this refers to the number of individuals looking for jobs versus the number of jobs available.

Labor market The individuals who are looking for jobs and the number of jobs that are available in a given geographic area.

Fringe benefits Pay and/or employment benefits beyond what is normally required by local and federal government regulations. Examples include vacation pay, health insurance, tuition reimbursement, retirement plans, and child care assistance.

Human resources A support department in a large hotel or restaurant environment where a professional staff oversees job recruitment, reference checks, interviews, job placement, and training.

Back-of-house Refers to areas of a restaurant or a hotel that guests normally do not see. Examples include housekeeping, kitchen, storage and receiving areas, and dishwashing.

Front-of-house Refers to areas of a restaurant or a hotel that guests normally see and where guests and employees normally interact. Examples include front office, bell services, restaurant waitstaff, and host/hostess station.

Demographics The characteristics of a target market population in terms of income, education levels, occupation, age, and sex.

Baby boom generation U.S. demographers have put this generation's birth years at 1946 to 1964. Approximately 76 million people were born in the United States during these 18 years.

Motivations, needs, and expectations (MNEs) In the food and lodging service industry, these are an overview of what motivates guests to visit your establishment as well as what those guests' needs and expectations are once they choose to become your customer.

Turnover rates The loss of employees by an organization. Turnover represents those employees who depart either voluntarily or involuntarily.

1. Kinkead's home page: www.kinkead.com.
2. Christine Jaszay and Paul Dunk, *Ethical Decision-Making in the Hospitality Industry,* 2006, pp. 2, 3. (Reprinted by permission of Pearson Education, Inc., Upper Saddle River, NJ).
3. *Restaurant Industry Forecast* (Washington, D.C.: National Restaurant Association, 2005), 6–7.
4. Ibid.

CHAPTER 2

THE HOSPITALITY MANAGER'S LEGAL CHALLENGES

I can still remember the separate water fountains and segregated buses as a young boy growing up in Atlanta in the 1950s . . . The Civil Rights Act of 1964 was enacted to end this discrimination and begin to restore the full rights of citizenship for all Americans.[1]

Herman Cain, former CEO and president, the National Restaurant Association

CHAPTER OBJECTIVES

After completing this chapter, you will be able to

- Define Title VII of the 1964 Civil Rights Act.
- Identify the Equal Employment Opportunity Commission's (EEOC) role in discrimination lawsuits.
- Define sexual harassment.
- List the protected classes covered under Title VII.
- Define and give an example of a bona fide occupational qualification (BFOQ) defense.
- Define the Americans with Disabilities Act (ADA).
- Explain *disability, reasonable accommodation,* and *undue hardship* as defined by the ADA.
- Define the Age Discrimination in Employment Act.
- Define the Equal Pay Act.
- Define the Immigration Reform and Control Act.

 **HRM IN ACTION**   Most human resources professionals working in the hospitality industry will tell you that the very first step in the employee recruitment process should be the creation of a job description. A **job description** details the primary duties of a particular position. Creating this list of responsibilities first will force management to focus on the particular set of skills and characteristics an applicant should have in order to do the job well. However, before the manager even begins to create job descriptions, it's important all members involved in the recruitment process recognize that there are certain laws that regulate the hiring process in the hospitality industry. The following section focuses on the legal landscape of the hospitality industry, providing some important dos and don'ts with respect to issuing employment applications, conducting interviews and background checks, and, of course, writing job descriptions.

EMPLOYMENT LAW AND THE EQUAL EMPLOYMENT OPPORTUNITY COMMISSION

There are numerous federal and state employment laws that hospitality managers must obey as they go about the business of making daily, routine management decisions. One of the most important of these laws is **Title VII of the 1964 Civil Rights Act.** This law applies to businesses with 15 or more employees, including state and local governments. Title VII prohibits employment discrimination based on an individual's sex, race, color, religion, and national origin. Whether writing a job description, placing a help-wanted advertisement in the local newspaper, or conducting a job interview, it is essential that managers have a thorough understanding of Title VII to ensure that no employment discrimination of any sort occurs. The **Equal Employment Opportunity Commission,** commonly referred to as the EEOC, is the federal agency that provides oversight and coordination of Title VII as well as other federal EEO (equal employment opportunity) laws (see Figure 2.1).

In addition to the guidelines the law imposes on the hiring process itself, managers must understand that *all* matters that are employment-related are covered under Title VII. Determining whether to promote a specific employee, deciding who will receive a raise in pay, designing work schedules, training schedules, and even administering employee discipline are all management duties that will in one way or another fall under the broad spectrum of Title VII. Figure 2.2 provides examples of discriminatory practices as defined by the EEOC. In Chapter 9, we will cover in greater detail the types of questions that hospitality managers are prohibited from asking on the job application as well as during the job interview.

Figure 2.1   Hospitality operations must post notices advising employees of their rights under federal, state, and local EEO laws. *(Source: U.S. Equal Employment Opportunity Commission.)*

Equal Employment Opportunity is
THE LAW

Employers Holding Federal Contracts or Subcontracts

Applicants to and employees of companies with a Federal contract or subcontract are protected under Federal law from discrimination on the following bases:

RACE, COLOR, RELIGION, SEX, NATIONAL ORIGIN
Executive Order 11246, as amended, prohibits job discrimination on the basis of race, color, religion, sex or national origin, and requires employers to take affirmative steps to ensure equality of opportunity in all aspects of employment.

INDIVIDUALS WITH DISABILITIES
Section 503 of the Rehabilitation Act of 1973, as amended, prohibits job discrimination because of a disability and requires affirmative action to employ and advance in employment qualified individuals with disabilities who, with or without reasonable accommodation, can perform the essential functions of a job.

VIETNAM ERA AND SPECIAL DISABLED VETERANS
38 U.S.C. 4212 of the Vietnam Era Veterans' Readjustment Assistance Act of 1974, as amended, prohibits job discrimination and requires affirmative action to employ and advance in employment qualified Vietnam era veterans, special disabled veterans, recently separated veterans, and veterans who served on active duty during a war or in a campaign or expedition for which a campaign badge has been authorized.

Any person who believes a contractor has violated its nondiscrimination or equal opportunity obligations under one or more of the authorities above should immediately contact:
    The Office of Federal Contract Compliance Programs (OFCCP), Employment Standards Administration (ESA), U.S. Department of Labor (DOL), 200 Constitution Avenue, N.W., Washington, D.C. 20210 or call (202) 693-0100 (DOL's toll free TTY number, for individuals with hearing impairments is (800) 326-2577), or an OFCCP regional or district office, listed in most telephone directories under U.S. Government, Department of Labor, or access OFCCP's web site via the Internet at *www.dol.gov/esa/ofcp_org.htm*.

Previous Edition Useable

Private Employment, State and Local Governments, Educational Institutions, Employment Agencies and Labor Organizations

Applicants to and employees of most private employers, state and local governments, educational institutions, employment agencies and labor organizations are protected under Federal law from discrimination on the following bases:

RACE, COLOR, RELIGION, SEX, NATIONAL ORIGIN
Title VII of the Civil Rights Act of 1964, as amended, prohibits discrimination in hiring, promotion, discharge, pay, fringe benefits, job training, classification, referral, and other aspects of employment, on the basis of race, color, religion, national origin, or sex (including pregnancy). Religious discrimination includes failing to reasonably accommodate an employee's religious practices where the accommodation does not impose undue hardship.

DISABILITY
Title I and Title V of the Americans with Disabilities Act of 1990, as amended, protect qualified applicants and employees with disabilities from discrimination in hiring, promotion, discharge, pay, job training, fringe benefits, classification, referral, and other aspects of employment on the basis of disability. The law also requires that covered entities provide qualified applicants and employees with disabilities with reasonable accommodations, unless such accommodations would impose an undue hardship on the employer.

AGE
The Age Discrimination in Employment Act of 1967, as amended, protects applicants and employees 40 years of age or older from discrimination on the basis of age in hiring, promotion, discharge, compensation, and other terms, conditions or privileges of employment.

SEX (WAGES)
In addition to sex discrimination prohibited by Title VII of the Civil Rights Act, as amended, the Equal Pay Act of 1963, as amended, prohibits sex discrimination in payment of wages to women and men performing substantially equal work, in jobs that require equal skill, effort and responsibility under similar working conditions, in the same establishment.

RETALIATION
All of these Federal laws prohibit covered entities from retaliating against a person who files a charge of discrimination, participates in an investigation, or opposes an unlawful employment practice.

WHAT TO DO IF YOU BELIEVE DISCRIMINATION HAS OCCURRED
There are strict time frames in which you must file charges of employment discrimination. To preserve the ability of EEOC to act on your behalf and to protect your right to file a private lawsuit, should you ultimately need to, you should contact EEOC promptly when discrimination is suspected. If you believe that you have been discriminated against under any of the above laws, you should immediately contact:
    The U.S. Equal Employment Opportunity Commission (EEOC), 1801 L Street, N.W., Washington, D.C. 20507 or an EEOC field office by calling toll free (800) 669-4000. For individuals with hearing impairments, EEOC's toll free TTY number is (800) 669-6820, or access EEOC's web site at *www.eeoc.gov*.

Programs or Activities Receiving Federal Financial Assistance

RACE, COLOR, NATIONAL ORIGIN, SEX
In addition to the protections of Title VII of the Civil Rights Act of 1964, as amended, Title VI of the Civil Rights Act of 1964, as amended, prohibits discrimination on the basis of race, color or national origin in programs or activities receiving Federal financial assistance. Employment discrimination is covered by Title VI if the primary objective of the financial assistance is provision of employment, or where employment discrimination causes or may cause discrimination in providing services under such programs. Title IX of the Education Amendments of 1972 prohibits employment discrimination on the basis of sex in educational programs or activities which receive Federal financial assistance.

INDIVIDUALS WITH DISABILITIES
Section 504 of the Rehabilitation Act of 1973, as amended, prohibits employment discrimination on the basis of a disability in any program or activity which receives Federal financial assistance. Discrimination is prohibited in all aspects of employment against persons with disabilities, who, with or without reasonable accommodation, can perform the essential functions of a job.

If you believe you have been discriminated against in a program of any institution which receives Federal financial assistance, you should immediately contact the Federal agency providing such assistance.

EEOC-P/E-1 (Revised 9/02)

23

DISCRIMINATORY PRACTICES
What Discriminatory Practices Are Prohibited by Title VII?

Under Title VII, it is illegal to discriminate in any aspect of employment, including the following:

- Compensation, assignment, or classification of employees
- Transfer, promotion, layoff, or recall
- Job advertisements
- Recruitment
- Testing
- Use of company facilities
- Training and apprenticeship programs
- Fringe benefits
- Pay, retirement plans, and disability leave
- Other terms and conditions of employment

Discriminatory practices under these laws also include:

- Harassment on the basis of race, color, religion, sex, national origin, disability, or age.
- Retaliation against an individual for filing a charge of discrimination, participating in an investigation, or opposing discriminatory practices.
- Employment decisions based on stereotypes or assumptions about the abilities, traits, or performance of individuals of a certain sex, race, age, religion, or ethnic group.
- Denying employment opportunities to a person because of marriage to, or association with, an individual of a particular race, religion, or national origin. Title VII also prohibits discrimination because of participation in schools or places of worship associated with a particular racial, ethnic, or religious group.

Employers are required to post notices to all employees advising them of their rights under the laws EEOC enforces and their right to be free from retaliation. Such notices must be accessible, as needed, to persons with visual or other disabilities that affect reading.

Note: Many states and municipalities also have enacted protections against discrimination and harassment based on sexual orientation, status as a parent, marital status, and political affiliation. For information, please contact the EEOC District Office nearest you.

Figure 2.2   Discriminatory practices and conditions of employment covered by Title VII. *(Source: U.S. Equal Employment Opportunity Commission.)*

TALES FROM THE FIELD

I finished my degree in Baking and Pastry Arts and took a job as the pastry chef in a small privately owned restaurant. The restaurant was successful, and the owner gave me carte blanche in the pastry area. I brought my own recipes to the job and further fine-tuned them, and before long, the restaurant (and my recipes) was getting excellent reviews and write-ups. After about eight months, the owner fired me one day when I had called in sick due to some serious dental work I had to have done. I was shocked, but even more surprised when he told me that in order to receive my final paycheck, I would have to turn over all of my recipes to him . I refused, and he refused to release my check. I had to file a complaint with the state wage and hour board in order to get paid, but I did get paid, and as I understand it, the owner's business was then audited for other potential wage violations!

Melissa, 24, Murfressboro, Tennessee

ILLEGAL DISCRIMINATION

The word *discrimination* has typically gotten a bad rap. When we hear the word, we automatically think of it as something negative or ugly. Truthfully, we discriminate each and every day as we live our lives. For example, deciding which pair of socks to wear when we dress for work or school—or whether to wear any socks at all—is a form of discrimination. When we choose one pair of socks over the other, we are doing so based upon some selection criteria that we somehow deem relevant. Will the blue socks look better with the khaki slacks or would black socks look best? Discrimination then is simply about making choices. Title VII does not necessarily prevent hospitality managers from making informed choices in matters of employment; it prevents managers from making *illegal* choices, or decisions that are based upon some flawed or illegal selection criteria, such as race, religion, gender, and so forth.

There was a time in our nation's history—roughly 30 years ago—when society felt that certain types of people were best suited for certain types of jobs. A good example comes from our nation's airline industry, a relatively new industry in the grand scheme of things. Airline pilots had to be male, and stewardesses had to be female. It did not matter whether pilots and copilots were married or single, but stewardesses had to remain single—to get married meant losing one's job. When hiring stewardesses, the airlines were careful to select only those female applicants who were deemed the most attractive. There were strict height and weight requirements, and most airlines required that the applicant attach

Photo 2.1

The airline stewardess is now referred to as a flight attendant and is no longer required to be female and unmarried.

both a head-and-shoulders photo as well as a full-body photo to her application. It is not hard to imagine what probably happened to the applications of those less attractive.

In our more enlightened world today, these hiring practices seem ridiculous and unreasonable. While the estimated 4,000 female airline pilots flying today still only account for about 5 percent of all airline pilots, clearly, women are making inroads in the world of aviation. The term *stewardess* has been replaced with the more modern term *flight attendant,* and anyone who flies today will see that the modern flight attendant comes in all shapes, colors, ages, and sexes. A flight attendant's marital status is also no longer a job qualification.

Changes in employment practices such as these and many others were a result of the enactment of Title VII of the 1964 Civil Rights Act. According to Title VII, choosing one job applicant over another or making other employment decisions based upon an individual's sex, race, color, religion, or national origin is illegal. The penalties for illegal discrimination can be severe as well as expensive, and the fallout from such acts can also be a public relations nightmare.

BONA FIDE OCCUPATIONAL QUALIFICATION

When Title VII was enacted, Congress *did* realize that there would be legitimate occasions when management would need to choose a male applicant over a female applicant, or vice versa. Congress also knew that some positions might

Erica is a dining room manager for a small lodging operation based in the Midwest. Last week she placed a help-wanted ad for a host/hostess position in the local newspaper, and today she has set aside some time to review the applications that have come in thus far . All applicants in this hotel turn their completed applications in at the front desk, and Erica requested that any clerk taking an application make a few notations on the application about the general age, sex, and appearance of each applicant. Erica feels that younger, more attractive females are best suited for the hostess position in the restaurant, so she begins to sort through the applications, putting aside those in which the clerks' notations indicate older applicants, unattractive applicants, and male applicants. For those applications on which the clerks have failed to make notations, Erica attempts to weed out less-preferred applicants by ascertaining age based upon high school graduation year and so forth. Applications with first names that are clearly masculine are also put aside. Which of the *10 Ethical Principles for Hospitality Managers* is being violated? Can an action that is clearly in violation of a law still be ethical? How will Erica's hiring practices affect her hotel's standing in the community if her actions are discovered?

require that the job applicant be of a specific religion or national origin. Based on these realizations, Congress created what one might call a legal loophole. This loophole is known as **bona fide occupational qualification,** or simply **BFOQ**. Let's say that a manager of a resort hotel needs to hire a men's locker room attendant. Because of BFOQ, the manager could *legally* discriminate against any females who might apply for this job. It is important to note that the BFOQ defense is construed narrowly by the courts. Generally, two elements are necessary in order to qualify: (1) the job in issue must require a worker of a particular sex, religion, or national origin and (2) such a requirement must be necessary to the essence of the business operation. BFOQ is not a defense against a claim of racial discrimination.

THE HOOTERS RESTAURANT CHAIN

Some students preparing for careers in hospitality management may ask: "Well, how does Hooters [the restaurant chain] get away with hiring only female servers?" The answer is not a simple one. The restaurant chain was sued in 1992 when seven men from Illinois and Maryland claimed they were discriminated against when they applied to be servers at a Hooters restaurant. The EEOC initially took the case, alleging that Hooters employment practices of hiring only women to be servers, bartenders, and hosts were in violation of Title VII. Hooters claimed that because the restaurant chain was actually providing vicarious sexual recreation, female sexuality was a BFOQ. The EEOC alleged that all along Hooters was primarily a food business that marketed itself as a family restaurant rather than as an entertainment establishment.

The chain then launched a clever public relations campaign that featured a hairy, ugly "Hooters Guy," and the EEOC, which had initially demanded a $22 million fine from the restaurant chain, decided not to pursue the case. In 1997, the chain paid $3.75 million to the plaintiffs to settle the case and agreed to create gender-neutral host and bartender positions, but the settlement agreement allows Hooters to continue to lure customers with an exclusively female staff of "Hooters Girls."[2]

SEXUAL HARASSMENT

Sexual harassment is a form of sex discrimination that violates Title VII of the 1964 Civil Rights Act. There are numerous documented incidents in which hotels and restaurants have been fined hundreds of thousands of dollars for engaging in sexual harassment. The EEOC defines sexual harassment as "unwelcome sexual advances, requests for sexual favors, or other verbal or physical conduct of a sexual nature when this conduct explicitly or implicitly affect's an individual's employment, unreasonably interferes with an individual's work performance, or creates an intimidating, hostile, or offensive work environment."

Sexual harassment in the workplace generally occurs in one of two ways. A manager or a supervisor—someone in a position of power—sexually harasses an employee by virtue of the power held over that employee. This is known as **quid pro quo** or "this for that" type of harassment. Promising or withholding a raise or a promotion in return for sexual favors is an example of quid pro quo harassment. Another form of sexual harassment is known as creating a **hostile work environment.** This occurs when a manager allows employees to engage in telling dirty jokes or allows employees to circulate offensive pictures, Web sites, or e-mail messages. Allowing employees to make crude or suggestive comments of a sexual nature could also lead to a charge of hostile work environment by another employee.

It is important to note that the harasser's conduct must be *unwelcome.* It is important for the victim to inform the harasser directly that the conduct is unwelcome and that it must stop. If the unwelcome harassment continues, the victim should use any employer complaint mechanism or grievance system that is available. It is also important that hospitality organizations have a system in

Sexual harassment can occur in a variety of circumstances, including but not limited to the following:

- The victim as well as the harasser may be a woman or a man. The victim does not have to be of the opposite sex.
- The harasser can be the victim's supervisor, an agent of the employer, a supervisor in another area, a coworker, or a nonemployee.
- The victim does not have to be the person harassed but could be anyone affected by the offensive conduct.
- Unlawful sexual harassment may occur without economic injury to or discharge of the victim.
- The harasser's conduct must be unwelcome.

Figure 2.3   Circumstances in which sexual harassment may occur. *(Source: U.S. Equal Employment Opportunity Commission.)*

place that allows the employee to bypass the supervisor in case the supervisor is also the harasser. Figure 2.3 illustrates some other circumstances in which charges of sexual harassment may occur.

In January 2004, the EEOC settled bias suits with two Florida restaurants that were required to pay more than $500,000 in fines for the sexual harassment of female employees. ABC Pizza, a Tampa Bay area pizza chain, was found guilty of subjecting female employees to a sexually hostile working environment. The EEOC contended that the conduct was created by the restaurant's manager and was primarily directed toward two sisters who were ages 16 and 17 at the time they were employed with the company. The manager's conduct included inappropriate touching as well as crude sexual comments.[3] The other Florida case involved a Longhorn Steakhouse where an assistant manager subjected female employees to hip and lower back touches, breast grabbing, and inappropriate verbal comments. The company was forced to pay the three victims $200,000.[4] Both of these companies are now required to conduct annual training on Title VII with emphasis on sexual harassment.

Managers Must Establish Guidelines and Policies

Clearly, hospitality managers and supervisors must have well-established guidelines for preventing the sexual harassment of employees. Training is essential, and prevention is usually the best tool to eliminate this unlawful behavior. The EEOC recommends that managers clearly communicate to employees that sexual harassment will not be tolerated. Indeed, as a result of recent and expensive lawsuits such as those noted previously, most hospitality operations today have a zero tolerance policy with regard to sexual harassment. It is important that managers train their employees and clearly define what constitutes sexual harassment.

Employees should also be informed about an effective complaint or grievance system that allows victims to come forward and report harassment when it occurs. When an employee does complain, the manager must take immediate and appropriate action, including a fair investigation and disciplinary action when appropriate. As with all other areas of Title VII, managers are prohibited from retaliating against employees who may come forward and report illegal employment practices. Retaliation on the part of management could take various forms. Examples might include cutting an employee's work hours, demoting an employee, disciplining an employee for infractions that are normally overlooked, and transferring an employee to a less-desirable job or a location.

STATE AND LOCAL EMPLOYMENT LAWS

Title VII of the 1964 Civil Rights Act is a federal law, but many states, cities, and towns have enacted their own civil rights and equal opportunity employment laws and have added additional protected classes. For example, some states' and cities' civil rights laws not only make it illegal to discriminate based upon race, sex, color, religion, and national origin (Title VII), but they have also included such protected categories as marital status, disability, age, and sexual orientation. A state or local law must be at least as strict as the federal law, but it may also be stricter. It is important to note that the law that is deemed the *stricter law* is the one that must be followed. If ever in doubt, the prudent manager will always consult with an attorney who is well versed in federal as well as in any local laws that may apply to matters of employment.

AFFIRMATIVE ACTION PLANS

When organizations engage in illegal hiring practices, they could be required by the EEOC to implement affirmative action hiring procedures. This means that the EEOC now requires the organization to hire a certain number of female job applicants or a certain number of applicants who belong to a specific age group or race. Affirmative action is a term that is becoming more generalized, as it may be applied to a variety of federal, state, and private-sector programs aimed at achieving racial and gender diversity in the workforce.

THE AMERICANS WITH DISABILITIES ACT

President George H. W. Bush signed the **Americans with Disabilities Act (ADA)** into law in 1990, and the law went into effect in July 1992. This sweeping legislation covers five areas: employment, public transportation, public accommodations, telecommunication services, and public services. Future hospitality managers and supervisors will be most concerned with just two of the five areas covered: Title I, which governs areas of employment discrimination and is overseen by the EEOC, and Title III, which sets rules and guidelines for the public accommodation of disabled individuals (guests and customers) and is overseen by the U.S. Department of Justice. For the purposes of this textbook, our discussion will be focused only on Title I of the ADA—employment issues.

Photo 2.2

Title III of the ADA requires, among other things, that the hospitality business reserve a percentage of parking spaces for handicapped guests.

DISABILITY DEFINED

Under the provisions of Title I of the ADA, it is illegal to discriminate against people with disabilities in all employment and employment-related issues. The ADA defines a **disabled individual** as "any individual who has a physical or mental impairment that substantially limits one or more major life activities, has a record of such impairment, or is regarded as having such impairment." Protected groups under the ADA include individuals who use wheelchairs, walkers, and so on; individuals who are speech, vision, or hearing impaired; people with mental retardation or emotional illness; individuals with a disease such as cancer, heart disease, asthma, diabetes, or AIDS; and individuals with drug and alcohol problems who are in supervised rehab programs. It is estimated that there are more than 50 million Americans who qualify as being disabled under the ADA. Job applicants and employees who illegally use drugs are *not* covered under the ADA. See Figure 2.4 for EEOC guidelines in this area.

Drug and Alcohol Use

- Employees and applicants currently engaging in the illegal use of drugs are not protected by the ADA when an employer acts on the basis of such use.
- Tests for illegal use of drugs are not considered medical examinations and, therefore, are not subject to the ADA's restrictions on medical examinations.
- Employers may hold individuals who are illegally using drugs and individuals with alcoholism to the same standards of performance as other employees.

Figure 2.4   Illegal drug and alcohol use exceptions to the ADA. *(Source: U.S. Equal Employment Opportunity Commission.)*

Under the guidelines of the ADA, it is illegal for employers to discriminate against disabled individuals who are otherwise qualified to perform the **essential functions** of the job, with or without **reasonable accommodation,** so long as the individual does not pose a threat to the health and safety of others. It is important for hospitality industry managers to understand the importance of clearly determining a position's essential functions. This is best addressed when the job description is created, which we will review in a later chapter. For example, a cook would most certainly need cooking skills, which would be essential to successful job performance. What if the applicant for the position of a cook lacked the ability to hear servers' orders being shouted out? Would this disability be a legitimate reason for not hiring the applicant? Under the ADA's guidelines, probably not. As long as the applicant possesses the ability to perform the job's essential skills (cooking), the manager would most likely be expected to provide something reasonable that would accommodate the individual's hearing disability.

REASONABLE ACCOMMODATION

Accommodating an individual's disability is generally less costly and less intrusive than many managers realize. The EEOC has suggested that most reasonable accommodations cost less than $50, and there are many examples of reasonable accommodations that cost absolutely nothing. Minor changes in either work duties, procedures, work schedules, or in the physical work environment are often all that is required to make a reasonable accommodation. The ADA stipulates that an employer must provide work areas and equipment that are wheelchair accessible unless this is not **readily achievable** or unless it would cause **undue hardship.** Generally, whether something is readily achievable or would cause undue financial hardship is left up to the EEOC to decide.

The hospitality manager is required to provide a reasonable accommodation not only to the disabled applicant for employment but also to employees already on staff who are or who become disabled and cannot perform their original jobs.

AVOIDING ILLEGAL QUESTIONS AND PRACTICES UNDER THE ADA

Hospitality managers need to use caution during the job application and interview process to avoid any illegal practices with respect to the ADA. The ADA strictly limits the circumstances under which employers may ask questions about disability or require medical examinations of employees. Such questions and exams are only permitted when management has a reasonable belief, based on objective evidence, that a particular employee will be unable to perform essential job functions or will pose a direct threat because of a medical condition.

The manager may ask a wide range of questions designed to determine an applicant's qualifications for a job, but the manager may not directly ask about the existence, nature, or severity of a disability during an interview, unless previously disclosed by the candidate. A job offer may be conditioned on the results of a medical examination, but only if the examination is required for *all* entering employees in similar jobs. Medical examinations of employees must be job-related and consistent with the employer's business needs. Figure 2.5 provides some legal alternatives to some potentially illegal questions under the ADA.

Illegal Interview Questions with Legal Alternatives	
Examples of Illegal Questions	**Legal Alternatives**
Do you have a disability?	Are you able to perform the essential functions of this job? (The interviewer must have already thoroughly described the job.)
Have you ever been hospitalized? If so, for what condition?	
Have you ever been treated for a mental condition?	Can you demonstrate how you would perform the following job-related functions?
Have you had a major illness in the last five years?	Preemployment questions about illness may not be asked because they may reveal the existence of a disability. However, an employer may provide information on its attendance requirements and ask if an applicant will be able to meet these requirements.
How many days were you absent from work because of illness last year?	
Are you currently taking any medications?	

Figure 2.5 Illegal interview questions with legal alternatives under the ADA. *(Source: U.S. Equal Employment Opportunity Commission.)*

AGE DISCRIMINATION IN EMPLOYMENT

To prevent employment discrimination based upon an individual's age, the U.S. Congress passed the **Age Discrimination in Employment Act of 1967**. This law prohibits discrimination against individuals who are 40 years of age and older. The act was amended in 1986 to eliminate rules requiring mandatory retirement ages that were common in many industries. Enforcement of this law is handled by the EEOC, and violations can be time-consuming and costly. As with Title VII, exceptions based upon BFOQ are permitted, but they are extremely limited and would likely have no application in the hospitality industry.

EQUAL PAY ACT

In order to prevent huge disparities in pay and wages between men and women, Congress passed the **Equal Pay Act** in 1963. This law requires businesses to pay equal wages for equal work. Jobs are considered equal when both sexes work at the same place and the job requires substantially the same skill, effort, responsibility, and working conditions. Pay differences based on a seniority or merit system or on a system that measures earnings by quantity or quality of production are permitted. The law is interpreted as applying to "wages" in the sense of all employment-related payments, including overtime, uniforms, travel, and other fringe benefits. The EEOC handles equal pay violations, and the penalties can be severe. In a case from 1970, a federal court found that Wheaton Glass Company had violated the Equal Pay Act when it paid male factory workers 21 cents an hour more than female workers. The court ordered Wheaton to pay $900,000 in back pay and interest to more than 2,000 female employees.[5]

IMMIGRATION REFORM AND CONTROL ACT

The **Immigration Reform and Control Act of 1986 (IRCA)** was passed to control illegal immigration to the United States. This federal law imposes civil and criminal penalties on employers who knowingly hire illegal aliens. The law is administered by the Department of Homeland Security's U.S. Citizenship and Immigration Service, and penalties against businesses that knowingly use illegal labor can include fines of up to $10,000 per worker as well as potential criminal charges against the business or its owner. The law requires employers to verify the identity and employment eligibility of all workers hired after November 6, 1986. Hospitality managers accomplish this by requiring all employees to complete Form I-9, Employee Eligibility Verification. A Form I-9 is illustrated in Figure 2.6.

Form I-9 must be kept by the employer either for three years after the date of hire or for one year after employment is terminated, whichever is later. The form must be available for inspection by the authorized U.S. government officials. Currently, the debate in Washington, D.C. has heated up considerably over the "immigration issue" in which some members estimate that nearly four million immigrants are in the country illegally. Some members of Congress prefer a new law that would provide many of these immigrants with a "pathway to citizenship," while others call this route "amnesty" and suggest the criminalization and deportation of all illegal immigrants. The National Restaurant Association, which predicts a nationwide shortage of restaurant industry workers well into the year 2010, prefers legislation that would create a legal means for many of these immigrants to become guest workers in the United States. There appears to be no easy solution to the problem, but the impact of any legislation on the hospitality industry will be profound.

Department of Homeland Security
U.S. Citizenship and Immigration Services

OMB No. 1615-0047; Expires 03/31/07
Employment Eligibility Verification

Please read instructions carefully before completing this form. The instructions must be available during completion of this form. ANTI-DISCRIMINATION NOTICE: It is illegal to discriminate against work eligible individuals. Employers CANNOT specify which document(s) they will accept from an employee. The refusal to hire an individual because of a future expiration date may also constitute illegal discrimination.

Section 1. Employee Information and Verification. To be completed and signed by employee at the time employment begins.

Print Name: Last	First	Middle Initial	Maiden Name

Address (Street Name and Number)	Apt. #	Date of Birth (month/day/year)

City	State	Zip Code	Social Security #

I am aware that federal law provides for imprisonment and/or fines for false statements or use of false documents in connection with the completion of this form.	I attest, under penalty of perjury, that I am (check one of the following): ☐ A citizen or national of the United States ☐ A Lawful Permanent Resident (Alien #) A _____ ☐ An alien authorized to work until _____ (Alien # or Admission #) _____

Employee's Signature	Date (month/day/year)

Preparer and/or Translator Certification. *(To be completed and signed if Section 1 is prepared by a person other than the employee.) I attest, under penalty of perjury, that I have assisted in the completion of this form and that to the best of my knowledge the information is true and correct.*

Preparer's/Translator's Signature	Print Name

Address (Street Name and Number, City, State, Zip Code)	Date (month/day/year)

Section 2. Employer Review and Verification. To be completed and signed by employer. Examine one document from List A OR examine one document from List B and one from List C, as listed on the reverse of this form, and record the title, number and expiration date, if any, of the document(s).

List A	OR	List B	AND	List C
Document title:				
Issuing authority:				
Document #:				
Expiration Date (if any):				
Document #:				
Expiration Date (if any):				

CERTIFICATION - I attest, under penalty of perjury, that I have examined the document(s) presented by the above-named employee, that the above-listed document(s) appear to be genuine and to relate to the employee named, that the employee began employment on *(month/day/year)* _____ **and that to the best of my knowledge the employee is eligible to work in the United States. (State employment agencies may omit the date the employee began employment.)**

Signature of Employer or Authorized Representative	Print Name	Title

Business or Organization Name	Address (Street Name and Number, City, State, Zip Code)	Date (month/day/year)

Section 3. Updating and Reverification. To be completed and signed by employer.

A. New Name (if applicable)	B. Date of Rehire (month/day/year) (if applicable)

C. If employee's previous grant of work authorization has expired, provide the information below for the document that establishes current employment eligibility.

Document Title:	Document #:	Expiration Date (if any):

I attest, under penalty of perjury, that to the best of my knowledge, this employee is eligible to work in the United States, and if the employee presented document(s), the document(s) I have examined appear to be genuine and to relate to the individual.

Signature of Employer or Authorized Representative	Date (month/day/year)

NOTE: This is the 1991 edition of the Form I-9 that has been rebranded with a current printing date to reflect the recent transition from the INS to DHS and its components.

Form I-9 (Rev. 05/31/05)Y Page 2

Figure 2.6 Form I-9, Employment Eligibility Verification. *(Source: U.S. Department of Homeland Security, U.S. Citizenship and Immigration Service.)*

SUMMARY

- Employment laws affect virtually every aspect of the employee-employer relationship, so it is important to follow specific guidelines when asking job applicants to fill out applications and when interviewing prospective job candidates.
- Title VII of the 1964 Civil Rights Act prohibits discrimination on the basis of sex, race, color, national origin, and religion.
- Bona fide occupational qualification (BFOQ) is a legal defense against discrimination in the areas of sex, religion, and national origin, but the courts narrowly construe this defense; hospitality managers are not allowed to retaliate against employees who file discrimination claims.
- The Americans with Disabilities Act (ADA) prohibits discrimination based upon an individual being disabled, and this law applies to both job applicants as well as to current employees who are disabled or who may become disabled and who can no longer perform the essential duties of the job.
- A disabled applicant who otherwise can perform the essential functions of the job with or without a reasonable accommodation should be hired, so long as doing so does not cause the employer undue hardship.
- The Age Discrimination in Employment Act prohibits employment discrimination against those who are 40 years of age and over; the EEOC has oversight of this law.
- The Equal Pay Act prohibits sex discrimination as it relates to pay and salary issues and requires equal pay for equal work.
- The Immigration Reform and Control Act requires that employers verify and retain each worker's proof of identity and proof of legal status to work in the United States; this is done by completing and keeping on file the Form I-9.

PRACTICE QUIZ

1. Title VII of the 1964 Civil Rights Act prohibits job discrimination on the basis of age.

   A. True   B. False

2. Choosing a white applicant over an African-American applicant because of customer preferences would be in violation of Title VII.

   A. True   B. False

3. Title VII of the 1964 Civil Rights Act only impacts the hospitality manager's relationship with job applicants—not with current employees.

   A. True   B. False

4. The ADA requires that hospitality managers hire individuals who are disabled, regardless of the individual's ability to perform the essential functions of the job.

   A. True   B. False

5. The U.S. Department of Justice has legal jurisdiction over Title VII of the 1964 Civil Rights Act.

   A. True   B. False

6. With respect to the I-9 form, acceptable documentation must include which of the following:

   A. An item from List A, List B, and List C

   B. An item from List B only

   C. An item from List A only

   D. An item from List C only

7. Title VII of the 1964 Civil Rights Act prohibits discrimination based upon all of the following *except:*

   A. Race

   B. Color

   C. Age

   D. National origin

8. Refusing to hire a female applicant for the position of men's locker room attendant would be a legal defense of Title VII based upon

   A. Reasonable accommodation

   B. Bona fide occupational qualification (BFOQ)

   C. Essential duties

   D. Undue hardship

9. Which of the following individuals would currently *not* be covered under the ADA?

   A. An individual who is HIV positive or who has AIDS

   B. An individual who illegally uses drugs

   C. An individual who is in supervised alcohol rehab

   D. None of the above are covered under the ADA

10. Paying a female dishwasher less than a male dishwasher could be in violation of

    A. The ADA

    B. The Pregnancy Discrimination Act

    C. The Equal Pay Act

    D. Title VII of the 1964 Civil Rights Act

1. Eric Holmes has applied for the position of a reservations clerk in your hotel. The individual has no experience, but he types quickly and accurately and has good listening skills as well as a pleasant speaking voice. Eric has very limited eyesight; he is considered to be "legally blind" and is covered under the ADA. Discuss ways in which management in your hotel could accommodate Eric's disability with or without a reasonable accommodation.

2. The owner of the small restaurant that you manage has come to you with a new concept, and he wants you to adopt his idea as quickly as possible so as to boost lagging sales in the bar. He would like for you to begin hiring only attractive women to bartend as well as to serve cocktails in the bar. In order to do this, several employees—both male and female—would either have to be transferred to another department or let go. How would you respond to the owner and why? Write a report to the owner clarifying your point of view and be prepared to share your report with the rest of the class.

3. Write a sexual harassment policy for a small hospitality business. Be sure to define both quid pro quo and hostile environment harassment. What steps and procedures should employees take if they feel that they are victims of sexual harassment? What steps should management take when an employee makes a claim of sexual harassment?

4. Conduct an Internet search and find at least two examples—separate from those presented in the text—in which a hospitality operation has been sued for violation of either Title VII or the ADA. What are the circumstances of each case? What was the outcome? Be prepared to share your findings with the rest of the class.

5. Provide examples for ways in which a hospitality business could make a *reasonable accommodation* for each of the following job applicants:

   ■ An applicant for the position of dishwasher who has a hearing disorder.
   ■ An applicant for the position of sales manager who is wheelchair bound.
   ■ An applicant for the position of server who lacks use of the left arm.

Lee and Sue are college students, and they both work the 3 to 11 shift at the front desk of the Delmar Inn, a 250-room suburban hotel property located on the outskirts of a large Midwestern city. One afternoon as they are reporting for work, Joe Goodman, the front-office manager, tells them that the hotel is currently running a help-wanted ad in the local newspaper, and that if any applicants should come in, they should instruct them to fill out an application and then place the completed application in the in-basket on Joe's desk in the back office. Lee and Sue tell Joe "no problem," and they begin to settle in to their nightly shift routine. Joe wishes them a good evening as he closes the door to his office and leaves the hotel for the day.

Guest arrivals are somewhat slow and staggered, and Lee and Sue start to get bored pretty quickly until a few job applicants walk in and inquire about the help-wanted ad and ask to fill out applications. After accepting several applications and placing them in a pile at the front desk, Lee says to Sue, "Hey, we ought to put a few notes on these people's applications so that ol' Joe knows what he's dealing with when he looks them over in the morning." "Notes like what?" asks Sue. Lee snatches an application from the pile and says, "Well, take this one, for example. This gal was a babe!" Lee grabs a pen and writes on the upper right-hand corner of the application: *Awesome babe! Great bod!* "Oh, fun," giggles Sue, and she grabs an application from the pile. "I remember this woman," she says. "She was older than my mother!" Sue writes on the application: *Don't hire! Old hag!* "Cool," laughs Lee, and the two of them spend the next 30 minutes going through the applications and writing notes for Joe.

When they finish, they step back to admire their handiwork. Every application has a handwritten note on the upper right-hand corner: *Total Geek! Would NOT fit in!; Nice-looking guy, clean-cut! I'd date him!; Too much perfume! Bad dye job!; Don't hire this one! Looked foreign and spoke with a weird accent!; Strange-acting and has some kind of speech impediment!; Pretty lady but had three kids with her!;* and on and on. Finally, they put the applications in Joe's in-basket and return to their shift duties.

QUESTIONS ▶

1. When Joe sees the applications that Lee and Sue have accepted, what do you think his reaction will be? Explain your answer in detail.

2. List and briefly discuss all of the ways in which Lee and Sue's "helpful notes" to Joe could cause legal problems for the Delmar Inn? Be specific and cite examples.

3. If you were Joe would you terminate Lee and Sue or would you choose to administer some other kind of discipline? Explain your answer.

4. What kind of training should the hotel offer its employees to ensure that such activities do not occur again in the future? Be specific and explain your answer in detail.

KEY TERMS ▶

Job description A form that lists a job or a position within a hospitality industry business setting and that details the essential duties associated with that specific job or position.

Title VII of the 1964 Civil Rights Act A federal law that makes it illegal to discriminate against job applicants as well as current employees on the basis of sex, race, color, religion, or national origin.

Equal Employment Opportunity Commission (EEOC) The EEOC is the U.S. government agency charged with overseeing Title VII of the 1964 Civil Rights Act and Title I of the Americans with Disabilities Act.

Bona fide occupational qualification (BFOQ) A legal loophole, or a legal defense, to job discrimination based upon sex, national origin, or religion. There is no BFOQ defense to racial discrimination.

Sexual harassment A form of sex discrimination according to Title VII of the 1964 Civil Rights Act.

Quid pro quo This for that—you give me this, and I'll do that.

Hostile work environment An environment that is hostile can be created when management allows employees to tell off-color jokes, send off-color e-mails, or put up pictures or photos that someone could deem offensive.

Americans with Disabilities Act (ADA) A federal law that makes it illegal to discriminate against a job applicant or a current employee who is disabled.

Disabled individual The ADA describes a disabled individual as "any individual who has a physical or mental impairment that substantially limits one or more major life activity, has a record of such impairment, or is regarded as having such impairment."

Essential functions The primary, essential duties associated with a job position. These would be found on the job description and are important because of the Americans with Disabilities Act.

Reasonable accommodation Under the ADA, an individual who is disabled but otherwise qualified to perform the essential functions of a job may require a reasonable accommodation. This could be a minor adjustment of the individual's work schedule, an adjustment of policy or procedure, or the purchase of a device that would allow the individual to perform the duties of the job.

Readily achievable This term is associated with the ADA and generally refers to the adjustment of a task or a physical adjustment to the facility that is easily accomplished without great difficulty or expense.

Undue hardship A legal defense to the ADA that is generally left up to the interpretation of the courts. It could refer to a financial hardship or a business hardship.

Age Discrimination in Employment Act of 1967 This law prohibits discrimination against individuals who are 40 years of age and older.

Equal Pay Act The law requires businesses to pay equal wages for equal work without regard to the sex of the employee.

Immigration Reform and Control Act of 1986 (IRCA) All workers hired after November 6, 1986, must provide proper documentation and complete the Form I-9 to prove that they have the legal right to work in the United States.

NOTES ▶

1. Herman Cain, "Separate Water Fountains," Opinion Columns, 2004, http://www.herman-cain.com/news/press-opinion-042105.asp.
2. Ralph R Reiland, "Save Millions in Damages, Go Topless," *Restaurant Hospitality,* 81:11 (November 1997), 152-154.
3. EEOC press release, January 8, 2004, www.eeoc.gov/press/1-8-04-b.html.
4. Ibid.
5. *Schultz v. Wheaton Glass Co.,* 421 F. 2d 259 (3d Cir. 1970).

CHAPTER 3

WAGE AND HOUR LAWS AFFECTING SALARIED, HOURLY, AND TIPPED EMPLOYEES

A server who continues to improve himself or herself will qualify for a higher wage. Instead of $50,000 a year, it could be $60,000 a year.[1]

Charlie Trotter, chef/owner, Charlie Trotter's, Chicago

CHAPTER OBJECTIVES

After completing this chapter, you will be able to

- Describe the evolution of local and federal laws with respect to worker's rights, minimum wage, and child labor laws.

- Identify the importance of employee wages and salaries and their role in affecting workplace morale.

- Distinguish between exempt and nonexempt employees and their eligibility for overtime compensation.

- Understand the federal tip credit and tip pooling and their impact on an operation's labor costs.

- Recognize the effect that labor costs have on a hospitality operation's profits.

- Identify what is most important to employees when it comes to job satisfaction.

HRM IN ACTION To say that the hospitality industry is labor-intensive is an understatement. Unlike the manufacturing industry where state-of-the art machines and futuristic robots manufacture and assemble parts, the workflow in a typical restaurant or lodging operation is quite different. It takes a lot of worker bees to prepare, cook, and serve the food, not to mention the need for additional staff to clean up the mess at the end of the night and to put everything away in preparation for business the next day. Hotel beds are not made up daily by machines, and you won't find any robots scrubbing the toilets either.

The hospitality industry has the restaurant and lodging chains to thank for the relatively high levels of technology that we find in use today in modern restaurants and hotels, but even the chains understand that this is an industry driven by people performing tasks that are not always pleasant and for which they are not often well paid.

We learned in earlier chapters that the ability to attract and retain a quality workforce might be the single most important factor in determining the success or failure of a restaurant or a lodging operation. In this chapter, we investigate the importance of employees' wages and salaries and how these factors affect morale in the workplace. In addition, we review important wage and hour laws with which all hospitality managers and supervisors must be familiar. Many of these laws are frequently violated by hospitality organizations.

A BRIEF HISTORY

Your grandparents, and certainly your great-grandparents, probably never heard of such things as **minimum wage, child labor laws,** or workers' rights in general. That's because these concepts were not even invented until 1938—less than 70 years ago! Most of us today take labor laws that protect us from the evils of unregulated industry for granted. In fact, during the course of our nation's history, many workers have fought and often died for rights within the workplace. Figure 3.1 provides a glimpse at some of the events that make up our nation's tumultuous labor history.

During the **Industrial Revolution,** children sometimes as young as seven years of age were often forced to work for 14 hours a day, under conditions that are prohibited for people of any age in the workforce today. The government was under a lot of pressure to control this abuse of labor. The first attempt to establish more control over conditions and wages in the workplace was to determine a minimum wage in the United States. Establishing the first minimum wage came in 1933, when a $0.25-per-hour standard was set as part of the **National Recovery Act,** a law that was designed to promote recovery and

TALES FROM THE FIELD

The waitstaff at Charlie Trotter's Chicago restaurant are highly motivated and well paid. They are not working their tables for tips; however, they work for a regular paycheck in which their annual compensation can range anywhere from $40,000 to $80,000 per year. In addition, staffers also receive health and dental insurance, paid vacations, and a 401(k) plan. The restaurant is closed about three weeks a year, and employees schedule their vacations at that time. Employees can invest up to 15 percent of their salary in the 401(k) program, and Trotter's will match 25 percent of their contributions. Servers are eligible for annual merit-based raises, salary bonuses for exemplary service, and promotion to manager status. The top supervisors can earn about $120,000. Benefits, not to mention a regular wage as opposed to tips, are the exception for front-of-the-house employees in the hospitality industry where the rule of thumb is cash-and-carry.

Reprinted with permission from *Lessons in Service from Charlie Trotter* by Edmund Lawler. Copyright 2001 by Edmund Lawler, Ten Speed Press, Berkeley, CA, www.tenspeed.com.

February 24, 1912
Women and children were beaten by police during a textile strike in Lawrence, Massachusetts.

January 5, 1914
The Ford Motor Company raised its basic wage from $2.40 for a nine-hour day to $5 for an eight-hour day.

September 7, 1916
Federal employees win the right to receive worker's compensation insurance.

June 3, 1918
A federal child labor law, enacted two years earlier, was declared unconstitutional. A new law was enacted February 24, 1919, but this one too was declared unconstitutional on June 2, 1924.

June 25, 1938
The Wages and Hours (later Fair Labor Standards) Act is passed, banning child labor and setting the 40-hour work week. The act went into effect in October 1940 and was upheld in the Supreme Court on February 3, 1941.

June 10, 1963
Congress passes a law mandating equal pay to women.

October 6, 1986
One thousand, and seven hundred female flight attendants won an 18-year lawsuit (which included $37 million in damages) against United Airlines, the company that had fired them for getting married.

Figure 3.1   Highlights in twentieth-century labor history.

Month/Year	Minimum Hourly Wage
October 1938	$0.25
October 1939	$0.30
October 1945	$0.40
January 1950	$0.75
March 1956	$1.00
September 1961	$1.15
September 1963	$1.25
February 1967	$1.40
February 1968	$1.60
May 1974	$2.00
January 1975	$2.10
January 1976	$2.30
January 1978	$2.65
January 1979	$2.90
January 1980	$3.10
January 1981	$3.35
April 1990	$3.80
April 1991	$4.25
October 1996	$4.75
September 1997	$5.15

Table 3.1

History of Federal Minimum Hourly Wage. *(Source: U.S. Department of Labor.)*

reform, encourage collective bargaining for unions, set up maximum work hours and minimum wages, and forbid child labor in industry. However, in 1935 the United States Supreme Court declared the National Recovery Act unconstitutional, and the minimum wage was abolished. It was not until 1938 with the passage of the **Fair Labor Standards Act (FLSA)** that a federal law to set national minimum-wage and maximum-hour standards for workers was firmly in place. Table 3.1 details the history of the federal minimum hourly wage.

The law also placed many limitations on child labor. Some states have no unique child labor laws and, thus, simply adhere to the federal laws. Other states have stricter child labor laws of their own. In some states, almost all jobs are totally prohibited for persons under the age of 16. Currently, the federal minimum wage is $5.15 per hour. During his presidency, Bill Clinton gave states the power to set their minimum wages above the federal level. As of 2004, 12 states had done so, and on November 2 of that year, two additional states (Florida and Nevada) approved increases in statewide referendums. Figure 3.2 provides a comparison of state and federal minimum wage.

Effective January 1, 2006, minimum wage increased in the states of Hawaii and Vermont to $6.75 and $7.25, respectively. Some government entities, such as counties and cities, have set minimum wages that are higher than the state and the federal government as a whole. San Francisco's $8.82-per-hour minimum wage is the highest in the nation. While the San Francisco ordinance covers all workers in any company with more than 10 employees, the vast majority of these local ordinances does not cover all businesses operating within the city or county, but rather, narrowly focus on businesses that sell goods or services to local governments, or receive subsidies from that government. Examples of such subsidies include grants, loans, bond financing, and tax abatements, to name a few. These are called **living wages,** or livable wage ordinances, and their levels reflect the income needed to maintain a family at the poverty level in that area. The stricter law, or the one most favorable to the employee, is the law that must be followed.

January 2005 Comparison of State and Federal Minimum Wage

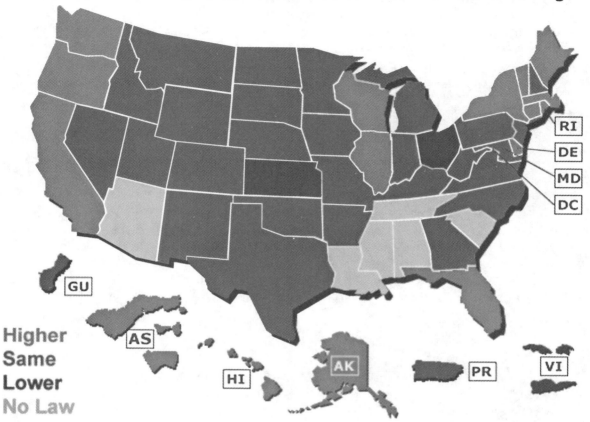

Higher
Same
Lower
No Law

| **Figure 3.2** | Comparison of state and federal minimum wage. *(Source: U.S. Department of Labor, Employment Standards Administration, Wage and Hour Division.)* |

TIP CREDITS AND TIP POOLS

A **tip** is a sum a customer gives as a gift or a **gratuity** in recognition of some service performed. Whether a tip is given, and how much, is determined solely by the customer. The history of leaving a tip or a gratuity is somewhat clouded. Some research suggests that tipping has its roots in the Roman Empire. Other experts claim that the word "tip" was medieval street talk for "hand it over." Regardless of its origins, leaving a tip for a hospitality industry service worker today is commonplace, and one's failure to do so will cer-

- *Restaurants and bars.* Restaurant servers are normally given between 15 and 20 percent of the total bill. Depending on the restaurant, you may also need to tip the sommelier or wine steward 10 to 15 percent. What you also have to remember is that your server tips all of the other servers who assisted them throughout your meal, such as the bushelp, the bartender, and others.

  In bars, 10 to 15 percent is considered average, but you should also take into consideration the complexity of your drink orders.

  At buffets where you serve yourself, you might be tempted to skip the tip, but remember that someone also has to clear your table, refill your drink, and bring you more plates. Ten percent is the usual amount to tip in these restaurants.

- *Hotels.* Gratuities to hotel staff vary from location to location, usually depending on the size of the metropolitan area. Typically, however, you should give bellhops at least $1 for each bag they carry (more if the bags are especially large, heavy, or awkward to carry), and more if they go above and beyond the call of duty to make your stay more pleasant.

  The standard tip for the maid is $1 to $2 per night. This, of course, depends a lot on the mess you make, the price of the room, and the extra services you request. The standard amount for the concierge is $5 to $10 depending on how helpful he or she was. If the concierge suggested and made reservations for you at a great restaurant, then you might tip more. Tips are not usually necessary for the doorman or the desk clerks, unless they do something out of the ordinary that you really appreciate.

- *Airports.* Standard practice is to tip skycaps $1 to $2 per bag for carrying and checking your luggage. The same goes for shuttle drivers if they help you with your bags. If they don't, which often happens, then no tip is necessary.

- *Parking and auto-related.* The usual amount for tipping valets is $1 to $2 per car when you pick the car up. If you ask for special care or for quicker retrieval, then you might also tip when you drop the car off.

Figure 3.3   United States tipping guidelines.

tainly result in a withering cold stare, if not worse. Figure 3.3 provides tipping guidelines in the United States, and Figure 3.4 provides tipping guidelines overseas.

A **service charge** is an amount of money added to the customer's bill by management. Under federal law, because service charges belong to the establishment, they should be considered part of the establishment's gross receipts and must be considered as income to the employer. Service charges may be retained entirely by management or distributed to employees in any amount management chooses. When restaurant management chooses to institute such a charge, customers should be notified in advance, either by a conspicuous notice on the menu or by some other clear and obvious means.

Australia

Keep your change! Except at upscale restaurants—where a 10 percent tip is common. Taxi drivers, hairdressers, and porters do not expect tips.

Brazil

Restaurants will typically add a 10 percent service charge to your bill, in which case it is customary to leave an additional 5 percent for good service. If no service charge is added, you should leave 15 percent for good service.

Britain

For the most part, service charges aren't included in restaurant or hotel bills, and a tip of 12 to 15 percent is expected for good service. In pubs and bars, tips aren't expected. For housekeepers, small change—up to 1 pound per day—is reasonable. Taxi drivers are generally tipped 10 percent, depending on the distance.

Canada

For restaurant staff and taxi drivers, a 15 percent tip is the norm. Porters and bellhops generally receive 1 Canadian dollar per piece of luggage.

France

Almost all restaurants will add a 15 percent service charge to the bill. It is customary to leave an additional 2 to 3 percent—or any remaining small change—for good service. If the service charge is not included in the bill, a 15 percent tip is the norm. Porters and bellhops are generally tipped 1.5 euro per bag. Taxi drivers are usually tipped 10 to 15 percent of the fare.

Germany

Tipping is not a traditional German custom, and overtipping is supposedly frowned upon, although it is doubtful anyone would refuse to take your money. Most hotel and restaurant bills include a service charge, and it is now customary to tip up to an additional 10 percent of the total bill if you receive good service.

Greece

Restaurant bills usually include a service charge of 15 to 20 percent, in addition to a "cover charge" for use of the table. It is also customary to leave the change from your bill (some on the plate for your waiter and some on the table for the busboy).

Italy

In major cities, restaurant bills usually include a 10 to 15 percent service charge. If not, a tip of 10 to 15 percent is appropriate for good service. Hotels will usually add a 15 to 20 percent service charge to your bill. Bellhops or porters are tipped 1.5 to 2.6 euro for carrying your bags to your room.

Japan

Tipping is not customary in Japan, and most service-industry employees do not expect tips. However, restaurants and hotels will usually add a 10 to 20 percent service charge to your bill.

Mexico

Except in resorts, most restaurant bills do not include a service charge. A 10 to 15 percent tip is customary. Porters and bellhops are generally tipped 9 to 10 pesos, while taxi drivers receive 5 to 10 pesos.

Figure 3.4 Overseas tipping guidelines.

Tips, on the other hand, belong to the employee and cannot be used to pay for uniforms or to reimburse management for shortages, breakage, walkouts, or other establishment losses. While a few states prohibit this practice, restaurant employers can pay most employees who receive tips less than the minimum wage by taking a "tip credit." The **tip credit** can be used whether the tips involved are received directly from customers or are received indirectly through a **tip pool** or sharing system. By using tip credits and tip pooling arrangements, a restaurant can obtain steep cuts in labor costs. For example, payroll outlays for minimum-wage servers drop from $5.15 an hour to $2.13 an hour. To obtain this $3.02 per hour in labor cost savings, however, the restaurant must adhere to strict notice and administrative requirements. It is important to note, however, that some states prohibit employers taking a tip credit against minimum wage. The prudent hospitality manager will always consult with a local labor attorney to ensure that the establishment is in full compliance with local and state laws. This information can normally be obtained from a specific state's department of labor.

Regular Tips   For purposes of the tip credit, an eligible employee is one who is in an occupation that regularly and customarily receives $30 or more per month in tips, and the employee actually receives that amount. In the restaurant and lodging industry, food and beverage servers and bartenders are obviously in this category. Other positions, such as food runners and hosts or bellhops and housekeepers are not always regularly and customarily tipped.

Tip Retention   For the tip credit to apply, an employee must be able to retain all of his or her tips, aside from any portion placed into a tip pool. Thus, if the restaurant uses a system in which the house takes a cut of an employee's tips, using the tip credit is not an option.

Slow Shifts   To prevent an employee's total compensation from falling below the minimum wage, the restaurant must have a system for monitoring employee tips and compensating employees when business is slow or whenever tips are not at least equal to the tip credit. If the restaurant takes the full $3.02-per-hour tip credit, covered employees must each receive at least $3.02 per hour in tips. If they don't, the restaurant has to make up the difference.

Advance Notice   Finally, an employer seeking to take a tip credit must provide advance notice to the affected employees. Some restaurant employers rely on a posting in the break area or on the employee bulletin board, but a better practice is to use a notice system that creates a written record that the notice has been received and read. This can be either a written receipt for the **employee handbook** (which itself contains a tip credit notice) or a stand-alone tip credit notice that contains an employee acknowledgment to sign and date. In either case, a copy of the record should be maintained by restaurant management.

Tip Pools   The tip credit can be expanded beyond the core of servers and bartenders through the use of a tip pool. When employees who receive tips contribute a portion of their tips to other employees, this is considered a tip pool. When a tip pool is purely voluntary in the sense that it is not the result of management involvement or coercion, the employees are free to share their tips with any other employees, such as the back-of-the-house staff. If, however, management requires employees to contribute to the tip pool or is involved in the collection of contributions, then the tip pool is deemed mandatory and will be legal only if the sharing is limited to certain employees. Mandatory tip pools can include only employees who are in positions that are regularly and customarily tipped. Back-of-the-house staff, such as cooks, dishwashers, and managers, is generally ineligible because these workers are not regularly and customarily tipped. Keep in mind that penalties can be severe. The consequences of ignoring this restriction may result with the employer losing both the tip pool program and the tip credits. When this occurs, back-pay awards are distributed to each employee for the full amount taken as a tip credit. Nevertheless, the risks associated with a mandatory tip pool are generally outweighed by the benefits of making the tip credit apply to more employees. For example, a bus person typically does not have enough customer contact in most restaurant settings to receive a separate tip directly from the customer. Rather, direct tips generally go to the servers and bartenders. As a result, the bus person's direct tips are almost never enough to cover the $3.02-per-hour tip credit, making it impossible to take the credit for that position. By redistributing customer tips from highly tipped positions, however, a tip pool provides the bus person with sufficient indirect tips to allow the employer to take the full tip credit. When a tip pool is instituted, the bus person's hourly labor costs drop substantially from $5.15 per hour to $2.13 per hour. Food and beverage service employees employed by hotels might also participate in a tip pool. Lodging positions such as bell staff and housekeepers, which are not customarily tipped, would most likely not. It is important to note that some state wage and hour laws may prohibit mandatory tip pools enacted by management, so the prudent hospitality manager would consult a local labor law attorney before implementing such a plan.

ethical dilemma

Dale was recently hired as a kitchen manager in a restaurant that is part of a large national chain. Management generally frowns on paying overtime, and, consequently, the kitchen staff must work quickly and efficiently to get out on time so that no one goes beyond his or her prescribed work schedule. Dale has noticed that on certain nights when the sous chef, who is on salary, is closing, he asks certain workers to clock out, yet remain for the 30 or 40 minutes required to complete the kitchen's closing procedures. Dale later learns that to "compensate" the employees who have remained while off the clock, the sous chef awards them with a six pack of beer he has taken from the bar. Dale is reluctant to mention this practice to higher management or even to the sous chef, realizing that the practice is an effective way—albeit an unusual one—to control overtime and that a six pack of beer is much less costly to the organization than would be average kitchen wages paid at time-and-a-half. Which of the *10 Ethical Principles for Hospitality Managers* is being violated? Should Dale end the practice or allow it to continue? How will Dale's decision affect his position with the organization? How will his decision affect his relationship with the sous chef and the hourly workers in the kitchen?

Overtime   Once a mandatory tip pool has been set up and the restaurant is ready to take a tip credit for all eligible staff members, there is the problem of calculating **overtime**. For purposes of determining the regular wage rate for a tipped employee, management simply adds the tip credit back into the hourly wage actually paid to the employee. For the bus person, the correct hourly wage rate for overtime purposes is $2.13 per hour plus the tip credit of $3.02 per hour, for a total of $5.15 per hour. Thus, **time-and-a-half** (the overtime wage rate) for the busperson would be about $7.73 per hour.

Of course, this does not mean the restaurant will actually be paying the bus person $7.73 per hour for each hour worked over 40. The restaurant still will get to take the $3.02-per-hour tip credit (assuming the bus person makes enough in tips) for each overtime hour. This will lower the effective hourly overtime wage to $4.71 per hour.

Despite having to strictly comply with another set of regulations, a properly administered payroll system using both tip credits and tip pools, when permitted under state law, can dramatically lower labor costs. Given the ever-growing pressure to scrutinize margins in the restaurant industry, these are savings management cannot afford to overlook.

As pointed out earlier, the Fair Labor Standards Act (FLSA) provides that when any state law or municipal ordinance establishes a minimum wage higher than the federal minimum wage, the law that benefits and is most favorable to the employee must be followed. The same principle applies to the tip credit. Some states have laws that prohibit employers from taking a tip credit or that limit the tip credit to an amount less than that authorized by the FLSA. Figure 3.5 provides IRS contact information.

Call the IRS hotline at (800) TAX-FORM, or visit www.irs.gov for copies of any of the following:

- IRS Form 4070A, Employee's Daily Record of Tips. Helps employees keep track of daily tips.

- IRS Form 4070, Employee's Report of Tips to Employer. Employees can use this form to report tips to employers once per month.

- IRS Form 8027, Employer's Annual Information Return of Tip Income and Allocated Tips. Filed annually by large food and beverage establishments.

- IRS Publication 531, Reporting Income from Tips. Explains reporting laws to tip earners.

The National Restaurant Association also offers materials to help restaurant owners and managers explain the do's and don'ts of tip reporting to employees. Call the association at (800) 424-5156 for more information, or visit www.restaurant.org.

Figure 3.5 Federal tax reporting documents for tip earners. *(Source: Internal Revenue Service; National Restaurant Association.)*

CHANGES IN OVERTIME LAW

As noted earlier, the FLSA contains provisions that determine overtime pay as well as the proper classifications of an employee as either **exempt** or **nonexempt.** In August 2004, these rules were changed for the first time in more than 50 years. An exempt employee is one who is not eligible to receive overtime. Employees who are classified as nonexempt must be paid a minimum of one and one-half times their normal rate of pay for each hour worked over 40 during a normal work week.

As you might expect, there has been a lot of controversy regarding these changes. Some felt that the new law would eliminate the overtime pay that many workers were accustomed to receiving. Others believed that unscrupulous

Photo 3.1   The restaurant's salaried general manager in the center would be classified as exempt and ineligible to receive overtime pay, whereas the waiters would be classified as non-exempt and would be eligible for overtime pay.

business owners would "reclassify" nonexempt positions as exempt, forcing those workers to put in more hours for less pay. Nearly one year later after the dust had settled, many human resources professionals said that with a few minor exceptions, things had not changed that much at all. Some businesses have acknowledged that they have reclassified a few positions as nonexempt, but many more businesses claim that they have now converted nominally exempt employees to nonexempt, entitling those employees to time-and-a-half pay for hours worked over 40 per week.

Any small-business owner with gross annual revenues over $500,000 must comply with the Department of Labor's new overtime rules. Failure to comply with these new regulations could result in the business owner being charged with the willful violation of the act. The penalties for such a charge can be severe; the statute of limitations is three years, and the monetary damages awarded to the employee double.

THE NEW RULES

Almost all employees who make less than $455 a week ($23,660 a year) are eligible for overtime. The old rule set overtime for anyone who made less than $250 a week. The new rule applies whether the employee is blue-collar or white-collar, or whether he or she supervises people. The exceptions to this rule are teachers, doctors, and lawyers. They do not get overtime, no matter what they are paid. Employees who earn between $23,660 and $100,000 a year and who are in most executive, professional, or administrative positions are not eligible for overtime. Managers are not entitled to overtime if they oversee two or more people and have the authority to hire, fire, or recommend that someone be hired or fired. Administrative employees who have decision-making power and run some sort of operation are also not eligible for overtime pay.

The new federal overtime regulations require that each of the following three tests be met for an employee to qualify as exempt from federal overtime pay requirements:

- Test 1—Salary-Basis Test. Is the employee paid on a salary basis? The employee must receive a predetermined and fixed minimum salary that is not subject to reduction because of variations in the quality or quantity of work performed.

- Test 2—Salary-Level Test. Executive, administrative, and professional employees must earn a minimum weekly salary of $455 ($23,660 per year) to be considered exempt from federal overtime requirements.

- Test 3—Duties Test. What are the employee's duties? To be exempt, white-collar employees must perform a job that primarily involves executive, administrative, or professional duties.

EXECUTIVE (MANAGERIAL) EXEMPTION

In the hospitality industry, many managers and even some supervisors would be exempt because they fall under the executive or managerial exemption. Figure 3.6 provides an overview of the duties test as it applies to the executive or managerial exemption from federal overtime requirements.

In many hospitality operations, managers, assistant managers, and even some supervisors perform not only exempt duties, such as scheduling employees, managing inventory, and authorizing bill payment, but they may also perform nonexempt duties, such as helping out in the kitchen, manning the cash register, or checking in guests at the front desk. Does performing nonexempt duties such as

DUTIES TEST

An employee is considered an exempt executive if

1. The employee's *primary* duty is management of the enterprise of which the employee is employed or of a *customarily recognized department or subdivision thereof.*
2. The employee customarily and regularly directs the work of two or more other employees.
3. The employee has the authority to hire or fire other employees, or his or her suggestions and recommendations as to the promotion, hiring, advancement, or any other change in status of employees are given *particular weight.*

Figure 3.6	Executive exemption duties test. *(Source: U.S. Department of Labor, Employment Standards Administration, Wage and Hour Division, Fact Sheet #17A.)*

these mean that the manager should be paid overtime? The Department of Labor says that in order to be exempt, managerial employees should not spend more than 50 percent of their time at work performing nonexempt duties.

ADMINISTRATIVE EXEMPTION

The second major exemption from federal overtime rules is for certain administrative employees. The new rules make only modest changes to the old rules in this area. In general, the rules require that exempt administrative employees have a primary duty of performing office or nonmanual work directly related to the management or general business operations of the employer. The new regulations also require that exempt administrative professionals exercise "discretion and independent judgment."

PROFESSIONAL EXEMPTION

Professionals—including both **learned professionals** and **creative professionals**—might be exempt from federal overtime pay requirements if they meet certain duties tests and pass the salary-basis and salary-level tests. For example, the new rules provide two new ways that a chef might be classified as exempt:

1. Chefs, such as executive chefs or sous chefs, who have obtained a four-year academic degree in a culinary arts program generally meet the du-

ties requirement for the "learned professional" exemption. This exemption would not be available to cooks who perform mostly routine mental, manual, mechanical, or physical work.

2. A chef who is considered a "creative professional" could be exempt from federal overtime requirements, but the Department of Labor notes that there is a "wide variation in duties of chefs, and the 'creative professional' exemption must be applied on a case by case basis with a particular focus on the creative duties and abilities of the particular chef at issue." Most likely, this exemption would extend only to truly "original" chefs, such as those who work at five-star or gourmet establishments, whose primary duty requires "invention," "imagination," "originality," and "talent."

It is important to remember that many states have their own overtime regulations that may or may not exactly coincide with those of the federal government. The prudent business operator will always seek the legal advice of informed counsel before entering the murky waters of state and federal employment law.

LABOR COSTS, PROFITS, AND EMPLOYEE MORALE

Aside from the hospitality industry, there are very few other industries in which labor costs, profits, and employee morale are so closely related. Most employees want to engage in meaningful work, and, of course, everyone wants to be fairly compensated. Owners and managers must always keep a keen eye on the operation's bottom line, balancing the need to earn a fair return on investment with their employees' needs for adequate wages, salaries, and benefits. Many hospitality operations do not manage this tightwire act very well, and they consequently go out of business. Plenty of others, however, manage quite nicely and, as a result, become very successful.

In most full-service restaurants today, the cost of labor is the single largest cost. In some establishments, the combined costs of salaries, wages, and employee benefits can be anywhere from 38 to 42 percent of sales. This means that for every one dollar that a customer brings through the front door, 38 to 42 cents of that dollar must go to pay wages, salaries, and fringe benefits. Owners and managers who strive to have profitable operations must manage labor costs very closely, ensuring that the ratio between labor costs and sales revenue stays within acceptable boundaries. However, what is acceptable to one operation versus another operation will largely depend upon the type of operation, as well as on the target market to which the operation primarily caters.

When so much emphasis is being put on labor costs these days, it would be fair to assume that most managers, owners, and even the employees themselves must rank wages and salaries very high on their list of matters of importance.

From the list below, please identify the single most important challenge facing your business today.

1. Gas and energy prices
2. Food costs
3. Building and maintaining sales volume
4. Competition
5. Labor costs
6. Recruiting and retaining employees
7. Insurance costs
8. Operating costs
9. Economy
10. Other

Figure 3.7   Challenges most likely to keep restaurant operators awake at night. *(Source: National Restaurant Association.)*

Interestingly enough, however, they do not! A recent National Restaurant Association "Industry Tracking Survey" asked restaurant operators to rank 10 challenges. These challenges are listed in Figure 3.7 in no special order. Take a moment to review these. How do you think these challenges stacked up in order of importance?

If you guessed that "labor costs" was the single most important challenge, you're probably with the majority of your fellow students. However, though most people probably would not have guessed "recruiting and retaining employees," the majority of respondents in this survey cite this as the challenge that "keeps them up at night."[2]

When asked, most employees will not cite "wages and salaries" as their number one job satisfier. In fact, most employees will tell you that "meaningful work" or a feeling of "being in on things" is what matters most to them when it comes to job satisfaction. It is important for managers to keep in mind that the wages and salaries that they choose to pay their employees will mostly be dictated by certain laws as well as by market conditions. That being said, their control over these things is relatively minimal, and that's good news for managers. If managers asked their employees what is most important to them as a job satisfier, employees would likely *not* rank salaries and wages very high on this list, noting instead such things as leadership styles, management styles, and other nonwage-related working conditions—all things that managers have complete control over. They have the ability to foster job satisfaction among their employees.

SUMMARY

- The hospitality industry is extremely labor intensive, and it requires a lot of workers to produce the quality products and services that more sophisticated travelers and diners have come to expect.
- Today's labor force is protected by a myriad of federal, state, and local laws with respect to minimum rates of pay, child labor law issues, exempt and nonexempt employee classifications, and overtime rates of pay for all hours worked over 40 in one workweek.
- Restaurants may legally pay tipped employees $2.13 per hour and may take a $3.02 tip credit. This payment method is legal but requires close attention to payroll matters and proper documentation in order to avoid running afoul of the law.
- While it stands to reason that most employees want to receive fair wages for a fair day's work, most would not rank wages as their number one job satisfier; rather, most employees see open communication between employees and management as well as a feeling that their work matters to the overall operation as being more important job satisfiers.

PRACTICE QUIZ

1. Restaurant and lodging chains have been quicker than independently owned and operated hospitality operations to adopt new technologies in the workplace.

   A. True   B. False

2. Minimum wage, child labor laws, and workers' rights in general have been in place in the United States since the mid-1800s.

   A. True   B. False

3. With regard to federal minimum wage, in which a state law is in conflict with the federal guidelines, the federal guidelines must *always* take precedent.

   A. True   B. False

4. The federal law that sets minimum-wage and overtime pay guidelines is the Fair Labor Standards Act (FLSA).

   A. True   B. False

5. The custom of requiring employees to "pool" or share their tips is illegal, and management should avoid this practice at all times.

   A. True   B. False

6. A service charge is

A. The same as a tip given to an employee by a customer and it belongs to the employee.

B. The same as a *gratuity*.

C. An amount of money added to the customer's bill by management and it belongs to management.

D. None of the above.

7. An employee who is classified as exempt

A. is not allowed to work overtime.

B. does not have to be paid time-and-a-half for overtime.

C. must be paid time-and-a-half for overtime.

D. None of the above.

8. An employee who is classified as nonexempt

A. Is not allowed to work overtime.

B. Does not have to be paid time-and-a-half for overtime.

C. Must be paid time-and-a-half for overtime.

D. None of the above.

9. Almost all employees who make less than $_____ per week are eligible for overtime.

A. 250.00

B. 325.00

C. 455.00

D. 635.00

10. Which of the following is *not* one of the tests required by the federal government when determining whether an employee is exempt from federal overtime pay requirements?

A. Salary-Basis Test

B. Wage and Hour Test

C. Salary-Level Test

D. Duties Test

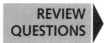
REVIEW QUESTIONS

1. Interview the manager of a local hospitality business to determine whether the operation utilizes a tip pool. Is it mandatory and required by management, or is it a system put into place voluntarily by the employees? If mandatory, how does management determine the best way to distribute the tips in the pool? If voluntary, how do the employees choose to distribute their tips? What are the benefits to management if it decides to implement a mandatory tip pool? What are the benefits to the employees who decide to voluntarily participate in a tip pool? Be prepared to share your findings with the rest of the class.

2. As the manager of a small lodging operation, you have decided to implement a mandatory tip pool policy in the bar and the restaurant of your operation. Your reason for doing this is to lower labor costs by taking a $3.02- per-hour tip credit for each individual in the pool. Write the new policy and be sure to clarify which employees will be required to participate. Explain your policy in detail.

3. You manage a local restaurant where the minimum hourly wage for tipped employees is $2.13 per hour. Overtime is calculated at 1.5 times the regular rate of pay for each hour worked over 40 in a workweek. You are allowed a $3.02-per-hour tip credit for each tipped employee. You are calculating payroll for Suzie, your bus person, who worked 47 hours last week. What will Suzie's gross pay (before taxes and other required withholding) be for the 47 hours that she worked? Be sure to show your calculations as backup for how you arrived at your answer.

4. Many consumers complain that hotels and restaurants should pay *all* of their employees a decent wage and that the practice of expecting customers to leave a 15 to 20 percent tip should be abolished. Do you agree or disagree? Why or why not? Explain your answer in detail.

5. The sous chef in your hotel has been paid an hourly wage of $14.50 per hour since she was hired two years ago. You would now like to make this a salaried, exempt position. You will expect the sous chef to work 50 hours per week, and she will no longer be eligible for overtime. Would you be able to apply the professional exemption to this position? Why or why not? What other information would you need to determine before you take this action? Explain in detail.

HANDS-ON HRM ▶

For the past three years, Mona has been a general manager at Duke's Restaurant, which belongs to a large, well-known chain that has more than 1,000 units nationwide. Lately, Mona and some of the other general managers in her region have begun to complain to the district manager about the method in which the company classifies exempt and nonexempt employees. Specifically, they feel that even though they are paid fixed salaries, they should be paid overtime, because the company requires each of them to log approximately 60 hours per week.

The managers complain that Duke's routinely requires them to spend most of their time at work doing chores such as washing dishes, sweeping floors, picking up litter in the parking lots, cooking food, and serving food to customers. They also claim that during the small amount of time that they are actually allowed to "manage," they are given little discretion and make few genuine management decisions.

The district manager, while empathetic to their concerns, explains that this has been Duke's policy for years and that the only way to advance to the position of district manager is to "follow the rules, run a tight ship, and not stir up trouble within the ranks." After months of frustration, the managers decide to pool their resources and hire a labor lawyer to help them determine whether they have a case. During their first meeting with the attorney, Mona says, "Our titles are impressive, but what we really do for the majority of each work day is serve meals, cook food, wash dishes, and clean up our restaurants." "They only pay us $24,000 a year," another manager adds. "I barely make $7.50 an hour when you add it all up."

After careful consideration, the attorney tells them that he does believe that they have a case. He explains that based upon what they have told him, Duke's may be in violation of the Fair Labor Standards Act. He advises them to continue with their duties as they normally would, and that he will get back in touch with them as soon as he has had a chance to consult with his senior partners in the law firm.

As Mona and the other managers return to their normal routines, they each are somewhat relieved that they have finally found someone who seems to take their concerns seriously. While they don't want to hurt their company, they do feel that if Duke's has in fact been breaking the law, then the company should "make things right" with their restaurant managers. A few weeks after meeting with the labor lawyer, Mona and the other managers involved detect a definite difference in the way the district manager has been interacting with each of them. He has visited their stores more often than usual, and during those visits, he has seemed abrupt and more businesslike than normal. They are each shocked as the week comes to an end and the district manager pays them another visit; this time he is accompanied by the company's director of human resources who hands each general manager a termination letter that immediately severs their employment with the company.

QUESTIONS ▶

1. Is Duke's in violation of the Fair Labor Standards Act with respect to the way the company classifies exempt and nonexempt employees? What other information might you require in order to make this determination? Why?

2. Even though the labor attorney had not yet filed a lawsuit with the courts, was it wise of the company to terminate each of the general managers? Why or why not?

3. If the general managers win their lawsuit against the Duke's Restaurant chain, what could be the outcome for the chain? For the general managers?

4. What policies or procedures should a restaurant follow when determining the overtime classification status of its general manager?

Minimum wage The current federal minimum wage is $5.15 per hour.

Child labor laws Federal, state, and local laws that set minimum-age requirements as well as other requirements for employees under the age of 18.

Industrial Revolution Refers to the time period of roughly late-eighteenth to early-nineteenth century, which saw many social and economic changes due to a shift from an economy based primarily on manual labor to one based on industry and manufacturing.

National Recovery Act A law designed to promote recovery and reform, encourage collective bargaining for unions, set up maximum work hours and minimum wages, and forbid child labor in industry.

Fair Labor Standards Act (FLSA) Federal legislation passed in 1938 that governs overtime laws, child labor laws, and other labor-related issues.

Living wage Also referred to as livable wage ordinances. It is similar to minimum-wage laws set by state and federal government; these ordinances carry the same weight but normally are enacted by cities and other municipalities.

Tip A sum of money given to a service employee by a guest in recognition of good service.

Gratuity A sum of money given to an employee by a guest in recognition of good or quality service. Term is interchangeable with tip.

Service charge A fee set by management that is normally kept for the house and not given to the employees in the form of a tip or gratuity.

Tip credit Currently the difference between $2.13 an hour and the federal minimum wage, which is currently $5.15 per hour. Tipped employees are paid $2.13 per hour, and the employee takes the remaining $3.02 per hour as a tip credit against the $5.15-per-hour minimum wage.

Tip pool When tipped employees share a portion of their tips with other front-of-house employees such as bus help.

Employee handbook A book that provides workplace rules, regulations, and guidelines that employees must follow.

Overtime Nonexempt employees must be paid at a rate of one-and-one-half their normal rate of pay for each hour worked over 40 in one week.

Time-and-a-half The rate at which a nonexempt employee must be paid for each hour worked over 40 in one week.

Exempt employee These employees do not have to be paid overtime for hours worked beyond 40 in any given week.

Nonexempt employee Employees who are classified as nonexempt must be paid time-and-a-half their normal rate of pay for each hour worked over 40 in one week.

Learned professional Based on certain Department of Labor guidelines, employees who meet these requirements could be exempt from federal overtime laws.

Creative professional Based on certain Department of Labor guidelines, employees who meet these requirements could be exempt from federal overtime laws.

NOTES ▶

1. Reprinted with permission from *Lessons in Service from Charlie Trotter* by Edmund Lawler. Copyright 2001 by Edmund Lawler, Ten Speed Press, Berkley, CA, www.tenspeed.com.
2. "Restaurant Industry Operations Report," Washington, D.C.: National Restaurant Association, 2004.

4

COMMON LAW, NEGLIGENT HIRING, AND EMPLOYEE RIGHTS

Scrutinize employee applications and do not hire on the spot. Make them come in for a second interview, which creates an aura of privilege to work there—as it should be. Check references. Ask for written references, if possible.[1]

Maren L. Hickton, Maren Incorporated, Pittsburgh, Pennsylvania

CHAPTER OBJECTIVES

After completing this chapter, you will be able to

■ Recognize the importance of prescreening job applicants and the negative consequences that may occur if this phase of the hiring process is not completed.

■ Understand the concepts of negligence, liability, and reasonable care.

■ Define common law and apply it to the employment relationship.

■ Define at-will employment.

■ Understand the rights of individuals in the workplace.

■ Identify the various circumstances that provide an employee with the grounds for filing a suit against his or her employer.

HRM IN ACTION — Hotels and restaurants are increasingly diligent about screening job applicants before giving them access to customers' credit card numbers, handing them pass keys and allowing them to transport luggage to guest rooms, and sending them to customers' homes to deliver hot pizzas and other home delivery items. According to a recent article in *Hospitality News,* "9.6 percent of job applicants have some kind of criminal record."[2] While criminal background checks as well as preemployment drug screenings are becoming the norm for large hotel and restaurant companies, smaller operations are slower to jump on the bandwagon, most likely due to the associated cost and the amount of time required to properly prescreen all job applicants. Unfortunately, cutting corners when prescreening potential employees can be extremely detrimental to small hospitality business owners. Consider the following:

- A restaurant manager raped his 16-year-old female coworker. He had a history of sexual abuse, but his employer chose not to do a background check. Judgment against the restaurant: $6.5 million.[3]
- A hospital employee murdered a coworker. He had two previous convictions for assault. Judgment against the hospital: $864,000 (National Institute for the Prevention of Workplace Violence).[4]

It is essential that managers and supervisors understand the potential liability of hiring a bad apple. Clearly, both the time and dollar investment necessary to conduct routine background checks on potential employees is minimal in comparison to the potential financial loss that could ensue if a staff employee commits unlawful acts.

COMMON LAW AND ITS IMPACT ON THE WORKPLACE

You may be somewhat familiar with the concept of **common law,** or perhaps you have heard the terms "common-law marriage" or "common-law spouse." Common law is the traditional, unwritten law of England and has been around for centuries. It is primarily based on custom and usage, and it evolved over a thousand years before the founding of the United States. Today, almost all common law has been enacted into various statutes by all states with the exception of Louisiana, which is still influenced by the Napoleonic Code. This makes sense when you consider that the state of Louisiana was not founded by the British but by French and Spanish settlers.

The common law, as applied in civil cases, was devised as a means of compensating someone for wrongful acts known as **torts,** including both intentional torts and those torts caused by **negligence.** In the common law, a tort is a civil wrongdoing for which the law provides a remedy. Loosely defined, negligence is doing (or not doing) what a sane, reasonable person would (or would not)

TALES FROM THE FIELD

My wife and I had a pizza delivered from a well-known national chain. It was about 11 in the evening, and a few moments after the driver had delivered our pizza, there was banging and yelling at our front door. I went to the door, and there stood the driver, all bloodied, telling a story about how he had just been mugged on the way back to his car that was parked at the curb. We let him in and called his store as well as the police. We later learned that the driver routinely carried a loaded pistol in his pocket while making deliveries, and during the attack, he was able to get the pistol out and get off a wild shot that zinged into the tree branches before the mugger disarmed him and ran away with the pistol. The police located the driver's gun in our neighbor's yard the next morning, and the driver was terminated for carrying a loaded firearm on the job.

Ken, 58, Louisville, Kentucky

Photo 4.1

Placing a warning sign on a recently mopped restaurant floor is an example of providing "reasonable care."

do under like or similar circumstances. If a restaurant employee spills a beverage on the dining room floor and fails to properly clean it up and a customer subsequently slips and falls, the restaurant could be held liable for the customer's harm and injuries. In this simple example, the law holds that a "reasonable person" could easily **foresee** a slip and fall accident and should, therefore, know to take the actions necessary to ensure safety by protecting the area and quickly cleaning up the spill to prevent an accident.

In most jurisdictions, it is necessary to initially demonstrate that a person had a legal duty to exercise care in a given situation, that he or she breached that duty, and that his or her negligence or breach was the **proximate cause** for the harm or injury. It is important to remember, however, that *all* innkeepers, restaurant and bar owners, and managers have a legal duty under common law to provide reasonable care to protect guests, customers, and their own employees from harm or injury. It is also important to note that owners and managers do not need to insure their guests' and customers' safety; rather, they are obligated to prevent foreseeable acts from occurring. In other words, the law does not expect us to protect people from acts that are not foreseeable.

McDonald's Coffee Too Hot?

In the infamous McDonald's hot coffee lawsuit in which the 81-year-old plaintiff was initially awarded $2.7 million (later reduced on appeal to $480,000), the McDonald's Corporation primarily lost the case on the issue of foreseeability. Figure 4.1 details some important elements of this 1994 case.[5]

As the McDonald's coffee lawsuit illustrates, it is clear that in spite of its aging demeanor, the common law still has teeth. While the purpose of this book is not to inform you about the legal relationship you will have with your guests and customers, it is important to recognize and understand the legal implications that common law will have on your relationship with your employees.

The facts of the case, which caused a jury of six men and six women to find McDonald's coffee was unreasonably dangerous, are as follows:

1. For years, McDonald's had known there was a problem with its coffee— the coffee was served much hotter (at least 20 degrees more so) than at other restaurants.

2. McDonald's knew its coffee sometimes caused serious injuries—more than 700 incidents of scalding coffee burns in the past decade have been settled by the corporation—and yet the company never consulted a burn expert regarding the issue.

3. The woman involved in this infamous case suffered very serious injuries—third-degree burns on her groin, thighs, and buttocks that required skin grafts and a seven-day hospital stay.

4. The woman, an 81-year-old former department store clerk who had never before filed a suit against anyone, said she wouldn't have brought the lawsuit against McDonald's had the corporation not dismissed her request for compensation of her medical bills.

5. A McDonald's quality assurance manager testified in the case that the corporation was aware of the risk of serving dangerously hot coffee and had no plans to either turn down the heat or to post warning about the possibility of severe burns, even though most customers wouldn't think it was possible.

6. After careful deliberation, the jury found that McDonald's was liable because the facts were overwhelmingly against the company. When it came to the punitive damages, the jury found that McDonald's had engaged in willful, reckless, malicious, or wanton conduct and rendered a punitive damage award of $2.7 million dollars. *(The equivalent of just two days of coffee sales, McDonald's Corporation generates revenues in excess of 1.3 million dollars daily from the sale of its coffee, selling 1 billion cups each year.)*

Figure 4.1 A summary of facts in the McDonald's coffee-burn case.*(Source: Liebeck v. McDonald's Restaurants, No. CV-93-02419, 1995, N.M. Dist. August 18, 1994.)*

EMPLOYEE RIGHTS UNDER COMMON LAW

Hotel and restaurant owners and managers have a legal duty under common law to exercise reasonable care in the practice of supervising the activities of others. Some of the potential legal pitfalls that may occur as a result of management's failure to do so include lawsuits based on the following:

- Wrongful discharge
- Constructive discharge
- Assault and battery
- Intentional infliction of emotional distress
- False imprisonment
- Defamation by libel or slander
- Invasion of privacy
- Negligent hiring
- Negligent retention

WRONGFUL DISCHARGE

Most U.S. employees can generally be categorized as at-will employees. An **at-will employee** can be terminated at any time, for any reason or no reason at all, and the courts will generally not intervene to protect the ex-employee from allegedly unfair treatment by the employer. At-will employees may also leave their jobs at any time and for any reason. However, things are not always as simple as they seem. Most employees of the U.S. federal government are not at-will employees but can be demoted or fired in an effort to promote the efficiency of the service. Similarly, most employees of state governments are not at-will employees. On the contrary, most members of labor unions are covered by a written contract called a **collective bargaining agreement,** which contains a clause specifying that their employment can be terminated only for just cause. While in most states the employment laws continue to respect the spirit of at-will employment, there are a number of exceptions that have evolved over time. For instance, if you are operating in an at-will state, it does not necessarily mean that you can fire your at-will employees for no reason at all. State and federal laws regulate terminations. For example, Title VII of the 1964 Civil Rights Act states that it is illegal to fire an employee due to his or her race, gender, ethnicity, color, or religion. If you terminate an employee for an illegal reason, you are liable under state and federal laws, even if you are in an at-will state. In addition, even if you are in an at-will state, you should still have a justifiable, nondiscriminatory business reason for any discharge. Why? Because if an employee submits a claim for a **wrongful discharge** based on one of the many statutes or legal theories available, the employer is normally required to state a legitimate reason for the discharge. While it's not illegal to fire someone for no reason in at-will states, it is not smart. An employer should always have a legally defensible reason for any discharge. Figure 4.2 provides additional exceptions to at-will employment.

Many state courts have recognized two basic exceptions to the employment at-will rule, as follows:

1. An employer may not terminate an employee at will if the termination would violate public policy.
2. An employer may not terminate an employee at will in which there is an implied contract between the employer and employee.

Public Policy Exception

A majority of the states have adopted the public policy exception to the employment at-will rule. This exception is based on the theory that employees should not be fired for reasons that violate public policy. For example, an employee fired as retaliation for opposing an employer's illegal activities, reporting fire or other safety hazards, or for other kinds of "whistle-blowing activities" may be an illegal termination.

Implied Contract Exception

Employers are usually careful not to state or imply that there is any contract of employment for an individual employee. When an express-employment contract does not exist and the employee is terminated, courts will often infer contractual obligations from the circumstances between a particular employer and employee. In many states, the contractual obligations have been found in an employer's oral or written assurances that employees would only be discharged for cause. Courts often have inferred these promises from an employer's words and actions. For example, a contractual promise has been inferred when statements like these were made by the employer:

"You will be employed as long as your performance is satisfactory."

"You will be terminated unless your performance improves."

It is always best to have a legitimate reason for discharge, but do not attempt to create one if it does not exist. Make sure that the reasons for discharge are legal.

Figure 4.2 Exceptions to the employment at-will rule.

ethical dilemma

Emma is the housekeeping manager of a popular inn located in New England. Lisa, one of the inn's long-time room attendants, has been calling in sick a lot lately, and when Lisa is at work, her mood seems angry; she often has to be sent back to re-clean parts of her rooms. Emma calls Lisa in for a private consultation, and she learns that Lisa was recently diagnosed with HIV. Lisa asks Emma to keep the information confidential, and Emma promises that she will, even though she feels that she needs to advise the inn's general manager, Mrs. Fee. After thinking about the situation for a few days, Emma decides to tell Mrs. Fee about Lisa's diagnosis. After hearing the news, Mrs. Fee seems more concerned with the inn's reputation than she does with Lisa's HIV status. She tells Emma to "keep a close eye on Lisa," and if her attendance does not improve, she should "write Lisa up and then let her go." Which of the *10 Ethical Principles for Hospitality Managers* has been violated? Was it necessary for Emma to inform Mrs. Fee about Lisa's HIV status? What should Emma do if Mrs. Fee forces her to terminate Lisa?

CONSTRUCTIVE DISCHARGE

Constructive discharge often occurs in harassment and discrimination cases. An employee can sue on the basis of constructive discharge if he or she is forced to resign to escape intolerable work conditions. In these situations, the employee is not actually fired, but rather the employee quits his or her job, usually as a result of unbearable treatment in the workplace by managers, supervisors, or coworkers. While the law of constructive discharge is complex and varies depending on the jurisdiction of the employer, these suits often occur when one or more of the following workplace conditions exists:

- Intolerable hostility toward an employee
- Intolerable employment discrimination
- Sexual harassment
- Retaliation for reporting a wrongdoing or for whistle blowing
- The humiliating demotion of an employee

Some managers use these techniques to rid their workplace of unwanted employees, rather than take the time to properly and fully document legitimate reasons for terminating an employee.

Physical contact such as touching or brushing up against an employee or even an intent of physical contact such as blocking a pathway or standing in forced close proximity could result in **assault and battery** charges. **Intentional infliction of emotional distress** occurs when a manager or supervisor's treatment is deemed particularly abusive and the employee can demonstrate some form of hardship as a result of the treatment. This may occur during the termination process, with managers loudly firing an employee in front of other employees and/or customers. The best way to avoid a constructive-discharge lawsuit is to treat employees in a fair and just manner and keep the lines of communication open. It is also important for management to set a proper tone and example and to clearly communicate what will and will not be tolerated to all employees.

FALSE IMPRISONMENT, DEFAMATION, AND INVASION OF PRIVACY

McDonald's Corporation was named as a defendant in a $30-million lawsuit for **false imprisonment** and sexual misconduct when a McDonald's restaurant manager in Kentucky, acting on the directions of a man on the telephone who identified himself as a police officer, took an 18-year-old female employee into the back office of the restaurant, forced her to strip naked, and held her against her will for several hours. When the restaurant became busy and the manager was needed at the front of the store, she called her boyfriend into the office to stand guard over the female employee. The manager's boyfriend molested the teenage employee and has since pleaded guilty to sexual abuse, sexual misconduct, and unlawful imprisonment; he was sentenced to a five-year prison term. The McDonald's manager will stand trial mid to late 2006, and the man who allegedly posed as a police officer and phoned the restaurant was arrested; his trial date is scheduled for late 2006. McDonald's Corporation, the defendant in the civil lawsuit, claims it is innocent. This tawdry episode played out on national television when the ABC news show *20/20* obtained copies of the actual videotapes recorded by the restaurant's own in-house security system.[6] Under the law, "the act of the employee is the act of the employer," so McDonald's could potentially be liable in this case.

DEFAMATION OF CHARACTER

When managers communicate false information about current or former employees, either verbally or in writing, and that information casts a negative light upon the character of that individual, charges of **defamation by libel** (written) or **defamation by slander** (verbal) often result. As you will learn in a later chapter, civil charges such as this are often the reason that hospitality businesses are reluctant to provide any kind of employment reference—good or bad—on current and former employees. A good rule of thumb when providing references is to say only what is true and what can easily be defended in court. Avoid subjective statements such as "she is not eligible for rehire," as these have no real, concrete meaning. What does that mean? Did she steal the cash register or was she late for work on one too many occasions?

Employee personnel records tend to be locked tightly in the offices of professional human resources departments of large hotel and restaurant operations. These documents are kept under lock and key to ensure that the personal employee information doesn't fall into the wrong hands. However, if this does occur, a lawsuit based on **invasion of privacy** is likely to follow. Where are these sensitive records kept in smaller operations? In an unlocked file cabinet shoved somewhere in a back office perhaps, where anyone with the desire to snoop can dig into employees' personal information? Whether you are affiliated with a larger hospitality operation or a smaller business, it's a good rule of thumb to properly protect and safeguard employee personnel files and strictly limit access on a bona fide need-to-know basis.

Photo 4.2

Employee personnel records are confidential and should be kept in a secure place at all times or a hospitality business could be sued for "invasion of privacy."

With the advent of modern technology and the ability to install closed-circuit TV monitoring cameras throughout the operation, it is also important to note that the courts have consistently ruled that employees have a reasonable expectation of privacy in employee locker rooms and restrooms. Employees at the Sheraton Boston Hotel were secretly videotaped before and after their shifts by cameras hidden in their locker room. Managers claimed they were trying to catch a busboy they suspected of selling cocaine, although they never found any evidence of illegal activity. The Sheraton employees in this case shared a $200,000 settlement for invasion of their privacy.[7]

NEGLIGENT HIRING AND NEGLIGENT RETENTION

Under the legal doctrine of **respondeat superior,** employers are liable for the indirect or vicarious job-related actions of their workers. Roughly translated, it means, "The act of the employee is the act of the employer." Respondeat superior is often difficult to prove because it requires an injured person to prove the worker's wrongful conduct was within the course and scope of his or her job. Because intentional misconduct is simply not part of most employees' job descriptions, this is often very difficult to prove.

But hotel and restaurant owners and managers could be found liable for **negligent hiring,** if they knew or should have known that hiring a particular individual could potentially put customers or other employees at risk of harm or injury. It is important that you not confuse the two because the second asserts that management itself did something wrong through their negligence in hiring the employee and indirectly permitted the employee to harm the victim.

The concept of negligent hiring has been successfully utilized to protect three classes of people: coworkers, customers, and the public at large. Obviously, the concept of the public at large greatly expands the number of people who can sue your hospitality business for the wrongful acts of an employee. As a manager or owner, your obligation to conduct a thorough background review is particularly strong when an employee is allowed access to a customer's home or business, as is the case with many restaurants that provide delivery service. The definition of *home* also includes a temporary residence such as a motel or hotel room, so bell staff, room service waitstaff, as well as members of the housekeeping and engineering departments should undergo thorough preemployment screening. Employees who have access to customer's credit card numbers or other such valuables should also be thoroughly screened.

While no court has provided a list of jobs for which background checks are required, it seems clear that the greater the contact with the public, the greater the need for a rather detailed preemployment screening. Clearly the prudent hotel or restaurant operator will take the necessary steps to prevent the kind of litigation described in some of the preceding scenarios. Figure 4.3 provides some guidelines in establishing a policy for conducting preemployment background checks.

Negligent retention occurs when an employee is "retained," rather than fired after he or she has demonstrated some propensity for violent behavior or other such conduct that could possibly cause harm or injury to coworkers, guests, or the public at large. An example of this would be a valet parking attendant who takes a customer's car for a quick joyride before properly parking it. Management decides to give the employee a second chance and instead of terminating the employee, a written report is placed in the employee's personnel file. Two weeks later this same employee pulls the same stunt, but this time he causes an accident where an innocent third party is injured or, even worse, killed. Manage-

---

ESTABLISHING A COMPANY POLICY

The courts suggest a two-step process when establishing a policy for conducting preemployment background checks.

1. The company should review the job description to determine the position's risk to third parties. If it is determined that the position has the potential for the employee coming into contact with third parties, then some level of background check should be initiated.

2. Given the risk factors, if the duties of the job dictate that a background check should be conducted, then the depth, breadth, and scope of the background check should also be determined at the same time. These decisions should then be written into the company's personnel manuals.

Important: By utilizing this two-step method (and no other), the employer is able to avoid any later criticism that some or all of the background check was based on the applicant's race, religion, or other statutorily protected criteria.

Figure 4.3   Process for establishing a background screening policy.

ment's decision to retain rather than to terminate the employee contributed to the accident, so management is liable because they knew or should have known the employee's potential for this type of behavior.

Finally, remember that the purpose of this book is to emphasize the importance of attracting, hiring, training, and retaining the very best employees so that you can deliver quality products and services to a demanding and industry-savvy customer base. Aside from the legal minefield that you may encounter by running afoul of some of these laws, you must also consider the negative effects one simple lawsuit could have on your business. The negative public-relations fallout that would certainly occur in the wake of one simple lawsuit would have dire effects on both the quality of job applicants and the overall success of the operation. Remember, the community of hospitality employees in your area is smaller than you think, and these professionals love to talk and share war stories. Getting branded with a bad reputation for poor human resources practices would greatly diminish your ability to attract top talent in the future.

SUMMARY

■ Owners and managers of hospitality businesses have a common-law duty to provide reasonable care in preventing harm or injury to their customers, guests, and employees.

- When an incident is foreseeable, managers who fail to provide reasonable care may be held liable if someone is harmed or injured.
- Employees also have rights under common law because management has a legal duty to exercise reasonable care in the practice of supervising the activities of others.
- Areas in which an employee could have a legal cause of action against his or her employer include wrongful discharge, constructive discharge, assault and battery, intentional infliction of emotional distress, false imprisonment, defamation by libel or slander, and invasion of privacy.
- Where instances of negligent hiring and/or negligent retention occur, management is not only liable to its employees but also to its guests, customers, and members of the public at large.
- Because of the potential for financially devastating lawsuits, most experts agree that some level of preemployment screening is necessary in order to prevent hiring a bad apple.

1. All states in the United States follow British common law.

   A. True   B. False

2. Many smaller hospitality operations find preemployment screening to be too expensive or too time consuming.

   A. True   B. False

3. According to *Hospitality News,* more than 65 percent of all job applicants have some kind of criminal record.

   A. True   B. False

4. Common law requires that hotel and restaurant managers insure their customers' safety and security regardless of whether or not incidents that could cause harm or injury are foreseeable.

   A. True   B. False

5. The McDonald's Corporation won the infamous hot-coffee lawsuit because most people thought the lawsuit was stupid.

   A. True   B. False

6. Employees working in at-will states can be terminated

   A. at any time.

   B. for any reason.

   C. for no reason.

   D. All of the above.

7. Employees working in just-cause states can be terminated

    A. for any reason.

    B. for a proper and just reason.

    C. for no reason.

    D. All of the above.

8. Constructive discharge occurs when the following occurs:

    A. A manager fires an employee for stealing.

    B. a manager fires an employee for harassing another employee.

    C. an employee quits or resigns due to intolerable work conditions.

    D. A manager fires a whistle blower for reporting drug use at the restaurant.

9. Defamation by libel occurs in

    A. written form.

    B. verbal form.

    C. written or verbal form.

    D. contract form.

10. Managers who fail to properly secure and protect sensitive employee personnel files could be sued for

    A. slander.

    B. defamation of character.

    C. invasion of privacy.

    D. wrongful discharge.

REVIEW QUESTIONS

1. Joe has applied to be a line cook in your restaurant, and he has considerable experience as well as solid references. His position will require that he occasionally drive the company van to assist with off-site catering events. After conducting a routine background check, you discover that Joe has two DUI offenses on his criminal record; one dates back to seven years ago, and the second offense occurred three years ago. Should Joe's history of drunken driving offenses eliminate him from the running for this position? Why or why not? If Joe is hired, could the restaurant later have legal troubles with respect to negligent hiring? Explain your answers.

2. Sally worked as a room attendant in your hotel for six years. You terminated Sally two months ago because you suspected her of stealing guest's valuables while she cleaned the guest rooms. You have no direct proof that Sally stole, but you did discover a ring and a camera in her locker during a routine locker inspection. The items that you discovered were later identified as belonging to one of your guests, and you felt that you were on solid

ground by terminating Sally. Now you have received a call from the director of housekeeping of a hotel in a nearby town where Sally has applied for work. The housekeeper would like to check Sally's references and is calling you because you were listed as her most recent employer. What information will you provide on the past employee? Is there any information that you would not provide? Explain your answer in detail.

3. Conduct a general Internet search and find four or five examples of recent lawsuits brought against a hotel or restaurant. Try to narrow your search to include only lawsuits having to do with employment issues or lawsuits having to do with the establishment failing to provide reasonable care. What were the outcomes of the lawsuits that you researched? What might the business have done prior to the lawsuit that may have prevented it? Be prepared to share your findings with the rest of the class.

4. You are the general manager of an old-fashioned ice cream parlor located within a hotel. In addition to the usual menu items, you make and sell frozen ice cream cakes, which you proudly display in a reach-in freezer in the dining area of your store. It is a slow evening with only a few guests sitting in your establishment. You direct two of your staff members to clean the reach-in freezer. To do so, they remove the cakes and the metal racks. The cakes are temporarily stored in the walk-in freezer in the kitchen, and the employees have stacked the racks against a booth in the dining room. What potential liability could be incurred in this scenario? What should you do to ensure you are providing reasonable care for the safety of your guests? Be specific and give examples.

5. Conduct a general Internet search and locate two or three companies in the hospitality industry business that provide preemployment screening. What kinds of services do the companies offer? If you owned a small lodging or food service operation, what kinds of preemployment screening would be most beneficial to you? Least beneficial? Explain your answers in detail.

HANDS-ON HRM ▶

Lindsey is an experienced hotel night auditor who has been employed full time at the Argos Hotel for nearly six years. Her employment record at the Argos has been exceptional. She rarely misses work, both guests and management recognize her positive attitude toward customer service, and her attention to detail in her nightly paperwork is impeccable. Management has really come to rely on Lindsey, but now there is a problem. An internal audit has uncovered evidence of theft, and the finger of guilt points directly at Lindsey.

Mr. Jacobson, the hotel's general manager, is sick with grief when he realizes that he must call Lindsey into his office and confront her with the hard evidence that she has stolen nearly $2,000 over the past six months. When confronted, Lindsey breaks down sobbing and admits to everything.

She tells Mr. Jacobson that her youngest child has had serious health problems and she and her husband have been struggling financially. She begs to keep her job and even promises to pay the money back. Mr. Jacobson is saddened, but he tells Lindsey that he is going to have to terminate her employment immediately. He says that he does not believe that the company wishes to file any criminal charges against Lindsey, but that she will need to collect her belongings and be escorted immediately from the building.

A few weeks later, Mr. Jacobson's secretary comes into his office and says that she has Erica Stovall, the human resources director at the Wyandotte Hotel, an upscale property located in a town about 20 miles away, on the line. Stovall is calling to get an employment reference for Lindsey, who has submitted an application to the Wyandotte for the position of full-time night auditor. "Oh no," Jacobson thinks to himself. "Why in the world did she ever list me as a reference?" He takes a moment to compose himself and then says to his secretary, "Okay, put her through."

QUESTIONS ▶

1. Since it is unlikely that Erica Stovall will ask Mr. Jacobson whether or not Lindsey is a thief, should Jacobson volunteer this information? If so, how should he present this information? If not, explain your answer.

2. If Mr. Jacobson chooses not to volunteer the information, could his hotel possibly face any liability in the future if the Wyandotte Hotel hires Lindsey and later learns the truth? Explain.

3. If Mr. Jacobson decides to tell Erica Stovall that Lindsey was terminated for theft, what might be the legal ramifications, if any, for the Argos Hotel? Explain your answer.

4. What steps and procedures should the Argos Hotel implement in the event that any future employees are caught stealing and have to be terminated? Please explain in detail.

KEY TERMS ▶

Common law The traditional, unwritten law of England that has been around for centuries and forms the foundation of many current U.S. laws and statutes.

Tort A civil wrong for which the law allows some form of legal remedy.

Negligence Failing to do (or not do) what any sane, reasonable person would (or would not) do under like or similar circumstances.

Foresee To be able to determine in advance. Normally associated with common-law negligence in which events need only to be prevented if they are foreseeable.

Proximate cause In negligence lawsuits, the breach of one's legal duty to provide reasonable care must be the proximate cause, or main reason, for the harm or injury.

At-will employee Employees in at-will states may be terminated for any reason at any time.

Collective bargaining agreement A type of employment contract used by labor unions.

Wrongful discharge Firing an employee for reasons that violate public policy, terms of a contract, or a covenant of good faith and fair dealing.

Constructive discharge When an employee feels compelled to quit his or her job due to intolerable work conditions.

Assault and battery Assault (the threat of violence) and battery (actual physical violence) against another person.

Intentional infliction of emotional distress Treating an employee in an outrageous manner with the intent of causing mental or physical distress.

False imprisonment Preventing or threatening to prevent an employee to move freely.

Defamation by libel False information communicated in writing to a third party with the intent to harm a person's character.

Defamation by slander False information communicated verbally to a third party with the intent to harm a person's character.

Invasion of privacy Accessing information about an employee without a bona fide need to know that information.

Respondeat superior The act of the employee is the act of the employer.

Negligent hiring Hiring an individual who harms or injures another when a proper background check would have shown the individual's propensity for violence or other unacceptable behavior.

Negligent retention Retaining an employee who harms or injures another when termination of that employee would have prevented such harm or injury from occurring.

NOTES ▶

1. Maren L. Hickton, "Service: Problem Employees," *Restaurant Report, LLC* (Miami, FL) www.mareninc.com.
2. Kelly Smith, *Hospitality News,* May 2003, p. 27.
3. Ibid.
4. Ibid.
5. *Liebeck v. McDonald's Restaurants,* No. CV-93-02419, 1995 (N.M. Dist. August 18, 1994).
6. Andrew Wolfson, "Bullit County Man Pleads Guilty in McDonald's Strip-Search Case," *Courier-Journal* (Louisville, KY) February 3 2006, sec. 1A.
7. *Clement v. ITT Sheraton Boston Corp.,* Suffolk Cty, Case No. 93-0909-F, Massachusetts Superior Court.

CHAPTER 5

WORKING WITH UNIONS

Professionals join unions because they feel that their work is being devalued.[1]

Kate Bonfenbrenner, director labor education research, Cornell University

CHAPTER OBJECTIVES

After completing this chapter, you will be able to

- Understand how the U.S. government shapes the union-management framework through laws and their interpretation.
- Identify illegal management and union activities as defined by the National Labor Relations Act (NLRA).
- Define the National Labor Relations Board's (NLRB) role in enforcing the NLRA.
- Define *right-to-work state*.
- Outline the typical organization structure of a local union.
- Identify key hospitality industry unions and their areas of geographic relevance.
- Describe the typical steps taken to resolve grievances.
- Identify the steps taken in the union organization process.
- Understand the reasons why some employees may desire to join a union.
- Describe actions that a manager can take to provide a positive work environment.

 **HRM IN ACTION**   While the lodging and food service industries of today are not heavily unionized overall, hospitality managers and supervisors who accept jobs within large operations in major metropolitan areas such as New York, Chicago, Las Vegas, and Atlantic City will need to know how to effectively deal with employees who belong to unions because unions are now beginning to infiltrate the hospitality industry and will most likely be prevalent in the near future. A **union** is an organization of workers formed for the purpose of advancing its members' interests with respect to wages, benefits, hours of work, and other conditions of employment.

Although the size and power of the U.S. labor movement has changed in recent years, labor unions remain a powerful political and economic force, particularly in highly industrialized regions and within industries that have a high percentage of unionized workers. The electric utility, manufacturing, trucking, telecommunications, and aerospace industries, and the government are, for example, highly unionized. Employee unions aimed at organizing the hospitality industry workforce have had success in major U.S. cities, especially in the lodging sector, but they have typically not organized smaller properties scattered in less-populated regions because it is not economically feasible for them to do so.

STATES AND METRO AREAS WITH A LARGE UNION CONCENTRATION

According to a 2005 report from the Working for America Institute, hotel union representation is very unevenly distributed geographically.[2] The percentage of workers represented by unions is highest in Hawaii, Nevada, New York, New Jersey, Illinois, California, Rhode Island, the District of Columbia, Alaska, and Washington. These states include 85.6 percent of all union hotel workers. The report also identifies Atlantic City, Boston, Chicago, Detroit, Honolulu, Las Vegas, Los Angeles, New York, San Francisco, and Washington, D.C., as the 10 metropolitan areas that have the largest segments of union representation.

Photo 5.1   Las Vegas hotels and restaurants are the most heavily unionized in the nation.

TALES FROM THE FIELD

I grew up in a small town where none of the hotels or restaurants were unionized, although sometimes when employees got angry with management over some policy or something, there was often some joking around about 'time to bring in the union.' When I left school and took a hotel job in California, I was surprised that I would be required to join the hotel's union whether I wanted to or not, since California is not a 'right-to-work state.' I didn't mind paying the dues so much, but I really didn't feel like I was benefiting all that much. I mean the wages and salaries paid at our hotel were competitive with other places I had interviewed with in other states, so I didn't really get it until management decided to outsource the food and beverage operations at our property. That meant that a lot of my coworkers and I would have lost our jobs. The union stepped in pretty aggressively, and management dumped its plan. Now I can definitely see that there is some benefit to belonging, and I'm really glad I did in that situation.

Thomas, 26, San Francisco, California

It is the hospitality industry managers' and supervisors' responsibility to maintain positive employee relations, whether their employees are represented by a union or not. However, if a union exists, managers find that their roles change because both unions and management must comply with the new rules that emerge based on the union-management framework. Some changes are mandated by law, while others come from written agreements between the union and management officials. Some hospitality operations try to avoid unions altogether due to the constraints that a unionized workforce puts on an organization.

THE NATIONAL LABOR RELATIONS ACT

The **National Labor Relations Act (NLRA),** also known as the Wagner Act, was signed into law by Congress in 1935 during the Great Depression. This law was intended to minimize the disruption of interstate commerce caused by strikes, which at times erupted into violent confrontations as workers trying to form unions fought with the police and the private security forces defending the interests of antiunion companies. Prior to the NLRA becoming law, employers had been free to spy on, interrogate, discipline, discharge, and blacklist union members.

This law gives employees the right to join labor unions without employer interference. It allows employees to form labor organizations and to bargain with management about wages, hours, and other working conditions. Congress also created the **National Labor Relations Board (NLRB)** to enforce this right. The

Five types of conduct that are deemed illegal under the National Labor Relations Act:

1. *Interference.* Management may not interfere, restrain, or coerce employees who desire to act collectively or refrain from such activities.

2. *Dominate.* Management may not dominate or interfere with the formation or administration of any labor organization by contributing money or other support to it.

3. *Discriminate.* Management may not discriminate against anyone in hiring, stability of employment, or any other condition of employment because of their union activity or lack of involvement.

4. *Retaliate.* Management may not retaliate, discharge, discipline, or otherwise discriminate against employees who have exercised their rights under the act.

5. *Refuse.* Management may not refuse to bargain in good faith with employee representatives.

Figure 5.1   Unfair labor practices as defined by the NLRA. *(Source: National Labor Relations Board.)*

NLRB ensures that employers don't take part in **unfair labor practices** that might discourage or prevent employees from organizing or negotiating a union contract. Figure 5.1 outlines the five types of conduct deemed illegal under the NLRA.

THE TAFT-HARTLEY ACT AND RIGHT-TO-WORK LAWS

Although most unions did not abuse their power after the NRLA was passed, some did, so Congress passed the **Labor Management Relations Act (LMRA)** in 1947. This law is more often referred to as the **Taft-Hartley Act,** and it amended the NLRA passed earlier by prohibiting unfair labor practices by unions. The LMRA makes it illegal for unions to force employees to join them, and it outlaws picketing and strikes under certain circumstances. This law also allows the individual states the right to pass **right-to-work laws,** which ensure that new employees are not required to join an already established union as a condition of retaining their jobs. States without such laws are known as **nonright-to-work states,** and employees in these states may be required to join the union and pay union dues if the **collective bargaining agreement** between the employer and the union require all new employees to do so. If the collective bargaining agreement does not contain such provisions, a new employee will not be required to be a member of a union or pay it monies as a condition of employment. The map in Figure 5.2 highlights which states in the United States are currently right-to-work states. Because state laws often change, before relying on the stipulations of a particular state's right-to-work statute, you should check the most recent edition of that state's laws.

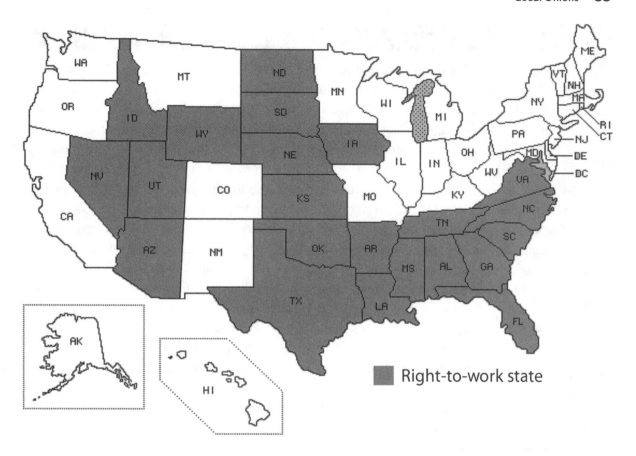

Figure 5.2   Right-to-work states are shown in gray on this map of the United States. *(Source: Image courtesy of the National Right to Work Legal Defense Foundation, Inc.)*

LOCAL UNIONS

For hospitality managers and supervisors, **local unions** are probably the most important part of the union structure. They provide the local members, the revenue, and the power behind the entire union movement. The organizational structure of a local union would most likely include a president, a secretary-treasurer, a business agent, a grievance committee, and a bargaining committee. The steward is the first level in the union hierarchy and is normally elected by the workers to help employees present their problems to management. The union steward may also represent the first step in the **grievance process** should an employee or the union feel that some element of the union contract has been violated. Grievance procedures are normally outlined in the union con-

ethical dilemma

Lynn lives in a large city and belongs to Local 19 of the International Banquet and Catering Employees Union. All of the venues in town are unionized, and when a large event is booked, waitstaff and bartenders must be obtained from the local union. The union's business agent, Carl, called Lynn and scheduled him for a big bartending job at the city's convention center. Lynn agreed to take the job, but he overslept and failed to show up to work at the event. The local union's procedure in such a matter is to put the case before the local's executive committee so that they can determine the union member's penalty for such irresponsible behavior. In this case, the executive board decides to suspend Lynn for the next 30 days, which means he will not be placed on any calls. This proves to be a major financial hardship for Lynn, as he is not allowed to work in any of the city's venues while he is on suspension. Near the end of his suspension, a friend who works in a local hotel calls Lynn and asks him to bartend for a large upcoming event. The friend assures Lynn that even though the hotel is a union shop, that Lynn will be working in an out-of-the way banquet room, and that it will be highly unlikely that local union officials will even know he is there. Should Lynn take the job, or should he turn it down and wait until his suspension is completed? Which of the *10 Ethical Principles for Hospitality Managers* would Lynn potentially violate if he takes the hotel job? How will his decision affect his relationship with the hotel? With the local? With his friend?

---

tract, and they may vary from operation to operation, but they often follow a step-by-step procedure such as the following:

Step 1: The employee with the complaint meets with the supervisor and the union steward to discuss the grievance. Most grievances are resolved at this step.

Step 2: If the grievance is not settled, there is a conference between the union steward, the employee, and the supervisor's boss or another manager such as a human resources manager in a larger operation.

Step 3: If the grievance continues to be unsettled, representatives from top management at the operation and top union officials try to settle it.

Step 4: If still unsettled, the grievance is given to a neutral third party such as an **arbitrator** or **mediator**. A mediator listens to both sides and suggests ways to resolve the grievance but has no authority to force either side to accept any of the proposed terms. In arbitration, both parties must agree, in advance of the actual arbitration, that the decision given by the arbitrator will be final and binding.[3]

NATIONAL UNIONS

Most local unions are chartered by larger associations called **national unions,** which organize and help the locals. National unions provide their locals with legal assistance and expert advice and help them with negotiations, training of local officials, and handling grievances. Locals must share their dues with their national union, and they must obey its constitution and bylaws. One of the largest and best-known hospitality industry labor unions is the Hotel Employees and Restaurant Employees International Union (HERE). In 2004, HERE merged with the Union of Needletrades, Textiles, and Industrial Employees (UNITE), and the combined union, now known as UNITE HERE, represents more than 440,000 active members throughout the United States and Canada. This labor union represents workers in hotels, casinos, food service operations, airport concessions, and restaurants. Some major UNITE HERE hospitality industry employers include the following:

- Aramark
- Boyd Gaming
- Caesars Entertainment
- Harrah's Entertainment
- Hilton Hotel Corporation
- Hyatt Regency Hotels and Resorts
- Mandalay Resorts
- MGM Mirage
- Starwood Hotels and Resorts
- Walt Disney World Company
- Wynn Resorts

HERE includes one of the fastest growing private-sector Local Unions in the United States—Local 226 in Las Vegas, which has increased its membership from 10,000 members in 1987 to 50,000 members today through an effective organizing program.[4]

MULTIUNION ASSOCIATIONS

Several national unions joined together to form **multiunion associations** as social problems began to affect them. The **AFL-CIO** is the most prominent multiunion association; it was formed when the American Federation of Labor and the Congress of Industrial Organizations merged. It is not a union in and of itself; rather, it is an association of unions. Its membership is composed of af-

Change to Win Coalition member unions represent more than 5.4 million workers, including the following:

- International Brotherhood of Teamsters
- Laborers' International Union of North America (LIUNA)
- UNITE HERE
- Service Employees International Union (SEIU)
- United Food and Commercial Workers International Union (UFCW)
- United Brotherhood of Carpenters and Joiners of America
- United Farm Workers

Figure 5.3   Change to Win Coalition member unions represent more than 5.4 million workers.

filiated national unions. While most major unions in the United States are members of the AFL-CIO, its two biggest and most powerful unions, the International Brotherhood of Teamsters and the Service Employees International Union, chose to break away from the AFL-CIO in 2005 to start their own multiunion association known as the Change to Win Coalition. Five other unions soon followed, including UNITE HERE. The AFL-CIO still claims union membership consists of everyone from airline pilots to letter carriers and from screenwriters to theatrical stage employees, but the organization dwarfs these new start-up multiunion associations. When comparing overall membership numbers, the Change to Win Coalition of unions now represents more than 5.4 million members, many of whom are hospitality-industry related. Figure 5.3 lists the unions that have joined the Change to Win Coalition.

WHY EMPLOYEES JOIN UNIONS

Hospitality industry employees typically join unions because they feel that management is not being responsive to the issues they've raised relating to their job satisfaction. These issues may include wages, benefits, job security, seniority issues, unfair treatment by supervisors, the physical work environment, and whether the company offers a career path or upward mobility. In short, most employees within an organization tend to join unions when their concerns about their working conditions are ignored by upper management. Most hospitality business owners and managers try to avoid unionization so that they can maintain lower labor costs by paying their employees lower wages and achieve greater management flexibility in the day-to-day operations of their facilities. It is important to note that unions certainly do not mean the end of a hospitality organization's success or the end of sound management practices.

Although many successful hospitality operations include employees who are members of one or more unions, they continue to perform well financially. Perhaps the key to avoiding the unionization of your hospitality business employees is to pay your staff competitive wages and salaries and to provide a positive work climate so they have no reason to join a union.

THE UNION ORGANIZATION PROCESS

Unions do not just walk in to your operation and take over; there is a well-established legal process that must take place in order for a union to organize the workers of a lodging or a food service establishment. The steps and guidelines are outlined in the NLRA and overseen by the NLRB to ensure the union adheres to the prescribed guidelines. Your employees may contact a union, or union organizers may contact your employees. Employees who initiate contact with the union will normally be given **union authorization cards** to pass out to coworkers. These cards, when signed by 30 percent of the employees in the organization, authorize the union to represent the employees during negotiations. If and when 30 percent of the employees sign authorization cards, the NLRB has a hearing and will generally set a date for the union election. If the majority of ballots cast are in favor of the union, the union becomes the bargaining agent on behalf of the employees, and management is required by law to bargain in good faith.

EMPLOYERS MAY NOT RETALIATE

The NLRA prohibits employers from retaliating against employees who may be involved in union organization activities. The NLRB and a federal appeals court recently awarded a Kentucky nurse $400,000 after a six-year battle over her firing from a hospital. The hospital company had contended that she was dismissed because she flushed a heart patient's intravenous line with saline solution without approval from a doctor. The court determined that the hospital illegally fired her because of her union organization activities.[5] The court ordered the hospital company to pay the nurse lost wages and her legal expenses, and it ordered that she be reinstated to her position with full benefits.

THE UNION CONTRACT

Like any other contract, the collective bargaining agreement, or **union contract**, is a legal, binding document. Once both the representatives of the union and the company agree to the proposed terms and conditions, the contract is signed and cannot be changed except during previously agreed-upon renegotiation periods, usually after three or more years have passed. Management and the union do not necessarily have to agree on each and every term or condition included in the contract, but the law requires that each party bargain in good faith.

Clearly, the union will stress matters it sees as most beneficial to its members, and management will work hard to retain as much control and flexibility over business operations as possible. A union contract typically contains terms and conditions that affect some or all of the following areas:

- Wages, salaries, and employee benefits
- Holidays and vacations
- Overtime pay, sick days, leaves of absence, and personal days
- Seniority matters
- Training and new employee orientation
- Grievance procedures
- Disciplinary issues and probationary periods for new hires
- Employee performance evaluations, promotions, and transfers
- Union dues
- Whether new employees are required to join the union and pay dues (in a nonright-to-Work state)
- Layoffs and other reductions in the workforce

As the union-management relationship matures, each of the points listed is typically defined in greater detail.

MANAGEMENT CHALLENGES WHEN WORKING WITH UNIONS

In addition to the increased labor costs and reduced flexibility in day-to-day decision making brought about by the unionization of their employees, hospitality managers and supervisors will often encounter other challenges when their employees belong to a union. Once a union and a collective bargaining agreement are in place at a particular operation, the dynamic in the workplace changes, and routines and procedures that were once commonplace may no longer be allowed. Examples of such challenges include the following:

- Promotions, rewards, and who gets overtime may now be based on seniority.
- Rewards and recognitions may no longer be based on merit or achievement.
- Managers must deal with the union steward instead of directly with the employee on matters outlined in the union contract.
- Both management and the union compete for the employee's loyalty.

Some hospitality business owners and managers feel like they have taken on an additional business partner when employees choose to join a union, and in many ways, they have, whether they like it or not!

CREATING A POSITIVE WORK ENVIRONMENT

Effective hospitality managers and supervisors realize that most employees in the organization will have no interest in joining a union if the organization pays competitive wages and salaries and if management works hard to provide a positive work environment. Most employees want to feel like the work they do matters and that they contribute to the overall success of the organization. One of the best ways a manager can be responsive to employees' needs is to get to know the employees, understand their likes and dislikes about their jobs and the work environment as well as what motivates them to do their best. Other steps to take in creating a positive work environment include the following:

- Design jobs that are personally satisfying to workers.
- Develop plans that maximize individual opportunities and minimize the possibility for layoffs.
- Qualify potential employees and be sure to carefully match the right applicant with the right job position.
- Establish meaningful objective standards to help measure and evaluate individual performance.
- Train workers and managers to enable them to achieve expected levels of performance.
- Provide ongoing training for all employees to ensure professional development and growth.
- Evaluate and reward behavior on the basis of actual job performance.

Failure to implement sound management and supervision practices provides the justification and the motivation for workers to be less productive, to seek the help of government regulatory agencies, or to form unions.

SUMMARY

- The hospitality industry is not heavily unionized, but those who become managers and supervisors in metro areas where unionization is strong will need to understand the dos and don'ts of working with unionized employees.
- Hospitality operations located in major cities such as New York, Atlantic City, Boston, Chicago, Las Vegas, San Francisco, and Washington, D.C., are heavily unionized.

- Managers find that their roles change when their employees are unionized because both unions and management must comply with laws and regulations that govern the union-management framework.
- The National Labor Relations Act (NLRA), which was signed into law in 1935, gives employees the right to join unions without any employer interference. The National Labor Relations Board (NLRB) was created to enforce employee rights.
- The Taft-Hartley Act, also known as the Labor Management Relations Act (LMRA), prohibits unfair labor practices by unions.
- When a new employee joins an organization that is unionized, that employee may be required to join the union and pay dues whether he or she wants to or not. In most cases, right-to-work states have passed laws that prohibit this practice, but in non-right-to-work states, employees may be required to join the union and pay union dues.
- Unions are composed of local unions, national unions, and large multiunion associations such as the AFL-CIO. The steward is the first level in the union hierarchy and is normally elected by the unionized employees to be the liaison between employees and management.
- During the union organization process, employers may not retaliate against employees who are involved in the organization process; the penalties for such retaliation can be severe.
- Employees who feel that management has violated one of the terms or conditions set forth in the union contract may file a grievance. The grievance procedure normally follows a specific set of guidelines, depending upon the union and the organization.
- Employees often seek union membership because they feel that management is not responsive to their needs. Management should work hard to create a positive work environment as a way of dissuading employees from joining unions.

PRACTICE QUIZ

1. A hospitality manager may fire any employee who attempts to organize a union.

   A. True   B. False

2. The hospitality industry is not heavily unionized except in some major metropolitan U.S. cities.

   A. True   B. False

3. When a hospitality business is unionized, the union is responsible for maintaining positive management-employee relations.

   A. True   B. False

4. Employees who are satisfied with their wages and salaries and who feel like management takes an interest in them and their professional future will often have little interest in joining a union.

   A. True   B. False

5. New employees at unionized companies in nonright-to-work states may *not* be required to join a union or pay union dues.

   A. True   B. False

6. An example of a multiunion association is which of the following?

   A. The Airline Pilots Association

   B. The Hotel Employees and Restaurant Employees International

   C. The Change to Win Coalition

   D. The United Autoworkers Union

7. When a dispute goes into arbitration, the arbitrator's decision is which of the following?

   A. Binding

   B. Nonbinding

   C. A strong recommendation but cannot be enforced

   D. None of the above

8. Which of the following laws prohibits unfair labor practices by unions?

   A. The National Labor Relations Board

   B. The Department of Labor

   C. The Taft-Hartley Act

   D. The Wagner Act

9. According to the NLRA, which of the following statements is false?

   A. Management cannot terminate an employee because he or she joined a union.

   B. Management may not interfere with employees who desire to join a union.

   C. Management does not have to bargain with the union if it does not want to do so.

   D. Management may not discriminate against an employee for joining a union.

10. Which would most likely *not* be a term or condition found in a union contract?

   A. Wages and salaries

   B. Promotions

   C. Meal breaks and rest breaks

   D. Senior management salaries

1. If you live in an area with unionized hotels and restaurants, interview an employee and a manager at one of these establishments and compare and contrast their views on the reasons for unionization at the property. Do they feel that unionization has helped or hindered the employee-management relation process? If you do not live in an area where the hospitality businesses are unionized, do some Web research and locate two articles regarding unionization in the hospitality industry and present two opposing viewpoints. Be prepared to present your findings to the class.

2. Assume that you are the manager of a lodging or food service establishment. List and briefly discuss some routine management activities that may not be possible if the establishment's employees were represented by a union. As the manager, how might you overcome these obstacles?

3. List and briefly discuss some of the reasons that hospitality industry employees may seek union representation. Then list and briefly discuss some activities that management can undertake in order to create a positive work climate. Compare and contrast the two lists and write an action plan that addresses some of the employee concerns. Be prepared to present your findings to the class.

4. Write a position paper on labor unions in the United States. Are you in favor of labor unions and, if so, why? Are you against labor unions? If so, why? Do you feel that labor unions will become more commonplace in the hospitality industry? What evidence is there to support your assumptions? Be prepared to share your ideas with the rest of the class.

5. It has been argued that manufacturing companies would prefer to relocate their operations to a right-to-work state so that employees would not be required to join the union. Others have argued that this often has no bearing on a company's decision to relocate its operations from one state to another. What are your thoughts on this issue? Explain your answer in detail.

Eric Little works the 3-to-11 shift at the front desk of a medium-sized hotel located in the suburbs of a large, southern city. He used to like his job very much, but the hotel was recently sold and the new owners have literally moved in, taking a large upstairs suite, and they are changing everything. Wages have been frozen, people have been laid off, and, what's worse, the new owners are hiring their own friends and relatives to replace many of the hotel's oldest and most loyal employees. The owners each have a medical background and do not seem to know a lot about how to run a hotel.

One of the hotel's regular guests, Alan Craig, is a union organizer for the retail clerk's union whose headquarters is located in the state capitol, about 300 miles away. He has been staying at the hotel for three nights per week for over four months as he assists his union's organization of a local department store. Craig stops by the desk often to chat with Eric in the evenings when check-ins have slowed down. Over time, the two have developed a casual friendship and are on a first-name basis with each other.

Lately, Eric has begun to ask Mr. Craig questions about how a union works. Craig has thoroughly explained the organization process to Eric, focusing on the signing of the union cards and the employee vote. Craig has also emphasized that "your employer may not retaliate against those employees seeking to join a union." He has offered to bring Eric some literature to pass out to the other employees, and he has also let Eric know that he would be glad to help him to organize his coworkers into a local chapter if he would like.

QUESTIONS ▶

1. What risks, if any, will Eric be taking if he decides to accept Alan Craig's union literature and distribute it to the other hourly employees in the hotel?

2. How does the law protect Eric? The union?

3. Should the efforts Eric makes to organize the hourly employees pick up steam, how should the new owners react? What exactly would they be able to do (and not do) with respect to the union's efforts?

4. If you were the new owner, what changes might you make to your management style in an effort to lessen the hourly employees' interest in union representation?

KEY TERMS ▶

Union An organization of workers formed for the purpose of advancing its members' interests with respect to their wages, benefits, work hours, and other conditions of employment.

National Labor Relations Act (NLRA) A law enacted in 1935 that gives employees the right to join labor organizations or unions free of employer interference.

National Labor Relations Board (NLRB) A U.S. government agency created to enforce that employers abide by the NLRA.

Unfair labor practices Certain types of management conduct that might discourage or prevent employees from organizing or prevent negotiating a union contract. NRLA outlines types of management conduct deemed illegal.

Labor Management Relations Act (LMRA) *See* Taft-Hartley Act.

Taft-Hartley Act Also known as the Labor Management Relations Act. It is a law that prohibits unions from engaging in unfair labor practices.

Right-to-work laws Laws that have been enacted by individual states to prohibit unions from requiring that new employees join the union and pay union dues. Some state's right-to-work laws may not apply in this matter if a collective bargaining agreement requires new employees to join the union. States that have enacted these laws are known as right-to-work states.

Nonright-to-work state A state that has not enacted right-to-work laws.

Collective bargaining agreement An agreement or a contract that discloses the terms and conditions that shall apply to the union-management relationship within a particular operation.

Local union Usually part of a larger, national organization, the local union provides local members, revenue, and the power of the entire union movement.

Grievance process A process by which an employee will lodge a complaint against management, usually a result of a breach of some term or condition provided for in the collective bargaining agreement between management and the union.

Arbitrator Two parties who have a disagreement may elect to enter into arbitration; the arbitrator's decision in the matter is final.

Mediator Two parties who have a disagreement may elect to enter into mediation. The mediator may only make recommendations; the mediator's decision is not final.

National union The national labor organization affiliated with the local union.

Multiunion association When several national unions join together for a common cause. The AFL-CIO is an example of a multiunion association.

AFL-CIO The AFL-CIO is the most prominent multiunion association; it was formed when the American Federation of Labor and the Congress of Industrial Organizations merged.

Union authorization card When a local union is attempting to organize a company, 30 percent of the company's employees must sign a union authorization card, which states that the employee agrees to have the union serve as his or her collective bargaining agent.

Union contract *See* collective bargaining agreement.

NOTES ▶

1. "Union Collars Whiten," *Courier-Journal* (Louisville, KY) October 24, 2005, sec 3D.
2. *U.S. Hotels and Their Workers: Room for Improvement* (Working for American Institute: Washington, D.C., 2005).
3. Jack Miller, John R. Walker, and Karen Drummond, *Supervision in the Hospitality Industry*, 4th ed. (John Wiley & Sons: Hoboken, NJ, 2007).
4. Readers desiring additional information about the labor union, UNITE HERE, are referred to the union's Web site: www.unitehere.org.
5. Patrick Howington, "Norton to Pay Fired Nurse: Union Organizer Won Final Appeal," *Courier Journal* (Louisville, KY) February 8, 2006, 1D.

UNIT
2

THE EMPLOYEE
SELECTION
PROCESS

CHAPTER 6

JOB DESCRIPTIONS AND JOB SPECIFICATIONS

No restaurant can keep its doors open without the services and devotion of the first role in the list: the dishwasher.[1]

Michael Garvey, Heather Dismore, and Andrew G. Dismore, *Running a Restaurant for Dummies*

CHAPTER OBJECTIVES

After completing this chapter, you will be able to

- Identify the steps in the employee selection process.
- Distinguish between job descriptions and job specifications.
- Create a written job description.
- Create a written job specification.
- Use a job description and a job specification as a recruiting and a training tool.
- Explain the legal importance of well-written job descriptions and job specifications.

HRM IN ACTION By now you should have a good understanding of some of the challenges facing hospitality industry managers and supervisors today with respect to finding, developing, and keeping a talented pool of labor. This is by no means an easy task, and coupled with the added burden of adhering to a myriad of federal, state, and local laws governing nearly every single aspect of the employment process, it is no wonder that hotel and restaurant managers say that *recruiting and retaining employees* is the thing most likely to keep them awake at night. It does not have to be this way. Assuming that an operation is able to pay competitive wages and offer at least a few **employee benefits,** eager applicants should be lining up at the front door. For many small operations, unfortunately, management fails pretty miserably in this area, and they have the high **turnover rates** to prove it! Even large operations that have the luxury of staffing a professional human resources department could do a better job when it comes to creating a positive work environment, a place where employees actually enjoy coming to work.

THE EMPLOYEE SELECTION PROCESS

The **employee selection process** consists of locating, recruiting, and hiring the best candidates to fill any open positions that the hospitality business may have. The goal is for management to pick the best from among a pool of qualified job candidates. The processes used when selecting and hiring new employees are critical to the operation's overall success. One of the key elements in the employee selection process is to ensure that we are matching the right applicant with the right job, so the very first step is to develop a well-written **job description** for each position in the operation.

JOB DESCRIPTIONS

Job descriptions detail the duties that the position requires. In other words, what tasks will this employee be required to do? Before placing even the first help-wanted advertisement or conducting even one single interview, management should first develop a written job description for the position that needs to be filled. Why is this? Because this process *forces* management to thoroughly think about this particular position and to review each of the tasks that the successful applicant will need to be able to accomplish. Only after this is done will mamagement be ready to think about the *type* of individual who would be most suitable for the position.

When we say *type* of individual, we are not referring to blonde hair and blue eyes; these factors are probably *not* job related and, therefore, have no business in the decision-making process. You learned in an earlier chapter that illegal job discrimination can be costly indeed, so you want to avoid basing your hiring decisions on factors that could be deemed discriminatory. When considering the type of individual who would be the best match for the position, you want to consider factors such as knowledge, abilities, skills, education, training, or anything else that you consider to be truly job related.

For example, suppose you manage a small restaurant with a busy carryout business, and the clientele your restaurant primarily serves is Hispanic. Many of your customers speak only Spanish, and you need to hire an individual to take

TALES FROM THE FIELD

I worked in the hospitality industry for over five years before deciding to get my education. And even though I had held a lot of different kinds of jobs, I had never seen an actual job description until we talked about them in class one day and my instructor had some samples for us to look at. I had heard the term—you know: 'that's not in my job description'—but I never really knew what they were or how they were used. Now I work at a resort that belongs to our State Parks system, and we're required to have up-to-date job descriptions for every position here. I'm the first to admit that it does take some time to develop them properly, but they sure save a lot of time in the long run, especially when recruiting and hiring new employees. We even use them as a sort of training checklist, and that helps us ensure that we are covering all of the tasks that the employee needs to master during the training process.

Matthias, 32, Land Between The Lakes, Kentucky

phone orders and process food and beverage orders for carryout. Would it be justified to say that the best candidate for this position would need to be fluent in Spanish? You bet it would be! It would also be *legal*. The ability to speak and understand Spanish would certainly be job related in this example.

Many employees often quit their jobs because they are frustrated. They do not know exactly *what* they are supposed to do, *how* they are supposed to do it, or *how well* they are doing whatever it is they are supposed to be doing. A job description is a very useful tool for eliminating this kind of confusion and frustration. The best job descriptions define the job very clearly and tell employees the *what, how,* and *how well* of their jobs. A job description also provides management with a formal document describing what each employee is supposed to be doing. It acts as a standard that management can use to assess how well the employee is performing. This, in turn, can be used in the employee's **performance appraisal,** feedback, wage adjustment, and need-for-training decisions. The job description also helps the employees learn their job duties, and it highlights the results that management expects them to achieve. Such information is crucial if management wants to have productive workers and a positive work environment. Figure 6.1 illustrates a job description for a hotel banquet cook.

Essential Elements   Properly written job descriptions may also serve as a defense against discrimination claims because they list the minimum job qualifications, provide job applicants with a picture of what the job entails, and document the essential job functions. As you learned in Chapter 2, this type of documentation is important in order to adhere to the requirements of the Americans with Disabilities Act.

Job Title: Banquet Cook

DEPARTMENT: Banquets and Catering

REPORTS TO: Executive Chef

WAGE CATEGORY: Nonexempt

Job Summary:

Prepare, season, and cook soups, meats, vegetables, desserts, or other foodstuffs in the hotel banquet department. May order supplies, keep records and accounts, price items on menu, or plan banquet menu.

Job Duties:

Bake breads, rolls, cakes, and pastries.

Bake, roast, broil, and steam meats, fish, vegetables, and other foods.

Carve and trim meats such as beef, veal, ham, pork, and lamb for hot or cold service or for sandwiches.

Estimate expected food consumption; then requisition or purchase supplies or procure food from storage.

Observe and test foods to determine if they have been cooked sufficiently, using methods such as tasting, smelling, or piercing them with utensils.

Regulate temperature of ovens, broilers, grills, and roasters.

Wash, peel, cut, and seed fruits and vegetables to prepare them for consumption.

Weigh, measure, and mix ingredients according to recipes or personal judgment, using various kitchen utensils and equipment.

Figure 6.1

Job description: Banquet cook.

For example, if none of the **essential duties** on a job description for the position of hotel front-desk clerk require that the employee be able to lift 50 pounds, then it would be unwise to reject an applicant for the position just because he or she is unable to lift 50 pounds.

The foundation of any job description is the position's *necessary* functions. Tasks that are regularly performed and the goals of the job would be considered essential functions. For example, essential functions for a host/hostess position might include scheduling day and shift assignments for all dining room personnel, assigning service stations to all servers and bus help, graciously greeting guests upon arrival, escorting them to their table, providing menus, and notifying the server of their arrival. Management should examine and verify that each job description lists only the position's essential functions.

Once you have decided on a position's essential functions, you are ready to begin formulating the job description. Often, the bigger the job, the smaller the

POSITION DESCRIPTION

TITLE: Assistant Restaurant Manager

REPORTS TO: Owner/General Manager

WAGE CATEGORY: Exempt

Position Summary:

Oversees and coordinates the planning, organizing, training, and leadership necessary to achieve stated objectives in sales, costs, employee retention, guest service
and satisfaction, food quality, cleanliness, and sanitation.

Position Duties and Responsibilities:

1. Understand completely all policies, procedures, standards, specifications, guidelines, and training programs.
2. Ensure that all guests feel welcome and are given responsive, friendly, and courteous service at all times.
3. Ensure that all food and products are consistently prepared and served according to the restaurant's recipes, preparation, cooking, and serving standards.
4. Achieve company objectives in sales, service, quality, appearance of facility, and
   sanitation and cleanliness through training of employees and creating a positive, productive working environment.
5. Control cash and other receipts by adhering to cash handling and reconciliation
   procedures in accordance with restaurant policies and procedures.
6. Make employment and termination decisions consistent with General Manager
   guidelines for approval or review.
7. Fill in where needed to ensure prompt guest service standards and efficient operations.
8. Continually strive to develop staff in all areas of managerial and professional
   development.
9. Prepare all required paperwork, including forms, reports, and schedule in an
   organized and timely manner.
10. Ensure that all equipment is kept clean and in excellent working condition
    through personal inspections and by following the restaurant's preventative
    maintenance program.

Figure 6.2

Position description:
Assistant restaurant
manager.

job description. An hourly position could require quite a lengthy job description
that details many tasks. As one moves up the managerial ladder, the essential
functions become broader. In fact, job descriptions for management positions
are often called **position descriptions.** Figure 6.2 illustrates an example of a
position description for an assistant restaurant manager.

JOB DESCRIPTION

JOB TITLE: Bartender

DEPARTMENT: Beverage

REPORTS TO: Beverage Manager

WAGE CATEGORY: Nonexempt

Job Summary:

Mix and serve drinks to patrons, directly or through waitstaff.

Performance Standards:

Mix ingredients, such as liquor, soda, water, sugar, and bitters, in order to prepare cocktails and other drinks according to standardized recipes with 100 percent accuracy.

Serve wine and bottled or draft beer correctly as specified in Bartender Procedures Manual.

Collect money for drinks served and carry our posting and payment procedures with 100 percent accuracy as specified on the Check Payment Procedures Sheet.

Arrange bottles and glasses to make attractive displays.

Slice and pit fruit for garnishing drinks according to standardized recipes.

Order or requisition liquors and supplies using proper Bar Requisition Form.

Perform side work correctly as assigned, according to the Side Work Procedures Sheet and to the level required on the Sanitation Checklist.

Check identification of customers in order to verify minimum age requirements for purchase of alcohol with 100 percent accuracy and to the level required by state law.

Take beverage orders accurately from serving staff or directly from patrons.

Figure 6.3   Job description: Bartender.

Performance Standards

All job descriptions should have these basic elements: descriptive position title (what the job is), title of immediate supervisor, position summary (synopsis of the job), and tasks (duties). Some organizations break each task into a **performance standard.** A performance standard is nothing more than the *what, how,* and *to what standard* each task is to be performed. Figure 6.3 illustrates the use of performance standards in a job description for a bartender.

ethical dilemma

Marilyn Streepey has only been in her position as general manager of the Downtown Inn for three months, but already she knows that the hotel had some serious personnel issues. Her fears are confirmed when she receives her first batch of quarterly guest comment cards from the hotel's corporate headquarters. The guest ratings were very low, and after reading each card carefully, Marilyn determined that many of the employees either did not know how to do their jobs or were simply unwilling or unable to do their jobs properly. She called a staff meeting for the next morning, and at that meeting she instructed all of the department managers to prepare written job descriptions for each position in their respective departments. "A lot of these employees are simply lazy," she said to her department managers. "Once these job descriptions are created, I want every employee in each of your departments to sign one." "That way," she added, "when we have to start terminating people due to poor performance, at least we will be covered from a legal standpoint." If Marilyn and her department managers proceed, are they in danger of violating any of the *10 Ethical Principles for Hospitality Managers?* What would be the outcome for the department managers? For the affected employees? For Marilyn herself? What might be a better way to proceed if the goal is to increase employee performance?

Developing a well-written set of performance standards for each job position in the operation provides the foundation for a management system for the employees and the work they do. Performance standards are important to the training process as well as to the employee appraisal process. We will cover each of these topics in greater detail in Chapters 11 and 12, respectively. Well-written performance standards also provide the following additional benefits:

- Describe jobs in detail.
- Present an accurate picture of what the job entails during the interview process.
- Describe the day's work for each job.
- Train workers to meet standards.
- Evaluate a worker's performance.
- Provide feedback to workers on their job performance.
- Reward achievement and select employees for promotion.
- Be used as diagnostic tools to pinpoint ineffective performance and serve as a basis for corrective action.
- Discipline workers as a means of demonstrating incompetence.

Essentials for Success

It is unlikely that you have chosen a career in the hospitality industry because of your love of writing. No doubt, producing well-written job descriptions for each position in your operation with thorough and detailed performance standards seems like a daunting task. It is not surprising that very few small hospitality businesses take the time and trouble to do this. But it does not have to be this way. By now, you should realize the benefits of well-written job descriptions. Let's look at a few simple steps that we will need to take to establish effective performance and, thus, create effective and accurate job descriptions.

Step 1: Allow and even *encourage* all of your employees to participate in the process. No one knows best how to do a job, but you are likely to get the best input from those who do the job everyday. Brainstorming sessions will normally produce better results than one person writing it alone, and you may be surprised to find that your employees will actually set higher standards of performance than management alone. Remember, effective managers and supervisors do not hand down rules as Moses, delivering the Ten Commandments. Rather, effective managers are good facilitators who are capable of leading others and who accomplish tasks with the help of others on the team.

Step 2: As the leader, you will be in charge at all times. It is you who must make the final decision on the tasks to be included and their relative importance. But you must work together as much as possible in identifying the *whats, hows,* and *how wells.* Under your leadership, performance standards will represent a joint acceptance of the work to be done and the responsibility for achieving it. As a manager or a supervisor, your leadership role must continue as you facilitate the learning of skills, giving feedback, and providing additional training as necessary. Frequent evaluations, whether formal appraisals or saying "Hey, you're doing a great job," must be an integral part of the system. If you neglect this aspect of a performance standard system, the system will soon deteriorate.

Step 3: There must be a built-in reward system of some sort, with rewards linked to how well each worker meets the performance standards. People who do not want to work hard must understand that the better shifts, the promotions and raises, and other rewards will go to those whose work meets or exceeds the standards set. Do not make the mistake of thinking that rewards are only about money and other material things. Often a handwritten note or a word or two of praise can be just as meaningful. People feel that you are recognizing them as individuals and appreciating their contributions. We will examine effective employee reward systems in a later chapter of the book.

Photo 6.1   Management should review the job duties of each employee's job description with all new employees.

JOB SPECIFICATIONS

Unlike the job description that lists each of the essential tasks of a particular position along with the standards of performance associated with each task, the **job specification** details the personal characteristics that a qualified applicant should possess. Those of you who have spent any time working in a professional kitchen may be familiar with **food specifications,** usually called food specs. Simply calling up your meat purveyor and ordering some bacon may result in your receiving a product that is entirely unacceptable for your restaurant. A food spec is a way for you to communicate in a precise way with a purveyor so that your operation receives the *exact* item requested every time. Like bacon, people have various and assorted characteristics that may or may not make them suitable for a particular position in your operation.

Photo 6.2   A job specification for the position of bartender might list personal characteristics such as "friendly" and "outgoing."

Once you have a clear understanding of the tasks that each position must fulfill, it is a relatively simple matter to determine what kind of person would best be able to accomplish those tasks. Knowledge, skills and abilities, work experience, and education and training are all examples of the kinds of personal characteristics found in a job specification.

The qualifications you list on the job specification must not discriminate in any way on the basis of race, national origin, sex (unless BFOQ), age (unless BFOQ), marital or family status, religion, or disability. Because of newer disability laws such as the ADA, job specifications now often include the position's physical and mental characteristics.

A job specification for the position of bartender may have some of the following characteristics.

REQUIRED KNOWLEDGE FOR BARTENDERS

Customer and Personal Service—Knowledge of principles and processes for providing customer and personal services. This includes customer needs assessment, meeting quality standards for services, and evaluation of customer satisfaction.

Sales and Marketing—Knowledge of principles and methods for showing, promoting, and selling beverage products or services. This includes marketing strategy and tactics, product demonstration, sales techniques, and sales control systems.

Law and Government—Knowledge of state and local alcohol laws.

Mathematics—Knowledge of arithmetic and the ability to add, subtract, multiply, and divide quickly and with accuracy.

SKILLS REQUIRED FOR BARTENDERS

Service Orientation—Actively looking for ways to help customers and employees.

Active Listening—Giving full attention to what other people are saying, taking time to understand the points being made, asking questions as appropriate, and not interrupting at inappropriate times.

Social Perceptiveness—Being aware of others' reactions and understanding why they react as they do.

Speaking—Talking to others to convey information effectively.

PHYSICAL AND MENTAL ABILITIES REQUIRED FOR BARTENDERS

Memorization—The ability to remember information such as words, numbers, recipes, and procedures.

Manual dexterity—The ability to quickly move your hand, your hand together with your arm, or your two hands to grasp or manipulate beverage containers or to assemble drinks.

Speech recognition—The ability to identify and understand the speech of another person.

Wrist-finger speed—The ability to make fast, simple, repeated movements of the fingers, hands, and wrists.

Extent flexibility—The ability to bend, stretch, twist, or reach with your body, arms, and/or legs.

Trunk strength—The ability to use your abdominal and lower-back muscles to support part of the body repeatedly or continuously over time without "giving out" or fatiguing.

Arm-hand steadiness—The ability to keep your hand and arm steady while moving your arm or while holding your arm and hand in one position.

Oral comprehension—The ability to listen to and understand information and ideas presented through spoken words and sentences in English.

JOB SPECIFICATION

JOB TITLE: Regional General Manager

REPORTS TO: Vice President, Operations

WAGE STATUS: Exempt

Skill Factors:

Education:	Bachelor's degree required.
Experience:	At least one year as a hotel manager or other professional assignment in hotel operations.
Communication:	Oral and written skills should evidence ability to capsulize hotel data succinctly. Must be able to communicate effectively with diverse workforce, including foreign-born employees.

Effort Factors:

Physical Demands:.	Limited to those normally associated with clerical jobs: sitting, standing, and walking.
Mental Demands:	Initiative and ingenuity are mandatory, because the job receives only general supervision. Judgment must be exercised on hotel features to be emphasized, operations to be studied, and methods used to collect property data. Decision-making discretion is frequent. Analyzes and synthesizes large amounts of abstract information into property reports.

Working Conditions:

Travels to hotels in the region from 6–12 days per month. Travels around each hotel to collect lodging data and performance reports. Meets with general managers to discuss performance results. Works mostly in an office setting.

Figure 6.4   Job specification: Regional general manager.

Job specifications may or may not offer the detail to the extent provided in the bartender example. Figure 6.4 illustrates a job specification for a regional manager for a small hotel chain. While it is not as detailed, it still provides an excellent overview of the necessary skills and abilities required for this position.

ONE SIZE DOES NOT FIT ALL

It is perhaps tempting to find a generic job description or job specification that might fit your operation's needs or even a template from one of the dozens of Web sites that provide such information. This is not a terrible thing, but it should be used as only the starting point for developing your own, personalized job descriptions and job specifications. Your forms must accurately represent the unique activities, responsibilities, and desired results for each position in your own operation.

SUMMARY

- Job descriptions and job specifications are excellent tools for recruiting, training, and retaining a qualified labor pool. A well-written job description should be the very first step in the employee selection process.
- The job description lists the tasks or duties associated with a specific position in the operation. Well-written job descriptions often include standards of performance so that employees not only know what to do but how to do it and how well to do it.
- The job specification details the personal qualities or characteristics that an ideal applicant should possess in order to be successful in a given position. Qualifications such as education, training, experience, skills, and abilities are also included on the job specification.
- It is important for legal reasons that neither the job description nor the job specification discriminates with regard to race, religion, or national origin. Age of the applicant and the sex of the applicant could be a basis for the decision-making process so long as those issues are bona fide occupational qualifications and are clearly job related.

PRACTICE QUIZ

1. Most hospitality industry managers cite recruiting and retaining employees as their number one challenge.

   A. True   B. False

2. Having plenty of blank applications on hand and placing help-wanted ads in local newspapers and other publications should be the first step in the employee selection process.

   A. True   B. False

3. Personal characteristics such as eye and hair color are perfectly acceptable on a job specification.

   A. True   B. False

4. Performance standards not only clarify what the employee is to do, but they also state how to do it and to what extent (how well) it is to be done.

   A. True   B. False

5. Job descriptions should detail the personal qualities or characteristics that an applicant should possess in order to be successful in a specific position.

   A. True   B. False

6. Job descriptions and job specifications should not illegally discriminate in which of the following areas?

   A. Race

   B. Religion

   C. National origin

   D. All of the above

7. Which of the following details the tasks to be performed in a specific position?

   A. Work flow analysis

   B. Job specification

   C. Performance standard report

   D. Job description

8. Which of the following is *not* a basic element found on the job description?

   A. Descriptive position title

   B. Title of immediate supervisor

   C. Educational levels and personal abilities required for the position

   D. Tasks and duties performed in the position

9. Performance standards can be used for which of the following?

   A. To describe the day's work for each job

   B. As a basis for rewarding achievement

   C. To describe a job or a position in detail

   D. All of the above.

10. The best job descriptions have which of the following features?

    A. They are well written and include performance standards.

    B. They have been created through brainstorming by management and staff.

    C. They are specific to the operation.

    D. All of the above.

1. Create a job description for a typical position in either a lodging or a food service setting. Include not only a summary of the position but also a list of the position's duties. Of the duties you have listed, which would you consider being "essential functions" and why? What was the most difficult aspect of creating the job description? Be prepared to share your job description with the rest of the class.

2. Based on the job description you created in the previous assignment, assume that an individual who is disabled according to the guidelines of the ADA (see Chapter 2) has applied for the job. Depending upon the individual's disability, of course, would you be able to accommodate the job applicant? Do you feel that you may need to make a reasonable accommodation for the applicant? Give an example of the type of accommodation you might be able to make. Share your findings with the rest of the class.

3. Create a job specification for either a restaurant greeter, hotel front desk clerk, or hotel bellhop. What special characteristics such as skills, abilities, education, knowledge, and work experience would you want to put on the job specification? Explain in detail and provide solid reasoning as backup for the personal characteristics that you have listed. What legal issues must you be concerned with when you create such job specifications? Are the characteristics you have listed bona fide and essential? Explain. Share your findings with the class.

4. From the job description that you created in question one, choose two or three of the duties that you listed and write a standard of performance for each duty. Be sure to explain the how, why, and to what extent each of the chosen duties must be performed. What are the benefits of adding performance standards to each duty listed on the job description? Are there any drawbacks? Explain in detail and be prepared to share your findings with the rest of the class.

5. Working with a team of one or two other students, find examples of poorly written job descriptions. You may have examples from past or current employers, you may be able to find examples on the Internet, or your instructor may be able to provide examples for you. You may also want to look in older, out-of-date human resources textbooks if you have access to any. What are the problems associated with the job descriptions that you have located? How should these errors be changed in order to make the job descriptions more effective? If you have located a job description that is significantly different than those described in this chapter, explain the differences as well as any benefits or drawbacks.

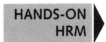

Jenna Hawkins has been trying to reach her best friend, Dee, for days. She is frantic and close to giving up when, finally, Dee answers her phone: "It's Dee. What's up, Jenna?" "My God, Dee," Jenna wails. "I've been calling and leaving messages for days. Where have you been?" "Oh, my mom got sick, and I had to go home and help out for a few days," Dee explained. "I can't afford the roaming charges, so I just turned my phone off, but I'm back now," she said. "Where's the fire?"

"Well, you know I just took that assistant manager's job at Poisson, the fancy seafood place downtown," said Jenna. "I'm in deep trouble; the general manager has been after me to write up a whole new set of job descriptions for the dining room staff, and I don't even know where to begin."

Jenna explained that during the job interview, the general manager had questioned her at length about her experience with job descriptions, and she had assured him that she was well versed in that area. "I basically lied," explained Jenna. "If I can't come up with some decent job descriptions by this Friday, they'll probably fire me."

"Well, we covered that about a year ago in culinary school," said Dee. "Why don't you come over tonight?" she offered. "I'll blow the dust off of some of these old books and you can just copy something from them."

Jenna had often teased Dee about going to culinary school. She felt that it was a waste of time and money. Personally, Jenna had gained her experience through the "school of hard knocks," and she often bragged to Dee about how much more money she was making than her friend. Dee would be graduating in another semester, and she still hadn't lined up a job, but Jenna was happy that her old friend was willing to help her out.

Dee had laid out two tattered textbooks on the coffee table, and when Jenna arrived, they sat down and began to go through them. "How old are these?" asked Jenna. "They look kind of dated." "Well, they were used when I bought them," said Dee. "And that was almost two years ago. I'm not even sure if they use these books at school anymore." "Well, it shouldn't matter," said Jenna. "How hard can this be?"

Dee explained what she remembered from her lectures on the subject of job descriptions to Jenna: Focus on the primary duties and responsibilities of the job, and note any special skills or characteristics that the employee should possess. "Well, there's not much to this," said Jenna, as she began to write some notes on a legal pad that Dee had taken out of her book bag. "Definitely, everyone needs a high school education," Jenna said. "I'd even prefer some college, but we won't get too picky."

"How about transportation," offered Dee. "You don't want anyone who doesn't own a car or live on the main bus route—they'd be calling out all the time." "I don't see anything like that on these examples in the book," said Jenna. "Are you sure that's okay?" "Of course," said Dee. "These are important characteristics that a successful job candidate should have, so it's okay to list them at the top of the job description." "Well, if you say so," replied Jenna. "You're the college girl."

After they had worked for about an hour listing some of the key personal qualities for each position in the dining room, Jenna said, "You know, the duties on this example in the book are pretty close to what we really do at Poisson." "I think I'm just going to copy these down and go with them." "I don't see any problem with that," said Dee. "Anything to save a little time."

Jenna thanked Dee as she carefully folded the notes she had written and tucked them in her purse. "Let's go have a beer," she said. "I don't have to go in till three tomorrow, so I'll have plenty of time to type these up before I have to get ready." "Sounds good," said Dee. "Your boss is really gonna be impressed."

QUESTIONS ▶

1. What are some of the key mistakes that Dee and Jenna are making with respect to designing the job descriptions for each position in the Poisson restaurant's dining room? Is it wise to copy job duties from a textbook in cases such as this? Why or why not?

2. Discuss the personal characteristics that Jenna plans to incorporate into the job descriptions? Can you foresee any potential problems for the restaurant should she decide to write these on the job descriptions? Explain in detail.

3. Do personal characteristics belong on a job description at all? If so, where should they be placed and how should they be written? If not, where do they belong and how should they be written?

4. Are there any important elements to a job description that Dee and Jenna failed to discuss at all? What are they? Why are these elements important?

KEY TERMS ▶

Employee benefits Job perks above and beyond salaries and wages. Examples include vacation pay, employee meals, tuition reimbursement, health insurance benefits, and so forth.

Turnover rates These are usually expressed as a percent and are determined by dividing the number of employees who have left the company (separated) by the number of workers normally employed by the operation.

Employee selection process Locating, recruiting, and hiring the most qualified candidates to fill the hospitality operation's available jobs.

Job description A form that details the essential tasks or duties required in a specific job or position.

Performance appraisal A system whereby management provides formal feedback to an employee on his or her work performance. These are often linked to wage increases and promotions.

Position description Identical to a job description but used for higher manager's positions as opposed to lower-level hourly positions.

Performance standard Details the what, the how, and the how well of a position's specific tasks.

Job specification A form that details the personal characteristics such as education level, training, work experience, and abilities required in an applicant in order to be successful in a specific job or position.

Food specification A written specification that details in a precise way the characteristics of a food product purchased by a restaurant from a purveyor.

 NOTES ▶

1. Michael Garvey, Heather Dismore, and Andrew G. Dismore, *Running a Restaurant for Dummies* (New York: John Wiley & Sons, Inc., 2004).

CHAPTER 7

THE EMPLOYEE HANDBOOK

When you have a good person and you create a good environment for that person, he or she doesn't come to work to do a bad job—they come to work to do a good job.[1]

Leonardo Inghilleri, vice president of human resources, the Ritz-Carlton Hotel Company

CHAPTER OBJECTIVES

After completing this chapter, you will be able to

- Describe the reasons for having an employee handbook in the workplace.
- List the key elements an employee handbook should include.
- Identify the legal ramifications of an employee handbook.
- Describe some of the uses for an employee handbook.
- Explain how a well-designed employee handbook can increase employee morale.

HRM IN ACTION "When do I get paid?" "Where am I allowed to park?" "Am I allowed to eat or drink here on my days off?" "Does the company provide an employee meal, or will I have to pay for that?" It is not at all uncommon for new employees and even seasoned veterans to have dozens of questions about their company policies and procedures. When hospitality industry employees ply their managers and supervisors with questions like these, it's extremely helpful to direct them to an **employee handbook** that clearly describes the established policies and procedures for a particular establishment. If your workplace doesn't provide employees with any written documentation of formalized policies and procedures, misunderstandings, low employee morale, and even expensive legal problems are likely to occur.

RATIONALE FOR EMPLOYEE HANDBOOKS

Perhaps one of the most important reasons to provide a handbook to employees is to alleviate employee confusion regarding the company policies and day-to-day operating procedures. Providing an employee handbook prevents employee confusion, because it provides everyone with the established policies and procedures for the operation. Employees are clear on what the restaurant or hotel's policies are, and they can refer to the handbook to answer any of their basic questions. A thorough and informative handbook will not only make the operation more effective because it helps to encourage consistency of procedures, but it will also improve employee morale, prevent disagreements among employees and between employees and upper management, and may even keep the company out of court, because no one is in the dark about company policies. Because all employees are well informed about the company's policies and procedures, they are more likely to promote the business within the community by spreading the word that it is a good place to work. Ultimately, this may result in a higher caliber of applicants for job vacancies and less employee turnover. Always a good proposition!

Another important reason for providing an employee handbook to employees is to provide a document of management's expectations. Most employees want to grow professionally and be successful; they are eager to know what is expected of them and how they can improve their job performance. A solid orientation and training program will go a long way in helping new and more seasoned employees achieve their goals (and subsequently help management achieve its goals), but a well-crafted employee handbook can serve as a valuable road map that assists the employee along the way.

The actual process of writing an employee handbook forces management to assess and improve its own leadership skills. Management must analyze the practicality and utility of policies in its own unique operation, and then, after concrete policies are established, it can lead employees more effectively because objectives for each position have been evaluated and set, benefits have been considered and perhaps retooled, and personnel policies are in place before contentious issues have an opportunity to arise.

TALES FROM THE FIELD

When I first graduated from culinary school, I took a job as a line cook in a medium-sized hotel operation. A few months after I started work, the chef was suddenly fired for cashing personal checks out of the restaurant's change bank, even though he had apparently been doing this every week for many months. The chef sued the hotel and won his job back—including back wages—because there was no specific policy about this in the hotel's employee handbook. Within two days, the corporate office amended the handbook to specifically include a policy which prohibited employees from cashing personal checks at the hotel.

Jeremy, 23, St. Louis, Missouri

EMPLOYEE HANDBOOKS ARE COMMON IN LARGE OPERATIONS

Large hospitality industry enterprises, such as hotel and restaurant chains, have provided employee handbooks to their full- and part-time employees for years to communicate rules, regulations, procedures, and policies. Newly hired employees in these enterprises are typically given the employee handbook within the first day or two on the job. They are asked to read the handbook, and then they are required to sign a document stating that they have not only received and read it, but that they also understand and agree to the policies and procedures contained therein. While this process may seem somewhat formal and perhaps even unnecessary for smaller, privately owned hospitality businesses, this is certainly not the case. Remember that the success of any lodging or food service operation is largely dependent upon whether these establishments are able to achieve consistency in the way they deliver products and services to their valued customers and guests. This important success factor is primarily dependent upon whether each and every employee is using the same set of guidelines set forth in the employee handbook. The employee handbook enables all operations, whether large or small, to maintain order within the organization because this manual helps to ensure that all employees are in sync with one another, abiding by the same policies and following the same procedures.

EMPLOYEES MUST SIGN FOR IT

Keep in mind that simply passing out an employee handbook to each member of the staff won't do. Employees must sign a statement that they have received the employee handbook, read it, and understand the company's policies and procedures. The employee should be allowed to keep one copy of the signed statement, and the other copy should go into the employee's personnel file. This procedure helps protect management from possible claims that a person was fired because he or she did not know the rules. A competent labor attorney can assist in drafting this form.

A WELL-CRAFTED EMPLOYEE HANDBOOK

A very large organization may have an employee handbook that is quite lengthy, with dozens of headings and subheadings. However, it is important to note that a well-crafted employee handbook does not necessarily have to be a big, thick, professionally printed manual. Many smaller hospitality operations can make do with something much simpler. It's not the look of the handbook that's important; it's what inside that counts.

It is not unusual for some organizations to provide a digital version of the company employee handbook in an effort to facilitate ease of use. Providing the employee handbook digitally also allows management to quickly and effectively make changes to the handbook when necessary. In cases such as this, newly hired employees log on to the company Web site, read the digitized version of the employee handbook, and submit their acceptance of the policies and procedures contained therein electronically. Figure 7.1 provides an example of the numerous headings and subheadings that may be found in a larger hospitality organization's employee handbook. Clearly, many of the employee handbook topics presented in Figure 7.1 would be unnecessary for a small restaurant or lodging operation. Even so, a smaller operation should expect to have an employee handbook that contains a minimum of 10 to 15 pages.

Because each operation is unique, management must develop and document its own unique book of policies, practices, and procedures relating to the hiring and employment of staff. The prudent operator will also hire a competent labor attorney who is familiar with local employment law to review the contents of the employee handbook before management adopts its contents and distributes it to its employees.

WRITE IT YOURSELF BUT HAVE AN ATTORNEY REVIEW IT

While it's true that management could turn the entire project of creating an employee handbook over to an attorney, the fees for doing so could be cost-prohibitive for a smaller hospitality operation. For those who do not feel that they are up to the task of writing an employee handbook from scratch, there are resources available to help management streamline the process a bit. Human resources consulting firms as well as industry trade groups such as the

Welcome to XYZ COMPANY
Disclaimer

Introduction
XYZ COMPANY Mission Statement

Employment
Equal Opportunity Employment
Eligibility for Employment
Familial Employment

Discipline
Criminal Convictions
Violence
Weapons
Alcohol, Drugs, and Illegal Substance Abuse
Sexual and Other Unlawful Harassment

Policies and Procedures
Attendance
Parking
Work Schedule Requirements
Bulletin Boards
Suggestion Box
Time Cards
Breaks
Workplace Dress Code
Medical Attention
Compensation
Overtime
Wage and Salary Disclosure
Payroll Schedules
Taxes, FICA, and Medicare
Tipped Wages
Individual Retirement Accounts (IRAs)
Performance and Evaluation Reviews
Visitors
Safety and Security
Smoking

Company Property
Confidential Information Security
Office Supplies and Postage
Company Vehicles
Company Equipment
Phone Systems, Voice Mail, and Personal Calls
Conservation and Recycling

Computer Related
Computers and Related Equipment
Internet
E-mail and Electronic Communication

Policies for Leave of Absence
Eligibility
Personal Leave of Absence
Sick Leave
Short-term Disability Leave
Unpaid Family and Medical Leave
Funeral Leave
Jury Duty
Military Duty
Severe Weather Closings

Benefits
Overview
Eligibility
Group Medical Insurance
401K Plan
Worker's Compensation
Holidays
Vacations
COBRA
Education—Tuition Reimbursement
Employee Discounts

Termination of Employment
Termination

Acknowledgment
Notice

Figure 7.1   Table of contents page from a sample employee handbook.

ethical dilemma

You recently took a job as a dining room supervisor in a medium-sized restaurant chain. You and one of the restaurant servers have become close friends, and she soon confides to you that she has been dating the bar manager for several months, even though this practice is a violation of written employee policies and procedures. If you inform upper management, both employees could lose their jobs, and you could lose a close friend. If you do nothing and it is later discovered that you knew about the relationship all along, you will appear unprofessional, and it may ruin any chances you may have had for a promotion. Which of the *10 Ethical Principles for Hospitality Managers* is being violated? Can this ethical dilemma be avoided? What will be the negative and positive consequences of your decision? Will any other parties be affected by your decision and, if so, in what way? You have decided that your final decision must be based on the best possible outcome for the greatest number of people. What is your decision?

National Restaurant Association and the American Hotel & Lodging Association can provide guidelines and templates that would at least provide management with a starting point. Remember, however, that each operation is unique, so guidelines and templates must be tailored to the specific operation in order to be effective. A competent labor attorney should always fine-tune the employee handbook before it is distributed to ensure that all wording, policies, and procedures are in accordance with federal, state, and local laws.

BE CLEAR, CONCISE, AND CONSISTENT

It is essential that the handbook be written in a clear, concise, and direct manner so that there is no chance for confusion. The handbook should detail the operation's own unique human resources policies. The fact is that many lawsuits occur because companies do not have documented consistent policies, which may potentially open the door to charges of discrimination or wrongful discharge. A good handbook will rectify this.

SETTING THE PROPER TONE IN THE INTRODUCTION

A well-crafted employee handbook almost always includes a welcome note or greeting from the company's owner or from management. Because many small operations view their employees as valued team members working toward

Photo 7.1   Supervisors can set a positive tone for new employees by answering questions after thoroughly reviewing the employee handbook with them.

achieving shared goals, the overall tone of the handbook should be positive. The employee handbook should serve as a positive tool for encouraging growth, improving employee morale, and aligning employee behavior with company policies. A friendly letter or greeting in which the organization's **mission statement** is outlined helps to set the proper tone for the manual and informs employees of the organization's primary goals.

LEGAL ISSUES AND DISCLAIMERS

Based upon what you learned about at-will employment in Chapter 4, it should come as no surprise that most organizations include a carefully worded **disclaimer** within the employee handbooks that indicate that the handbook should *not* be considered a contract of employment. When employees try to sue their employer, so long as there is an explicit statement indicating that the handbook and its contents do not represent a contract of employment and that the company retains the right to terminate employment at any time and for any reason, courts have repeatedly upheld the **employment-at-will** doctrine when employee handbooks are concerned.

A disclaimer should also appear within the handbook when there is any mention of firing an employee or instituting disciplinary procedures. Often, policy statements list specific courses of action that may be taken prior to terminating an employee. Sometimes this process is referred to as **progressive discipline.** Examples include a verbal warning, a written warning, suspension without pay, termination, and so forth. In some cases, however, an employee's actions may be so unfavorable as to warrant immediate termination. In order to protect the operation from a lawsuit filed by an employee who has been disciplined or terminated, a statement such as the following should appear within the employee handbook, along with the list of examples of unacceptable conduct: "This list is intended as an example only and is not intended to indicate all those acts that could lead to employee discipline."

With this statement, an employee would most likely not contest a termination because "stealing" was not specifically listed in the handbook. Figure 7.2 lists some of the typical disciplinary problems that often occur in hospitality operations. We will cover the employee disciplinary process more thoroughly in Chapter 14.

Examples of Discipline Problems

1. Insubordination
2. Sleeping while on duty
3. Time clock violations
4. Failure to report an accident
5. Violating safety/security regulations
6. Tardiness and absenteeism
7. Destruction of property
8. Theft
9. Fighting
10. Alcohol abuse
11. Drug possession or use
12. Sexual or other harassment
13. Improper conduct with a guest or customer
14. Lewd or immoral behavior
15. Presence on property during nonwork hours
16. Falsifying records
17. Smoking violations
18. Improper break violations
19. False statement on job application
20. Other rule violations

Figure 7.2

An excerpt from an employee handbook that provides examples of discipline problems.

PROBATIONARY PERIOD, TRIAL PERIOD, OR TRAINING PERIOD?

Another issue that management should be aware of when preparing an employee handbook is to avoid restrictive language. Words such as "will," "must," or "in all cases" may legally bind managers to actions they may not want to take in a given case or situation. **Collective bargaining** jargon such as "terms and conditions of employment" or "seniority" also may lead employees to interpret the employee handbook as an employment contract. Finally, avoid referring to periods of employment as "probationary" periods. Otherwise, the handbook may imply that employees are entitled to continue employment after the "probation" is over. Instead, use terms such as "orientation," "training," or "trial" period. As mentioned previously, given the legal ramifications of the employee handbook, it is important for management to have a competent labor attorney review the employee handbook before it is distributed as an official company document to employees.

WHAT TO INCLUDE IN THE EMPLOYEE HANDBOOK

While each hospitality business is unique, most small restaurant or lodging operations would want to include each of the following topics:

- *Company overview, mission statement, and welcome message.* Introduce the company with a few paragraphs about its history, growth, goals, ethics, and management philosophy.
- *Disclaimer.* A statement indicating that the employee handbook shall not be construed as an employment contract and that employment is at-will.
- *Equal opportunity employment statement.* State that an employee's religion, age, race, or sex has nothing to do with hiring, promotion, pay, or benefits.
- *Work hours.* Define the workweek and time allotted for meal and rest breaks.
- *Pay and performance issues.* General statements about when paychecks will be issued; the classification of employees (part time, full time, exempt, nonexempt); vacation pay, if applicable; overtime; and tip reporting requirements are normally sufficient.
- *Performance review and evaluation.* State when and how often employees will be evaluated. A statement about in-house versus external hiring policies may also be appropriate for this area.
- *Insurance and other benefits.* The handbook only needs to define who is eligible for insurance, how long a new employee must wait for coverage,

and what portion of premium cost is paid by the company. The organization's insurance company should provide separate literature that detail limits, specific coverage, copayments, and exclusions.

- *Leave of absence.* A policy about vacations and all types of leave (paid and unpaid) including sick, military, funeral, personal, family, medical, and jury duty. List paid holidays along with any pay differential, if applicable.

Most hospitality operations—large and small—would also include the following information:

- *Age requirements in compliance with child labor laws.* The laws may vary from state to state and may differ from federal child labor laws. The law that must be adhered to is the law that is stricter and more favorable to the employee.

- *Orientation and training periods.* Clarify policies that affect new employee orientation and training. Most states' labor laws require employers to pay their employees when they are required to be on property for training and orientation.

- *Work schedules.* This section may clarify the individual who is responsible in each department for preparing work schedules and any policies or procedures that may be required of those employees who need to request certain days off. Clarification of where and when work schedules are posted may also be included here.

- *Standards of conduct and disciplinary procedures (include a disclaimer).* Rules, policies, procedures, and regulations should be detailed in this section, as well as any progressive discipline policy that the organization has in place. A disclaimer stating, "these policies are not all-inclusive" is important.

- *Absences and tardiness policy.* Any policies the establishment has in place with regard to employee absences, no-show and no-call policies, or employee tardiness should be detailed here.

- *Employee meals.* Any procedures or policies that dictate employee meals while on the job should be detailed in this section. If employee meals are charged against an employee's wages, a competent labor attorney should be consulted to ensure the business is in strict compliance with federal, state, and local wage and hour laws.

- *Employee safety and security.* A general policy statement about the importance of adhering to safety standards as well as the operation's security standards should be included in this section. This is the first step in providing reasonable care to protect the organization's employees and customers from harm or injury.

- *E-mail and Internet use.* With the advent of technology, many operations now rely on the Internet as well as e-mail for various communication purposes. The organization's policy with regard to Internet usage and e-mail usage should be clarified in this section.

■ *Cell phones and camera phones.* Most organizations expect their employees to own a personal cell phone. This was often not a problem until manufacturers began to produce cell phones with built-in cameras. These devices can be abused by employees and could consequently land the operation in legal jeopardy. The organization's policy regarding these devices should be clearly presented in this section.

■ *Visiting the property while off duty.* Some lodging and food service operations forbid this practice, so whatever the operation's policy is in this regard, it should be clearly detailed in this section.

■ *Food service sanitation.* This is an especially important section for restaurants and lodging operations with food and beverage operations. General guidelines may be provided here with the statement that more detailed guidelines and appropriate health department codes are available at the actual job location.

■ *Dress code and uniform policy.* Some organization's policies regarding dress and personal appearance are quite rigid, while others are more relaxed. No matter what the policy, it should be clarified in this section.

■ *Alcohol service and awareness policy.* All establishments that serve and sell alcoholic beverages must adhere to federal, state, and local alcoholic beverage control laws. A clear policy as to the organization's adherence to such laws should be included in this section.

■ *Proprietary and confidential information.* In most lodging and food service establishments, this area of the handbook would pertain to confidential employee personnel files.

■ *Document for employee signature acknowledging the employee handbook and receipt of it.* Once the employee has signed the proper document and receipt, it would be placed in the employee's personnel file.

SUMMARY

■ An employee handbook is a valuable workplace tool that provides written documentation of workplace policies and procedures.

■ A well-crafted handbook will prevent misunderstandings, improve employee morale, and help the operation avoid expensive lawsuits.

■ A large hospitality organization may produce an extensive, professionally designed employee handbook, but for smaller operations, a 10- to 15-page self-produced handbook would be sufficient.

■ Management should always have a competent attorney review the employee handbook and its wording to ensure that it adheres to federal, state, and local laws.

■ The list of possible topics that may be included in a well-crafted employee handbook is extensive, so each operation should tailor the handbook and its topics to its own specific and unique needs and goals.

■ The employee handbook should be written in a clear and concise manner, and the overall tone of the writing should be positive.

■ Employees must be required to sign an agreement indicating that they have received, read, and understood the contents of the employee handbook. A copy of the signed receipt or agreement should be retained in each employee's personnel file to confirm that the employee is aware of the company's policies and procedures.

PRACTICE QUIZ

1. Seasoned employees who have been with an organization for a long period of time rarely have questions about company policies and procedures.

   A. True　　B. False

2. A well-crafted employee handbook can take the place of new employee orientation and training.

   A. True　　B. False

3. An employee handbook can have a positive impact on misunderstandings and employee morale.

   A. True　　B. False

4. Large hospitality organizations may digitize their employee handbooks and make them available to employees on the company Web site.

   A. True　　B. False

5. Even a well-crafted employee handbook would have no real impact on an operation's ability to attract and retain quality workers.

   A. True　　B. False

6. A successful employee handbook can do which of the following?

   A. Save management time

   B. Improve employee morale

   C. Prevent disagreements

   D. All of the above

7. Which of the following topics would most likely *not* be found in an employee handbook?

   A. Company overview and welcome letter

   B. Pay and performance issues

   C. A listing of each employee's address and phone number

   D. Leave of absence policy

8. The best reason to have a competent attorney review the employee handbook prior to its distribution to the employees is to ensure the following:

A. The writing is clear and concise.

B. The format of the handbook follows industry regulations.

C. The policies adhere to federal, state, and local laws.

D. The handbook can be digitized for delivery on Internet.

9. The sentence, "This list is intended as an example only and is not intended to indicate all those acts that could lead to employee discipline" is an example of

A. A rejoinder

B. A faux pas

C. An epitaph

D. A disclaimer

10. The writing tone of the employee handbook should be

A. Positive, so as to engender the spirit of teamwork and shared goals.

B. Formal because of the legal nature of the handbook.

C. Funny and witty to ensure that employees do not get bored while reading it.

D. Stern and severe so that employees know the company means business.

REVIEW QUESTIONS

1. Explain in your own words why an employee handbook requires a disclaimer asserting that the handbook is not to be construed as a contract of employment. What does this disclaimer have to do with at-will employment? Be specific and use examples from the lecture and the textbook where appropriate.

2. Many cities and some states now prohibit or restrict workplace smoking, and some states require that employers have a written smoking policy. Research the law in your own community and write a smoking policy that would apply to the employees in a typical lodging or food service establishment in your community. Compare your written policy with that of at least one other student. Print a copy of your local ordinance and compare your smoking policy with the ordinance. If you are in a community that has no specific legislation regarding smoking in the workplace, write a smoking policy that clarifies your operation's employee smoking policy. Be prepared to share your findings with the rest of the class.

3. Draft a form letter that each employee must sign when he or she receives a copy of the employee handbook. Be prepared to explain in class each of the elements of your form letter and how those elements will protect your legal rights as the business owner or manager.

4. Should a restaurant or a lodging operation have a written policy regarding employees' use of the Internet, e-mail, and camera phones? If so, why? If not, why not? If an organization chooses not to have a written policy, what legal problems might the organization encounter? Explain in detail.

5. If you have a copy of an employee handbook from either a current or previous employer, identify some of the key features of the handbook and explain how those features follow the information presented in this chapter. Are there features that are unusual or do not follow this chapter's guidelines? Explain in detail. If you do not have an employee handbook, conduct an Internet search and download a copy.

HANDS-ON HRM

Barry Dither's hands began to shake as he opened and read the first letter on the neatly stacked pile that his secretary, Mrs. Hickton, placed on his desk earlier that morning. Dithers, the general manager of the downtown Royal Arms Hotel, has dealt with a lot of mail during his eight-year tenure with the property, but he cannot remember any letter frightening him quite as much as this one. His hands were still trembling as he picked up the phone and rang his secretary's outer office: "Mrs. Hickton," he said in a shaky voice, "get Franks from human resources up here right away, and put in a call to our attorneys: we're being sued for $4.5 million dollars!"

Dithers read and reread the letter from one of the state's largest law firms. He was just starting to grasp the magnitude of it when Leo Franks, the hotel's director of human resources, burst into his office. "What is it, Barry?" asked Franks. "Mrs. Hickton said she thought you were about to have a heart attack." Dithers, without muttering a word, handed the letter to Franks. As Franks quickly scanned the letter's contents, he located a chair, looked up at Dithers, and said in disbelief, "Why, he's suing us for millions! This is crazy! That was a clean termination if ever there was one."

"Well, I'm no lawyer," said Dithers. "But even if we can win this, it's going to cost the company a ton of money. We could all lose our jobs over this." Dithers told the human resources director that the hotel's attorneys had asked that he immediately fax them a copy of the letter. "In the meantime," said Dithers, "we need to pull this guy's entire file and prepare a full report of just how all this went down."

Ten months ago, two female banquet servers accused Justin Elliott, one of the hotel's banquet managers, of using the camera on his cell phone to take lewd photographs of the female servers while they were setting up and breaking down the hotel's banquet rooms before and after functions. "He told me to get down under a table and pick up some trash that was on the floor," stated one of the servers in her report to human resources. "He knows these dresses we're required to wear get all hiked up when he makes us do that, and he usually just stands back and gawks and snickers at us making fools of ourselves." "This time it was different, though," the other server had noted in her report. "I saw him holding his cell phone down by his waist, and I knew right away that he was takin' pictures of us crawlin' around on the floor." The servers stated in their reports that they confronted Elliott about the pictures. "He just laughed at us, and he even showed us the pictures he'd taken," they stated. "He told us to get back to work and to quit complaining or he'd post them on his personal Web site for the whole world to see."

At the time, both Dithers and Franks had agreed that they would terminate Elliott immediately—no written or verbal warnings—immediate termination. Even though the banquet manager had been with the hotel for more than 10 years, neither executive felt that they could not run the risk of a sexual harassment lawsuit, if they allowed him to remain in his position. During the termination interview, they told Elliott that using his cell phone to photograph his female employees without their permission was particularly egregious and that he would be wise not to use the hotel as an employment reference in the future.

"I don't see the problem here," said Franks. "As I mentioned before, this was a clean termination if ever there was one." "I do," replied Dithers. "We never had a written policy about employees using their cell phones at work to take pictures of other employees until *after* this all happened." "But what about the sexual harassment issue?" argued Franks. "We got him dead in the water there, especially with the statements those two servers gave us." "Wrong again, Leo," said Dithers glumly. "We didn't even follow our own sexual harassment policy on this, and I can't find any documentation in Elliott's file that indicates that he even completed our updated sexual harassment training." "I'm going to pull my master copy of the employee handbook," said Franks, somewhat defeated. "We're going to have to go through it with a fine-toothed comb and update it big time!" "I wish to hell those attorneys would call," said Dithers.

QUESTIONS ▶

1. If Justin Elliott's lawsuit is claiming "wrongful termination" because the hotel's employee handbook did not specifically provide a policy regarding the use of cell phone cameras at work, what are his chances of prevailing? What arguments might the hotel's attorneys present in its defense?

2. Because of the increased use of technology in the workplace, what policies should the hotel have in writing with respect to employee abuse of these technologies? Should there be separate policies on Internet use, cell phone use, instant messaging, and e-mail use? Explain.

3. Why is it important that the hotel's general manager says that the hotel did not even follow its own sexual harassment policy? Had these managers decided to terminate the employee on the grounds of sexual harass-

ment (as opposed to using his cell phone camera); how should they have proceeded?

4. Explain the importance of documenting employee awareness training with respect to such things as sexual harassment, alcohol awareness, and so forth. If Elliott did in fact miss the updated sexual harassment training, how might this affect his lawsuit against the hotel? Explain in full.

KEY TERMS ▶

Employee handbook A booklet that explains key benefits, policies, procedures, and other general information about the company.

Mission statement A short statement or paragraph that clearly articulates an organization's goals and objectives.

Disclaimer A statement made to free oneself of legal liability or responsibility.

Employment-at-will A legal doctrine that holds that employees may quit or leave a job at any time for any reason and they may be fired from a job at any time for any reason.

Progressive discipline Disciplinary procedures that become progressively more severe as the infraction becomes more severe.

Collective bargaining A term associated with labor unions meaning to bargain or to negotiate.

NOTES ▶

1. Sandra Sucher and Stacy McManus, "The Ritz-Carlton Hotel Company," *Harvard Business Review* (March 2001).

CHAPTER 8

ADVERTISING AND RECRUITING

I encourage restaurants to employ single moms; they have plenty of energy. Compared to what some of them do as a single parent, working in a restaurant is considered a "break" one glad mom told me.[1]

Maren Hickton, restaurant industry consultant, Pittsburgh, Pennsylvania

CHAPTER OBJECTIVES

After completing this chapter, you will be able to

- Identify key factors that define the labor market and the labor pool.
- Demonstrate how the labor market and the labor pool affect management's ability to recruit qualified workers.
- Provide examples of how the Internet has helped to expand the labor market.
- Define employee turnover and explain the direct and indirect costs for the hospitality business.
- Identify a hospitality business's internal and external sources of labor.
- Identify recruitment strategies that allow hospitality managers to tap both internal and external labor sources.
- Demonstrate how cultural diversity awareness can improve employee recruitment strategies.

HRM IN ACTION Successful hospitality operations, both large and small, must deliver quality products and services to their valued guests and customers, and they must do this with the help of people. Because the hospitality industry is people-driven, it is essential that operators attract a qualified pool of job applicants, hire the right applicant for the right job, provide thorough and ongoing training, and communicate with staff in such a way that the

133

work environment itself becomes a key motivator in ensuring employee job satisfaction. A happy, self-motivated staff practically guarantees customer satisfaction, not to mention the overall success of the business.

THE LABOR MARKET AND THE LABOR POOL

In the world of human resources management, **employee recruitment** involves locating and maintaining a pool of qualified applicants to fill positions within the organization. Larger hospitality businesses normally have a professional human resources department who can develop strategies and implement plans for doing this. Smaller operations do not usually have this luxury and must, therefore, be very diligent in their recruiting strategies. Effective human resources planning allows management to staff the organization at the right time with the right people. All hospitality operations, both large and small, will have their efforts somewhat impacted by certain external factors that influence the **labor market.** The labor market is the geographical area in which the hospitality business focuses its recruiting efforts. The **labor pool** is made up of the individuals who live within the labor market and who possess the skills, attitudes, knowledge, and abilities that the hospitality operation requires. Factors such as the location of the operation will influence things like education levels, personality types, unemployment rates, competitor recruiting practices, median age of the population, and diversity levels, to name a few.

A hotel located in a wealthier suburb of a particular city that is not well served by public transportation may have difficulty attracting and retaining job applicants who reside in a downtown area, or further from the hotel. Often, in cases such as this, the hotel finds it must subsidize the employees' wages with a monthly bus pass or subway pass in order to successfully compete with downtown hotels and other businesses to retain their more qualified employees. Hospitality operations that are located in or near major metropolitan areas normally have more local recruiting opportunities than those operations that are located 50 miles or more from the nearest major city.

THE INTERNET EXPANDS THE LABOR MARKET

The explosion of Web-based job sites such as Monster.com has greatly expanded the geographical area in which organizations can now successfully recruit qualified employees. Organizations can post job openings on these Web-based job sites, and potential applicants located anywhere in the world can submit résumés electronically for consideration. These sites can be effective when locating top

TALES FROM THE FIELD

I worked in a restaurant while I was in school, and we were constantly short-handed. This caused a lot of problems because we never had enough help, and people who were hired to work only part time were putting in tons of hours and were constantly working overtime. Management complained about everything, and the morale was so bad that the employee turnover was like a revolving door. What bothered me the most was that we had a pretty steady stream of applicants, but a lot of them did not speak English very well, and because none of the managers could even utter a word of Spanish, these applicants were simply ignored. Right then, I decided to sign up for a couple of Spanish classes. I knew that if I wanted to own a restaurant some day, I needed to jump-start my cultural education so that I wouldn't be afraid of people who are different than me like these managers were.

Jessica, 26, Bloomington, Indiana

talent to fill middle- and upper-level management positions but probably have little to no impact when a restaurant needs to hire a dishwasher or when a hotel needs to increase its housekeeping staff. Today, large hospitality operations often maintain separate human resources areas as part of their own corporate Web sites so potential applicants can view job openings and apply for jobs online.

While still somewhat uncommon, smaller hospitality operations are also slowly starting to embrace the World Wide Web by professionally designing and maintaining their own Web sites. As time progresses, small restaurant and lodging operations will most likely post job openings and accept online applications via their own Web sites.

SMALLER OPERATIONS HAVE SOME ADVANTAGES

Because the competition for qualified applicants is so fierce, many small hospitality operations feel that the larger organizations hold all the cards because of their deep pockets and their ability to invest large sums of money into their recruiting, hiring, and training efforts. However, managers and owners of small operations often fail to realize that they actually have a distinct advantage over the big guys: That advantage is their actual "smallness," their ability to operate lean and mean, making quick but well-informed decisions and effectively adapting to changing market conditions. Figure 8.1 illustrates the many steps larger organizations must often take during the hiring process, once they've ac-

1. Applicant submits job application either online or in person at the human resources office.
2. Human resources conducts a short, prescreening interview either in person or by phone.
3. Unqualified applicants are eliminated from the pool at this time.
4. Most qualified applicants are scheduled for a more in-depth personal interview.
5. Three to five top candidates are selected from this pool for further consideration.
6. Preemployment tests for ability, aptitude, honesty, and personality are administered.
7. Specific department managers interview candidates who have made the cut thus far.
8. Additional interviews may be scheduled with other employees in the department in which the potential candidate will work.
9. Department manager advises human resources which candidate he or she chooses for employment.
10. Human resources makes a conditional job offer contingent upon the applicant successfully passing a preemployment drug test and a criminal background check.
11. A formal job offer is made and the candidate's start date is scheduled, as is a reservation for participation in new employee orientation.
12. New employee participates in orientation prior to beginning on-the-job training.

Figure 8.1   Preemployment screening activities for a large hospitality organization.

cepted a job application and before they are able to make an actual job offer. Smaller operations are able to interview, screen, hire, and even begin training the candidate within the same amount of time it takes many larger organizations to evaluate a job candidate's suitability for a particular position.

EMPLOYEE TURNOVER

When employees leave an organization either voluntarily or involuntarily, the cost to the organization can be substantial. **Employee turnover** is defined as the voluntary and involuntary **separations** of employees from employment within a given operation. **Turnover rates** are calculated by dividing the number of employees who have left the company, or separated, by the number of

TALES FROM THE FIELD

My professor told me that the 'new hotel in town' had called her seeking full- and part-time front-office staff. The hotel was hopeful that my professor could recommend quality students who may be interested in such positions. I thought, *What the heck,* and I applied that very afternoon. I spent the next four weeks interviewing with this department, that department, this manager, that supervisor, and I was even interviewed by a group of other front-office workers. Finally, the front-office manager told me that my school schedule conflicted with the hotel's needs, and that they would not be able to offer me a position at this time. I couldn't believe it. I wrote my school schedule down for them when I first turned in the application, and I made it clear that I would only be available for nights and weekends. What a waste of my time and their time. I applied for the same position at another nice hotel, and they made me a job offer within four days.

Audrey, 20, Louisville, Kentucky

employees within the organization. For example, a restaurant that employs an average of 26 full- and part-time employees and has had 32 separations in the past year would calculate its annual turnover rate as follows:

$$\frac{32 \text{ employee separations}}{26 \text{ employees (average)}} = 123 \text{ percent turnover rate}$$

Operations may choose to calculate their turnover rates on a monthly, quarterly, semiannual, or annual basis. In addition, the turnover calculations may focus on the entire organization, as above, or this calculation can pinpoint turnover rates within certain departments or divisions of the organization. For instance, a lodging operation may want to track its turnover rates in the housekeeping department, the food and beverage department, and the front-office department.

Clearly, industry turnover rates are higher in some areas of hospitality operations than in others. For example, entry-level, low-wage positions tend to turn over at a higher frequency than better-paying supervisory and management positions. A 1998 survey conducted for the American Hotel Foundation places the cost of turnover between $3000 and $10,000 per employee.[2] Another study conducted in the year 2000 put the cost of replacing a worker at a New York luxury hotel at more than $12,000.[3]

While some experts argue that it is difficult to assign an actual monetary cost to employee turnover in the hospitality industry, most agree that those costs are both direct and indirect. Examples of direct and indirect costs include the following:

DIRECT COSTS OF EMPLOYEE TURNOVER

- Recruiting costs including advertising
- Selection costs including time spent interviewing and prescreening applicants
- Prescreening costs such as drug tests and background checks
- Employee uniform costs
- Training and orientation costs

INDIRECT COSTS OF EMPLOYEE TURNOVER

- Lowered employee morale leading to a decrease in productivity
- Customer complaints due to poor food, product, or service quality
- Lost revenues due to poor customer satisfaction, prompting comps and discounts
- Lost productivity during training
- Negative customer word-of-mouth referrals due to poor product and service quality

Because it can be difficult for owners and managers to accurately assess the true-dollar cost of employee turnover, researchers at Cornell University have designed a free Web-based management tool that helps hotels and restaurants accurately weigh the cost of employee turnover. Figure 8.2 provides additional information about this tool.

Turnover Cost Evaluator can be accessed through Cornell University's Center for Hospitality Research Web site located at the following URL: www.hotelschool.cornell.edu/chr/research/tools/turnover/

New visitors to the site are asked to register, at no cost or obligation. The evaluator, codeveloped by Cornell Hotel School Professor Timothy R. Hinkin and Associate Professor J. Bruce Tracey, allows users to enter data that is specific to their organization and provides them with a detailed cost analysis of employee turnover. It can be used to assess the turnover costs associated with a number of line, supervisory, and managerial positions and allows users to modify their entries to examine a variety of scenarios. Currently the tool is focused on the lodging industry, but it contains a food-and-beverage section that can be used by restaurants as well.

Figure 8.2   Cornell University's Web-based management tool: Turnover Cost Evaluator. *(Courtesy of Cornell University Center for Hospitality Research.)*

IDENTIFYING POTENTIAL JOB APPLICANTS

Perhaps the best place to search for new talent is right under your very nose. In other words, your own employees are often an excellent source of referrals and can recommend candidates for future job openings. Eager, motivated employees are generally happy to recommend friends, relatives, classmates, or even neighbors who may be interested in full- or part-time work in your establishment. It is important to note that some organizations have a **nepotism** policy that prohibits the organization from hiring relatives of individuals who are already employed by the organization. Other organizations may be a bit more lax about this policy and will allow relatives to be hired but prohibit any employees from being directly supervised by their relatives. For example, if Aunt Sally is the dining room manager of the hotel, her nephew, Joseph, would be prohibited from working in a position where Aunt Sally would be his immediate supervisor. Still, there are plenty of other organizations that do not have any such policy. These organizations allow employees who are relatives to work within the same establishment and even in the same department, with other relatives serving as their immediate supervisors.

EMPLOYEE REFERRALS

Establishing an employee referral program within an organization may have several distinctive advantages over more traditional methods of advertising for new workers. Employees with hard-to-find job skills may know others who have similar skills and who do the same kind of work. Also, new recruits who have been referred to the organization by current employees will already have some knowledge about the organization based upon information provided by the employees who referred them. Thus, referred applicants may be more attracted and intrigued by the organization than casual walk-in applicants. Another advantage of an employee referring a friend is that the friend may potentially have similar work habits and attitudes to those of the current employee. However, even if their work habits are different, friends will often work hard to perform well in a new job so that they do not disappoint the person who recommended them for the position.

While soliciting employee referrals can be an excellent recruitment technique, hospitality managers must be careful that they do not intentionally or unintentionally discriminate when they use this method. Because this method tends to maintain the status quo of the current workers in terms of race, religion, sex, and other protected classes, the results have the potential to be viewed as discriminatory and could put the operation in legal jeopardy. Which is the best policy with regard to hiring friends and relatives? There really isn't any one-size-fits-all policy that would work in all operations. Whatever policies and stipulations work for your own unique operation should serve as the best policy for you.

PAYING A REFERRAL BONUS

Operations that successfully utilize employee referrals as a source for potential job candidates will often set up an incentive system for employees so that the employee who provides a referral receives some sort of incentive, often a cash reward, if the referral is hired and remains with the company for at least a specified amount of time (typically a minimum number of months). This sort of incentive system is commonplace in many fast-food chain operations, and offering some sort of bonus tends to work well for most types of operations, provided the ground rules for earning the bonus are clearly communicated in advance. An example of a referral bonus program appears in Figure 8.3.

When an organization that is attempting to fill open positions looks for candidates within the company, it is doing **internal recruiting.** Soliciting employee referrals is just one source of internal recruiting. Larger organizations may also post job openings internally, promote and transfer employees from within, solicit referrals from vendors, and even solicit referrals from former employees. When an organization says it "promotes from within," its goal is not only to maintain employee retention but also to encourage prospective applicants to pursue positions within the organization because there is opportunity for professional growth and upward mobility within the organization. Internal recruiting efforts may also include offering part-time employees full-time work.

When a hospitality business must look to outside sources for recruiting personnel, it is using sources of **external recruiting.** In this particular case, sources of external recruiting may include hospitality and culinary schools and colleges, trade associations, competitors, labor organizations, churches and synagogues, temporary agencies, advertising, and so on. In truth, the most successful operations generally focus their efforts both internally and externally in order to attract a diversified and qualified pool of job applicants.

RECRUITING IS MARKETING

Professor Robert M. Kok of Johnson and Wales University in Providence, Rhode Island, believes that for managers to be more effective as recruiters, both in terms of time and money spent and quality of applicants found, they need to focus on target groups of applicants first (i.e., sources), and then select the tools (i.e., methods or techniques) that allow them to communicate in the most ef-

> ## $200 BONUS IS YOURS
> ## EMPLOYEE REFERRAL BONUS PLAN
>
> Do you have a friend, relative, neighbor, classmate, or other known associate who you feel would like to join our XYZ Restaurant family? If so, you can earn a $200 one-time cash bonus if your recommendation works out. Here's how the program works:
>
> 1. Refer a friend or a relative for any job opening that you feel the individual would be qualified for.
>
> 2. The individual must meet all preemployment eligibility requirements and must possess the necessary skills and abilities to successfully perform the duties of the job.
>
> 3. If we hire your referral and the individual successfully completes his or her first 90 days of employment with a positive evaluation from his or her immediate supervisor, you will earn a $100 cash bonus!
>
> 4. If the individual remains with our restaurant for an additional 60 days and earns a favorable review from his or her supervisor, you will receive an additional $100 cash bonus!

Figure 8.3   Sample referral bonus plan for a restaurant employee.

fective ways with those targeted groups. Professor Kok believes that a major problem in recruiting effectively has been management's failure to think clearly as marketers. "Focus on your desired sources of employees first, then find the best methods/techniques to use in recruiting people from those source groups," says Kok.

WALK-IN APPLICANTS

People who simply show up at your door requesting a job application are known as *walk-in applicants*. Different hospitality operations handle walk-ins in different ways. It is not uncommon for the human resources departments of larger operations to require walk-ins to complete the application in the human resources

ethical dilemma

Josie just signed a franchise agreement with a new, up-and-coming restaurant chain that specializes in premium, deli-style sandwiches, homemade soups, and other similar fare, served in a dine-in or carryout environment. She's excited about owning her own business even though she knows the competition will be tough. She also realizes that one of her biggest challenges will be her ability to recruit and retain a qualified staff. With less than three months before her grand opening, Josie sets out to visit as many similar establishments in her immediate area as she can to observe how employees at different restaurants interact with customers. When she sees an employee who impresses her, she hands the employee a business card and lets the employee know that she is opening a brand-new place nearby and that she would love to schedule a personal interview with the employee. She quickly earns a reputation among other restaurant owners and managers as a "poacher" who is acting unethically by attempting to steal away the competition's valuable staff. Is Josie violating one of the *10 Ethical Principles for Hospitality Managers* and, if so, which one? If you were Josie, how would you react to the claims of the other owners and managers? Would you decide to continue offering jobs to employees at other restaurants or would you decide to stop?

office. Some large organizations limit the days and the business hours during which they will accept walk-in applicants. For example, one large hotel in Louisville, Kentucky, only accepts walk-in applicants on Tuesdays and Thursdays between the hours of 2:00 P.M. and 4:00 P.M. This policy may stem from the fact that the hotel prefers to have a human resources professional available to speak with each walk-in applicant personally in an effort to get an immediate feel for the applicant's suitability for a specific job opening. Other large organizations have gotten away from accepting walk-in applicants. Instead, they require all job applicants to submit an application online via the company's Web site.

WALK-IN APPLICANTS SHOULD BE WELCOMED

Smaller hospitality operations can seldom afford the luxury of discouraging walk-in applicants. Without exception, small food service and lodging businesses should accept applications all the time, whether the business has an immediate opening or not. It requires little time to hand a formal application to a walk-in job applicant, and even if there are no immediate openings, applications can be kept in an active file until suitable openings become available or the applications are too dated (six months or older) to be valid. If an applicant telephones Charlie Trotter's famous Chicago restaurant to ask whether the restaurant is accepting applications, Mitchell Schmieding, Trotter's director of restaurant operations, will routinely say no, but he will invite the applicant to fax him a résumé and cover letter or submit it to the restaurant's office. He explains to the applicant that he is happy to review a résumé because the restaurant will always consider a qualified applicant when an appropriate position becomes available.[4] Even though Charlie Trotter's restaurant is one of the most highly regarded restaurants in America and is in the enviable position of cherry-picking the very best applicants, Trotter understands that to restrict his recruiting efforts may be to overlook "a future star."

ADVERTISING FOR JOB APPLICANTS

Advertising is another effective method of recruiting to fill open positions. Many hospitality operators use advertisements as a key part of their recruiting efforts, since placing advertisements in local newspapers or magazines has the potential to yield a larger job applicant pool than the referrals provided by employees or through unsolicited walk-ins. Most *want ads* provide a brief job description, information about the employer, the benefits provided, and how to apply. They are probably the most widely used form of employment advertising. Ads may be placed in local newspapers, out-of-town newspapers, and even specialized trade journals, depending upon the needs of the organization. A hotel operation seeking to hire a general manager—a highly specialized recruit —may place an ad in *Lodging* magazine, a trade journal that targets professionals in the hotel and motel industry. The owners of Cincinnati's famed *Maisonette,* Mobil Travel Guide's longest-running five-star restaurant in the country, went all the way to France to search for a replacement for a retiring executive chef who had served the operation for many successful years.

HELP-WANTED ADS HAVE SOME LIMITATIONS

It is important to note that want ads do have some limitations. First, they are expensive. Because the number of words used determines the size of the ad, and the size of the ad determines its cost, most help-wanted ads contain short words and phrases that only outline the bare minimum job qualifications and tell applicants how to apply. In many daily newspapers, the ads have a short shelf life, and if the ad isn't worded well, you may not get responses from the most qualified applicants. In today's labor market, where there is an increased demand for job relevance, quality of work life, and other job satisfaction factors,

FULL-CHARGE LINE CHEF
For restaurant and catering operation needed immediately! Minimum 5 yrs exp required. Send letter of interest, including resume and salary history to: John Smith, 123 Any Street, Anytown, USA, 12345 or fax 555-1234 by Mon., Nov. 7, 2006.
NO PHONE CALLS PLEASE!

Restaurant

Mama Louise's

ALL FRONT-OF-HOUSE STAFF

Mama Louise's is seeking customer service oriented staff with outgoing personalities & the desire to grow with a dynamic company. We offer F/T, P/T, & a fun working environment. Apply 123 Any Street, Anytown, USA, 12345.

EEO

Figure 8.4

Comparison of sample help-wanted ads posted by restaurants.

the need for more descriptive job information and information concerning work environment, supervisory style, and organizational climate are necessary. Figure 8.4 provides a comparison of two different types of restaurant ads.

While both ads contain approximately the same number of words and spaces, the ad for Mama Louise's probably cost a bit more to place because of the use of bold and italic text, which do make the ad stand out. You may also have noticed the *EEO* in the bottom right-hand corner of Mama Louise's ad. This stands for "equal opportunity employer" and using the abbreviation allows the restaurant to save money on the cost of its ad. This should also serve as a reminder to you that the wording of the advertisement may not illegally discriminate or in any way violate Title VII of the 1964 Civil Rights Act. In fact, most newspaper publications today have strict policies that prohibit ad copy that illegally discriminates.

Ad copy, layout, and design should reflect an accurate image of the company and department represented. Because many of today's job applicants value quality-of-life issues, well-written ads may also need to reflect whether the company is

- Conservative or progressive
- Small, medium, or large
- Dynamic or static
- Expanding or stabilizing
- Centralized or decentralized

The key objective when placing a help-wanted ad is that you are trying to convince qualified applicants to apply. Be sure to emphasize the benefits of the job while being specific enough about the requirements and job responsibilities to weed out candidates who would not be right for the job.

| Photo 8.1 | Some hospitality businesses seek applicants outside the company by placing "want ads" in the classified section of local newspapers. |

Maren L. Hickton, owner of Maren Incorporated, a full-service hospitality consulting and marketing firm based in Pittsburgh, Pennsylvania, offers the following excellent advice with respect to finding qualified job applicants:[5]

> Hire carefully and seek employees through sources other than the local newspaper. Advertise for "professional servers for growing business" at employment agencies and other sources including culinary school internships. Scrutinize employee applications and do not hire on the spot. Make them come in for a second interview; this tactic creates an aura of privilege to work there—as it should be. Check references. Ask for written references. Award bonuses to employees who find you other good employees that last at least three months.

DIVERSITY—THE NEW WORKFORCE

Due to an ever-increasing demand for qualified workers in the hospitality industry, ethnically diverse groups, which have for so long been overlooked, are now getting much more attention from hospitality industry managers struggling to fill positions. Recent immigrants to the United States are settling more and more into smaller communities, and these individuals may represent a huge, untapped source of qualified labor. Senior citizens who are retiring in droves thanks to the aging baby boom generation are also an important part of this new workforce, as are single moms and even displaced homemakers. When considering the extent of cultural diversity in the United States, consider the following information supplied by the *2002 American Community Survey Profile.*[6]

ETHNIC BREAKDOWN

- 68 percent of Americans are white, non-Hispanic.
- 14 percent are of Hispanic origin.
- 13 percent are African-American.
- 4 percent are Asian.
- 1 percent is American Indian and Alaska Native.
- 2 percent reported two or more races.

DISABILITY AFFECTS 1 IN 5

- There are 49.7 million people with some type of disability in the United States in 2000.
- This represents 19.3 percent of the 257.2 million civilians age five and over.

WOMEN

- There are 140 million women in America, 51 percent of the general population.
- 13 percent of these women are African-American.
- 12 percent are Hispanic.
- 4 percent are Asian and Pacific Islander.

In its *2004 Report to Industry,* the Multicultural Foodservice and Hospitality Alliance suggests that the food service and hospitality industry employs more women and minorities than any other industry, on average.[7] Consider the following:

WORKFORCE

- 72 percent of the restaurant industry's workforce is composed of women and minorities.
- 17 percent of the restaurant industry's workers are Hispanic.
- 12 percent of the restaurant industry's workers are African-American.
- 3 percent of the restaurant industry's workers are women.
- 5 percent of the restaurant industry's workers are Asian.

SUPERVISORS

- More than 66 percent of supervisors in the restaurant industry are women.
- 16 percent of supervisors are African-American.

- 13 percent of supervisors are Hispanic.
- 6 percent of supervisors are Asian.

BUSINESS OWNERS

- Almost one out of four (24 percent) of eating and drinking establishments is minority owned.

TARGETING THE NEW WORKFORCE

Attracting potential applicants from the new workforce does not have to be difficult; it simply requires more aggressive recruiting practices. Instead of waiting for members of the new workforce to come to you, you have to go to them. One way to do this is to check your local phone book for the names of organizations that support members of the new workforce. Check local newsstands for newspapers and magazines that will help you target ads specifically aimed at these groups. Hospitality managers should take the time to explore their communities in order to find ways to reach these groups. Usually, you can locate members of diverse ethnic groups at community centers or job placement offices. In addition, community organizations, places of worship, and public agencies will often reveal an untapped labor market. You might also find recent immigrants looking for work in English as a Second Language (ESL) classes held at local high schools and universities.

Photo 8.2   An ESL class may be a good source for hospitality managers to find immigrants looking for work.

It is important to remember that the one-size-fits-all approach to advertising is not very effective when targeting the new workforce. Ads should be rewritten so that they market your business and show what you have to offer, not simply what you need. Take an inventory of everything that your business has to offer a potential applicant, and then use **hot buttons**—key items such as services or benefits—that will most appeal to your target audience.

HOT BUTTONS

Senior citizens may be attracted to your organization if you focus on the solid training that you provide and if you emphasize the importance of the experience that a typical senior brings to the table. Single moms may appreciate the flexibility in scheduling that your operation provides, as well as your overall benefit package. Immigrants who struggle with English may be attracted to a work environment that employs other such workers, and certainly, if someone in management is bilingual, then this can be seen as attractive as well. Many immigrants who struggle with English would welcome the opportunity to learn the language, so providing off-hours for instruction in ESL, either in your own facility or somewhere off-site, would be very attractive.

LANGUAGE SOLUTIONS FOR MANAGERS AND SUPERVISORS

The language and culture gap between staff and hourly employees in the hospitality industry often becomes the source of misunderstandings, accidents, frustrations, and high turnover.[8] Because nearly 20 percent of the restaurant industry's workforce is composed of people of Hispanic origin, the ability to speak and understand basic Spanish words and phrases could provide the hospitality manager with a real competitive advantage with regard to recruiting talented employees. A number of organizations provide excellent tools and products that can assist management in its day-to-day operations. The Multicultural Food Service and Hospitality Alliance is just one example with its very successful *QuickVue English to Spanish Workplace Language Guides.* The organization offers pocket translation guides as well as colorful posters that assist restaurant and hotel managers in communicating more clearly with Spanish-speaking employees and coworkers. The National Restaurant Association's Educational Foundation as well as the Educational Institute of the American Hotel & Lodging Association also offer tools, guides, and services to operations that struggle with language barrier issues.

SUMMARY

- Successful hospitality business operators must attract a qualified pool of applicants, hire the right applicant for the right job, and provide consistent and on-going training in order to ensure success for the employee and for the operation.

- The labor market and labor pool within that market will have an impact on the manager's ability to successfully recruit talented employees.

- The Internet has expanded the labor market with Web-based job sites as well as with large hospitality organizations that now post job openings and accept online applications on their own corporate Web sites.

- The direct and indirect costs of employee turnover can be substantial, and hospitality managers will often see a negative effect on their recruiting efforts if the operation's turnover is high.

- Potential job applicants can be recruited both internally and externally; each source of recruitment provides advantages and disadvantages, depending upon the unique aspects of the operation.

- Employee referral programs and employee referral bonus plans are an excellent example of internal employee recruiting methods.

- Small operations seldom have the luxury of being fully staffed, and these operations should accept walk-in applicants when it is possible.

- Advertising normally consists of placing a help-wanted ad in the local newspaper, but in order for a want ad to be targeted, it should be carefully written to ensure the operation attracts applicants with the necessary skills and abilities to fill the specific position.

- The new workforce consists of minorities, women, displaced homemakers, and recent immigrants; each of these groups provides an untapped source of talented employees, but the hospitality manager must be proactive in reaching this potential labor market.

PRACTICE QUIZ

1. Hospitality operations that are located 50 miles or more from the nearest major city will normally have less local recruiting opportunities than those locations nearer to major population centers.

   A. True   B. False

2. Many large hospitality operations maintain corporate Web sites, but job postings and the ability to submit an online application are still rare for such sites.

   A. True   B. False

3. Because large hospitality operations possess the financial resources to invest heavily in their recruiting and training efforts, smaller operations have no advantages whatsoever over larger organizations.

A. True   B. False

4. Employees who leave an organization on their own are classified as *voluntary separations.*

A. True   B. False

5. A hospitality business that has a strict no nepotism policy would prohibit the hiring of relatives of individuals already employed by the organization.

A. True   B. False

6. Which of the following would *not* be considered a direct cost of employee turnover?

A. Separation costs

B. Training and orientation costs

C. Costs associated with preemployment drug testing

D. Lowered employee morale leading to lost worker productivity

7. Which of the following should be emphasized when writing a help-wanted ad for a local newspaper?

A. A description of the job and the employer

B. The benefits of the job

C. How to apply for the job

D. All of the above

8. One disadvantage of using an employee referral system for recruiting new job applicants is

A. Friends and relatives of current employees should never be hired.

B. An employee referral system tends to maintain the status quo of current employees in terms of race, religion, sex, and other protected classes.

C. Employees will rarely recommend their friends and relatives, even if the employees are satisfied with their work environment.

D. Referrals rarely work out and the effort involved in setting up such an in-house program rarely pays off.

9. Identifying key items that your organization offers such as services or benefits and then presenting those key items in a way that they will appeal to a target audience of potential job applicants is known as

A. Internal recruiting

B. Labor pool analysis

C. Hot buttons

D. External recruiting

10. The No-Tell Motel maintains a year-round housekeeping staff of 23 full- and part-time employees. Voluntary and involuntary separations in the department for the year ending December 31 totaled 37. What is the No-Tell Motel housekeeping department's turnover rate for the year?

   A. 62 percent turnover rate

   B. 112 percent turnover rate

   C. 88 percent turnover rate

   D. 161 percent turnover rate

REVIEW QUESTIONS ▶

1. Your restaurant or hotel needs to hire entry-level workers to fill a variety of front- and back-of-house positions. You have determined to target the Hispanic and senior citizen labor pools in your immediate area. Develop two distinctive help-wanted advertisements that will utilize hot buttons to effectively target job applicants in each pool. You may wish to prepare your ad targeting Hispanics in Spanish, if possible. Remember that the length of the ad in terms of advertising copy will determine its cost: the larger the ad, the more expensive. Where will you place each ad? Why? Are there potential venues for your ad other than the local newspaper? Explain. Be prepared to present your ads to the rest of the class and to support your decisions with examples from both the lecture and text.

2. Telephone the advertising department of your local newspaper and determine the cost and pricing guidelines for a business that wishes to place a help-wanted ad. How does the day of the week on which the ad is to run impact the cost? Do using features such as bold and italics have an effect on the cost? Be prepared to share your findings with your classmates.

3. Assume you own or manage a small lodging or food service establishment. Write a nepotism policy for your establishment. If you choose to write a no nepotism policy, be sure to include sound reasoning and principles for your policy. If you choose to allow the hiring of relatives, be sure to qualify your policy in such a way as to clarify reporting relationships among supervisors, departments, and relatives, where applicable. Locate one other student in your class who has written a policy that is the opposite of your policy and attempt to convince the student to change his or her policy to reflect your own. Were you successful in changing the other student's mind? Why or why not? Be prepared to present your policy and findings to the rest of the class.

4. Conduct a search on the Internet and locate a hospitality-related business Web site in which job applicants may apply for position openings. Describe some of the key features of the company's Web site. Do you feel that the Web site the company uses is an effective way to recruit job applicants? Why or why not? Be prepared to share your findings with the rest of the class.

5. Aside from a large hospitality company that may host its own corporate Web site, there are dozens of specific employment Web sites such as Monster.com where any number of businesses may advertise job openings. Compile a list of at least five hospitality-specific job recruitment Web sites. From the list you have compiled, be prepared to discuss the features of each Web site. Examples include such areas as geographic span of the jobs, types of jobs advertised, types of companies that have placed ads, and so forth. Be prepared to share your findings with the rest of the class.

HANDS-ON HRM

Eric Masters recently began a new job as the rooms division director of a 400-room hotel located in an affluent suburb of a large, southeastern city. Since coming on board nearly eight months ago, Eric has noticed a persistent problem of understaffing in the hotel's housekeeping department. Guest rooms are rarely cleaned in a timely manner, and room attendants are often sent back to correct deficiencies uncovered by the department's floor supervisors. Guest comment cards are overwhelmingly negative toward the housekeeping department, and Eric realizes that he must get to the bottom of the problem before things get so far out of hand that the hotel's profit margin is seriously endangered.

Eric has scheduled a meeting with the hotel's executive housekeeper, Naomi Wilson. Naomi has been with the hotel for nearly 15 years. After working her way through the ranks of the housekeeping department and after completing an associate's degree at the nearby community college, she has held the position of executive housekeeper for the past nine years.

When Eric and Naomi meet, Naomi stresses that she can't remember a time when the housekeeping department has not been "stretched to its limit." "It's hard work," she explains to Eric. "No one wants to clean hotel rooms on this side of town for the wages we pay." "Just talk to Liz," Naomi continues. "She'll tell you how we've been working our employee referral system and placing help-wanted ads, but nothing seems to work." "That's a good idea," says Eric. "Let me ring her office and see if she has a few minutes to join us."

Liz Ribeiro, the hotel's human resources director, has been with the property for nearly as long as Naomi. When Liz joins the meeting, she explains to Eric that the hotel instituted an employee referral program more than 10 years ago. The plan started out successfully, but for the past few years, it has become increasingly difficult to administer as fewer and fewer people have been applying to fill the positions needed in the housekeeping department. "Perhaps it's time to rethink the employee referral system," says Eric. Liz explains that even though the pool of referrals seems to be shrinking, it does bring applicants into the hotel who are already somewhat familiar with the nature of the work and the hotel's expectations. "Besides," Liz adds, "this knowledge that they bring to the table helps us keep our training and orientation costs down."

"Well, clearly," says Eric, "we've got to be doing more." Liz tells Eric that she supplements the program by running ads every week in the newspaper. "I'm spending a fortune on advertising," she says, "but no one ever applies; every hotel in town is hiring room attendants."

"Okay," says Eric. "I'm starting to get the picture." He goes on to explain that in order to remain competitive and to increase guest comment scores, Naomi and Liz are going to need to come up with some creative strategies to locate and recruit qualified staff. "You will have my full support," promises Eric. "This is so important to our overall success that the vice president of operations has made this his top priority."

QUESTIONS ▶

1. What seems to be the primary flaws in the hotel's recruitment strategy? How have these issues led to the staffing problems that the hotel currently faces?

2. What creative strategies could be used that would allow the hotel to tap into labor supplies that have been ignored over the past few years?

3. Is it an asset or a liability that the hotel is located in an affluent suburb of a large city? Explain your answer. If the hotel's location is an asset, how could the hotel capitalize on this? If the location is a liability, what strategies might be employed to turn this liability into an asset for the hotel?

4. As they grapple with this challenge, what kind of support should Naomi and Liz expect from the hotel's general manager and from its vice president of operations? If they request financial resources, how should the money be spent?

KEY TERMS ▶

Employee recruitment The process of locating and maintaining a pool of qualified applicants to fill positions within the hospitality organization.

Labor market The geographical area in which the hospitality business focuses its recruiting efforts.

Labor pool The individuals who live in the labor market and who have the skills, attitudes, knowledge, and abilities that the hospitality operation requires.

Employee turnover The voluntary and involuntary separations of employment within an organization.

Separation A human resources term that refers to individuals who have left the organization, either voluntarily or involuntarily.

Turnover rate A comparison of the number of employees who have left the organization for any reason with the number of employees in the organization that is expressed as a percentage. The turnover rate is calculated by dividing the number of employees separated by the number of employees in the organization.

Nepotism In the work environment, the term normally refers to hiring relatives of individuals who are already employed by the organization. The term could be expanded to include close friends of employees as well.

Internal recruiting Identifying sources of labor from inside the organization.

External recruiting Identifying sources of labor outside the organization.

Ad copy The actual written message included in a print advertisement. Copy may also refer to the spoken message in TV or radio media.

Hot buttons Key items such as services or benefits that are presented within your recruitment material (e.g., want ads or job postings) that will most appeal to your target audience.

NOTES

1. Maren L. Hickton, "Service: Problem Employees," *Restaurant Report, LLC,* (Miami, FL). www.mareninc.com.
2. Robert H. Woods, William Heck, and Michael Sciarini, *Turnover and Diversity in the Lodging Industry* (Washington, DC: American Hotel Foundation, 1998).
3. Timothy R. Hinkin and J. Bruce Tracey, "The Cost of Turnover: Putting a Price on the Learning Curve," *Cornell Hotel and Restaurant Administration Quarterly* 41:3 (June 2000), 14–21.
4. Reprinted with permission from *Lessons in Service from Charlie Trotter* by Edmund Lawler. Copyright 2001 by Edmund Lawler, Ten Speed Press, Berkley, CA, www.tenspeed.com.
5. Maren L. Hickton, "Service: Problem Employees," *Restaurant Report, LLC* (Miami, FL) www.mareninc.com.
6. "Making the Case for Inclusion: The Multicultural Foodservice and Hospitality Alliance 2004 Report to Industry" (Cranston, Rhode Island: MFHA, 2004).
7. Ibid.
8. *QuickVue Guide for Hospitality* (Cranston, Rhode Island: MFHA, 2004).

CHAPTER 9

APPLICATIONS, INTERVIEWS, AND BACKGROUND CHECKS

You need two basic ingredients for good service. You need good training, but before that, you need the right people. Don't bother hiring and training the wrong ones.[1]

Nicholas Nickolas, restaurateur

CHAPTER OBJECTIVES

After completing this chapter, you will be able to

- Identify the purpose and value of a job application.
- Recognize the types of questions on a job application that may be illegal.
- Describe how a job application protects management's rights.
- Understand the importance of previewing a job application before inviting candidates for a personal interview.
- Identify various questioning techniques to be used during a job interview.
- Recognize areas of discussion during job interviews that are illegal.
- Identify the goals of a well-conducted job interview.
- Explain how to avoid charges of negligent hiring in the selection process.
- Define slander and libel.
- Explain the legalities of conducting a routine background check.
- Identify methods for conducting routine reference checks.
- List outside sources for conducting routine background and reference checks.
- Define employee bonding.

 **HRM IN ACTION** Almost everyone who is at least 18 years of age has first-hand experience with filling out a **job application** and sitting through a **job interview.** Have you ever wondered about what happens to that application when you leave it with the clerk at the front desk or with the host or hostess in the restaurant? Who is going to read it, how will that person decide which application warrants a closer look and perhaps an in-person interview, and which application should be rejected? When a job applicant is contacted to schedule a personal interview, how does management know which questions to ask, or, perhaps more importantly, which questions they are allowed to ask? How does management determine that a job applicant is right or wrong for a certain job simply by talking with him for only a few minutes?

It may surprise you to know that managers in some hospitality operations do a poor job qualifying potential employees. The reasons for this are as numerous and varied as the operations themselves. This is one of the primary reasons for the unusually high-employee **turnover rate** in the hospitality industry. One thing is certain: If we agree that matching the right applicant with the right position is fundamental to ensuring that we have a well-trained and motivated staff, capable of delivering high-quality products and services to our valued customers and guests, it's imperative that we do a much better job qualifying applicants.

THE JOB APPLICATION

Today's job application process does not even closely resemble that of a few years ago. In fact, in larger hospitality organizations, there may not even be an actual "form" for the applicant to complete in writing. Rather, the application process is automated and potential job applicants are required to fill out an "online application" via the organization's Web site—they don't even have to go to the facility to complete the application. Powerful computers then take over the screening process by sorting digital applications according to some predetermined selection criteria, spitting out only those applications that contain key words or phrases that suggest an applicant might be a good match for a given position. In very large hospitality organizations, this automation streamlines the process and allows busy human resources professionals to focus their attention on other things.

This luxury of having the job application process automated is something that few smaller hospitality industry operations can afford. For these operations, requiring a potential candidate to complete a good old-fashioned application form by hand and go through the personal interview process is still the way to go. And that's okay because when properly executed, this is a system that still works very well. In addition, having a handwritten application form allows management to make judgments about an applicant's attention to detail, neatness, and other factors that may be important and relevant to specific positions.

TALES FROM THE FIELD

I just love those managers who do all the talking during a job interview. I usually just sit there, smile, nod my head, and agree with everything they say, and before you know it, I've been offered the job—and usually on my terms! I've even been offered a job right on the spot: no application, no interview, no reference check, nothing. How do they know that I can even cook or that I'm not a mass murderer or something? I mean, I didn't take the job because I knew I wasn't right for it, but I probably would have if I'd been desperate enough, at least until something better came along.

Carrie, 24, Louisville, Kentucky

A FACT-FINDING FORM

Although large hospitality organizations may customize their job applications with corporate logos and such, most forms are, for the most part, standardized. They may be purchased at office supply stores or even downloaded from the Internet via computer and then copied as needed by the organization. Most such forms have had a legal review, eliminating potentially illegal questions, but if management is unsure, it would be prudent to have the application form thoroughly reviewed by a local labor attorney.

A well-designed job application provides a fact sheet about each job applicant. The application is standardized in that it asks relevant and job-related questions such as name, address, phone number, type of job wanted, work history, education, special skills, references, and so forth. Figure 9.1 represents a typical job application form.

Personal Data

All job application forms begin with a request for personal data. Requests for name, address, and telephone number are fairly universal. Some questions about an applicant's personal information, however, are considered inappropriate because of federal antidiscrimination laws such as Title VII of the 1964 Civil Rights Act. Questions regarding place of birth, race, religion, age, birth date, or national origin are good examples of the kinds of questions that may lead to a discrimination lawsuit. The ADA also prohibits questions related to a job applicant's medical history. In addition, privacy issues preclude asking for an applicant's social security number. If the applicant is later hired, however, then much of this information may be legally obtained.

APPLICATION FOR EMPLOYMENT

NAME:_____
     (FIRST)   (MIDDLE)   (LAST)

ADDRESS:_____
   (STREET/ PO BOX)   (CITY)   (STATE)   (ZIP)

TELEPHONE: Home_____Business _____ Cell_____

If hired, can you provide the necessary documents to verify that you are authorized to work in the U.S.? YES ❑   NO ❑

Are you 18 years of age or older?   YES ❑   NO ❑

Do you have a valid driver's license? YES ❑   NO ❑   If yes, what state? _____

Number _____

WORK PREFERENCE AND QUALIFICATIONS

Position for which you are applying: _____

Types of office machines/computer programs able to use: _____

_____

Typing Speed (WPM) _____

Please check language(s) you speak. ❑ English ❑ Spanish ❑ Other _____

Do you read and write this/these language(s)? YES ❑   NO ❑ If yes, please list language(s) _____

Do you wish to obtain a permanent position? YES ❑   NO ❑ Full-time ❑ Part-time ❑ Summer only ❑

	Names and Location of Schools Attended	Major Subject and/or Degree	Dates Attended
High School			
Junior College			
College/University			
Trade/Service School			

Figure 9.1 Sample application for employment with a simple disclaimer above the applicant's signature line.

List the names and addresses of all employers for at least the past 5 years, beginning with the most recent. **DO NOT INDICATE "SEE RESUME"**

DATES OF EMPLOYMENT AND SALARY RECEIVED		OCCUPATIONS	EMPLOYER INFORMATION
		Title:	Name:
	Month/Year	Duties:	Address:
To:			
	Month/Year		
			Telephone:
Salary:		Hours per Week:	Supervisor:
		Reason for Leaving:	Title:
From:		Title:	Name:
	Month/Year	Duties:	Address:
To:			
	Month/Year		
			Telephone:
Salary:		Hours per Week:	Supervisor:
		Reason for Leaving:	Title:
From:		Title:	Name:
	Month/Year	Duties:	Address:
To:			
	Month/Year		
			Telephone:
Salary:		Hours per Week:	Supervisor:
		Reason for Leaving:	Title:

May we contact the above employer(s)? YES ❏   NO ❏   If not, list which employers you would like us not to contact.

_____

Do you have relatives employed with this company? YES ❏ NO ❏   If yes, specify name(s).

_____

Have you ever been convicted of any offense other than a minor traffic violation? YES ❏   NO ❏   If yes, please explain, giving dates.

_____

Have you ever been employed by this company? YES ❏   NO ❏   If yes, indicate dates of employment.

From _____   To _____

REFERENCES: (People who know you well, either personally or in business, who are not related to you.)

Name	Phone #	Title	Address	City/State/Zip
Name	Phone #	Title	Address	City/State/Zip

I hereby affirm that the statements made in this application are true to the best of my knowledge and belief. I understand that if this application is incomplete or false statements are made, I may be disqualified from subsequent employment with the company.

_____   _____
Date   Signature

Employment Status   The job application form may also include some questions concerning the applicant's objective for employment and current job status. Questions concerning the position desired, the applicant's willingness to accept offers for other positions as well as her availability to start work, desired salary or wages, and whether she prefers part-time or full-time work and desired work schedule may also be posed in the job application form.

Education and Skills   The education section of the employment application is designed to help identify the job applicant's abilities and skills. Traditionally, education has been a major criterion used to evaluate job applicants, but the importance of an applicant's education level has been somewhat diminished because businesses must now demonstrate how an applicant's level of education is job related and necessary for adequate performance on the job. For instance, an earned degree in accounting may be a BFOQ for the position of hotel **comptroller,** but do applicants for the position of dishwasher need a college degree? Would a qualified applicant for a dishwasher's position even need a high school diploma? Most likely, he or she would not. Questions about specific skills may also be used to judge an applicant's qualifications for a particular position. The skills section of the job application form is perhaps the most useful tool to help employers determine the suitability of a candidate for a particular job. Remember, too, that in some cases education and experience may be interchangeable. For instance, some job listings may ask for a B.S. degree and one year of industry experience, or three years of experience and two years of college.

Work History   Typically, job applicants are asked to list their current as well as past employers, their titles and the positions held at each company, the duties and responsibilities required of each position, the contact information for each employer, reasons for leaving, and so forth. Normally, three to four years of job history will suffice; however, younger applicants are the exception because they may only have one year or less of actual work experience. This information is generally requested in reverse chronological order: The most recent job is listed first followed by the applicant's next most recent job, and so on. This format presents the employer with the most relevant job-related information first, and perhaps more importantly, this information provides the basis for much of the personal interview.

References   Aside from requesting that an applicant provide traditional references from friends or previous employers, an application may sometimes request additional information to determine the suitability of a job applicant. These additional ques-

TALES FROM THE FIELD

A large hotel with a national chain opened recently in my city, and their human resources department conducted a one-day job fair on our campus. They made over 75 **conditional job offers** that day, and I was one of the 'lucky' ones to receive an offer. A few days later, though, the human resources director called me and revoked the job offer because I told a lie on my job application. I said I'd never had a criminal conviction even though three years before, I'd had a DUI. She told me that it wasn't the DUI conviction that necessarily ruled me out; it was the fact that I'd falsified my application. That was a hard lesson because I'll never be able to apply to that company again.

Korey, 22, Louisville, Kentucky

tions may explore circumstances such as the applicant's criminal record, credit history, and whether she has any friends or relatives who are currently employed by the same company, and even whether applicant was ever previously employed by the organization. Criminal record and credit history may be important considerations if the job involves handling cash or other valuables. It is important to note, however, that management must be able to substantiate that this information is job related so that there is no violation of equal employment opportunity laws or credit reporting laws.

Signature Line

Job applicants are almost always required to sign and date their applications. A blanket authorization commonly appears above the signature line, which allows management to check references and conduct a criminal records check and/or request a credit report if this information is job related. Some applications will also include an "at-will" statement to ensure that the job application may not be construed as an employment contract. See Figure 9.2 for an example of an employment application waiver and signature line.

Another common provision of the signature line is a statement that the applicant affirms that, to his or her knowledge, the information provided within the application is true and accurate. Although many job applicants give little or no thought to this clause, falsification of a job application is grounds for termination in most organizations.

PLEASE READ CAREFULLY

APPLICATION FORM WAIVER

In exchange for the consideration of my job application by _____ (hereinafter called "the Company"), I agree to the following:

Neither the acceptance of this application nor the subsequent entry into any type of employment relationship, either in the position applied for or any other position, and regardless of the contents of employee handbooks, personnel manuals, benefit plans, policy statements, and the like as they may exist from time to time, or other Company practices, shall serve to create an actual or implied contract of employment, or to confer any right to remain an employee of _____, or otherwise to change in any respect the employment-at-will relationship between it and the undersigned, and that relationship cannot be altered except by a written instrument signed by the President/General Manager of the Company. Both the undersigned and _____ may end the employment relationship at any time, without specified notice or reason. If employed, I understand that the Company may unilaterally change or revise their benefits, policies, and procedures and such changes may include reduction in benefits.

I authorize investigation of all statements contained in this application. I understand that the misrepresentation or omission of facts called for is cause for dismissal at any time without any previous notice. I hereby give the Company permission to contact schools, previous employers (unless otherwise indicated), references, and others, and hereby release the Company from any liability as a result of such contract.

I also understand that (1) the Company has a drug and alcohol policy that provides for preemployment testing as well as testing after employment; (2) consent to and compliance with such policy is a condition of my employment; and (3) continued employment is based on the successful passing of testing under such policy. I further understand that continued employment may be based on the successful passing of job-related physical examinations.

I understand that, in connection with the routine processing of your employment application, the Company may request from a consumer reporting agency an investigative consumer report including information as to my credit records, character, general reputation, personal characteristics, and mode of living. Upon written request from me, the Company, will provide me with additional information concerning the nature and scope of any such report requested by it, as required by the Fair Credit Reporting Act.

I further understand that my employment with the Company shall be probationary for a period of sixty (60) days, and, further, that at any time during the probationary period or thereafter, my employment relation with the Company is terminable at will for any reason by either party.

Signature of applicant_____ Date: _____

This Company is an equal employment opportunity employer. We adhere to a policy of making employment decisions without regard to race, color, religion, sex, sexual orientation, national origin, citizenship, age, or disability. We assure you that your opportunity for employment with this Company depends solely on your qualifications.

Thank you for completing this application form and for your interest in our business.

Figure 9.2   A detailed application form waiver that the job applicant would sign and date when submitting a completed application form.

ANALYZING APPLICATION FORMS

When a vacant position needs to be filled, initially, a hospitality manager will most likely quickly analyze any completed application forms currently on file. Applications, especially those for hourly positions, tend to "age" very rapidly. That is, applicants find work elsewhere and are no longer available. If there are an insufficient number of qualified applicants, based on this analysis, it may be necessary to place a help-wanted advertisement within the classified section of the local newspaper or to initiate some alternate recruiting method. Small hospitality operations should *always* accept job applications, even if they are unsolicited or there are no vacant positions at the time. It is indeed a rarity to find a small restaurant or lodging business that has all of the employees it will ever need!

When management reviews a job application, it tends to make a number of general observations about the applicant. These observations reveal a lot about a potential employee, and it is often this kind of application preview that allows managers to determine whether to extend an invitation to the job applicant to take the next step: to participate in an interview, in-person with the employer. Some experts suggest that the following questions should be considered when looking over a job application:[2]

- Does the applicant meet the minimum qualifications in the job specifications? If not, no further review is necessary.
- Is the application neat and clean—or messy, with erasures and misspellings?
- Did the applicant follow instructions?
- Is the handwriting acceptable for the job in question?
- Are there any omissions? These should be explored carefully.
- Does the signature match the handwriting? People who read and write poorly, or not at all, sometimes obtain an application, take it home, and have someone else fill it out for them. If literacy is a job requirement, require that applications be completed in person on-site.
- How long was the person employed in each previous job? If the length gets shorter with each job, the applicant may have a problem that is growing in intensity.
- Are there gaps in the applicant's employment history that require further explanation?
- Do the responsibilities or job duties indicate a career that is improving, staying at the same level, or deteriorating?
- Do job choices indicate strong preferences for certain types of work?
- Do the reasons for leaving sound legitimate? Does the same reason occur? If so, this could indicate a problem.

PREPARING FOR THE JOB INTERVIEW

Once it has been determined that a personal interview should be scheduled with a particular applicant, it is always a good idea for management to review the application at least one more time in order to prepare for the actual interview. At this time, management should look for items that they may have in common with the applicant; this allows the manager conducting the interview to develop rapport with the applicant. This is also a good time to make notes about anything listed within the job application form that should be explored further during the interview. Keep in mind that any notes should be made on a

Résumé Mistakes

"Here are my qualifications for you to overlook."

"Education: College, August 1880–May 1984."

"Work Experience: Dealing with customers' conflicts that arouse."

"Develop and recommend an annual operating expense fudget."

"I'm a rabid typist."

"Instrumental in ruining entire operation for a Midwest chain operation."

Reasons for Leaving Your Previous Job

"Responsibility makes me nervous."

"They insisted that all employees get to work by 8:45 every morning. Couldn't work under those conditions."

"Note: Please don't misconstrue my 14 jobs as 'job-hopping.' I have never quit a job."

"Was met with a string of broken promises and lies, as well as cockroaches."

"I was working for my mom until she decided to move."

"The company made me a scapegoat—just like my three previous employers."

Personal Qualities

"I'm married with nine children. I don't require prescription drugs."

"I am extremely loyal to my present firm, so please don't let them know of my immediate availability."

"Number of dependents: 40."

"Marital Status: Often. Children: Various."

"I was proud to win the Gregg Typting Award."

Special Requests

"Please call me after 5:30 because I am self-employed and my employer does not know I am looking for another job."

Figure 9.3 Humorous mistakes that job applicants have made on resumes, applications, and during personal interviews. (*Source: www.slinkcity.com.*)

separate piece of paper rather than directly on the application, because it is a legal document that may be used by outside agencies, if the operation is ever faced with a lawsuit based on job discrimination.[3] While management might assume that the job applicant would arrive for the interview thoroughly prepared, research and some anecdotal evidence suggest just the opposite. Figure 9.3 lists some funny mistakes that job applicants have made on their résumés, their job applications, and even during the job interview.[4]

THE JOB INTERVIEW

In spite of the increased use of technology to sort through and prescreen applications, for many managers and supervisors in the hospitality industry, the personal job interview remains the preferred way to learn about an applicant and to match the right applicant with the right position. This is true because the interview forum is flexible; it can be adapted to accommodate a meeting with various types of applicants—unskilled or skilled, managerial or professional employees. An interview provides the opportunity for a two-way exchange of information where interviewers learn about the applicant and the applicant learns about the organization. A skilled interviewer can also judge a candidate's interpersonal skills and appearance and can even possibly assess an applicant's honesty.

PROCESS IS A TWO-WAY STREET

While there is not an optimal way to conduct a one-on-one job interview, hospitality managers in small restaurant and lodging operations should remember that the interview should consist of an exchange of information between the employer and the job applicant—the process is a two-way street; however, it is important to remember that the applicant should do about 70 percent of the talking. Organizations interview prospective employees and prospective employees interview organizations to gather valuable information to help both parties make informed decisions following the completion of the interview. This in-person interview is particularly important today, because the demand for hospitality industry employees far exceeds the supply of qualified applicants in many communities. While the information included in an application is informative for the employer, meeting an applicant in person can be much more telling to the employer in terms of the applicant's body language, interpersonal skills, and personality.

Photo 9.1   Managers who conduct interviews should find a quiet place free from interruptions.

When conducting personal job interviews, management should set aside sufficient time for the meeting and designate a meeting place where there will be no interruption. Certainly a busy restaurant operation should not schedule a job interview during the lunch rush! Choosing the proper setting in which to conduct the interview will go a long way to ensure that the interview is professional and informative. It is also very important that the person conducting the interview puts the applicant at ease. The most effective and informative job interviews occur when applicants are able to let down their guards and be themselves, allowing their true personalities to shine through.

CONDUCTING THE INTERVIEW

There are four broad questions an interviewer typically has in mind as she conducts the actual interview with the applicant: Can the applicant do the job? Will the applicant do the job? How does the applicant compare with others who are being considered for the job? Does the applicant fit the organization and its culture?

The Applicant Should Do Most of the Talking

Most seasoned interviewers suggest that a conversational tone be used throughout the interview process. The interviewer should control the topics discussed and the direction of the interview, but the applicant should set the pace for the discussion. It is unwise for the interviewer to begin with a full-blown description of the job and its duties. When this occurs, a clever applicant may easily tailor his answers to the organization's needs, and suddenly management will find itself in a situation like that described earlier in "Tales from the Field." In addition, when an inexperienced manager begins an interview in this manner, he often begins talking and sometimes does not know when to stop. While it is important to describe the job and its duties to the applicant to ensure the description is in line with the applicant's job expectations, it is more effective to do so later in the interview rather than earlier.

Don't Oversell the Position

It is very easy for a manager who is desperate to hire an employee to oversell the position to a particular applicant. It's important to avoid this tendency because it almost always leads to the new employee's disappointment with the actual position, and, consequently, higher employee turnover may occur. It is best to paint a very accurate picture of exactly what sort of tasks the position entails. For instance, some executive chefs are known to invite applicants into the hot kitchen during a busy lunch or dinner rush. If after 20 minutes or so, the chef turns around to find the applicant has high-tailed it out of there, it is better to know this now before wasting the time, money, and effort to bring the applicant on as a new employee only to have him or her leave after the first few days on the job. This process is called a "realistic job preview."

Check for Any "Knockout Factors"

The initial phase of the interview is a good time to verify that the applicant meets the position's primary requirements. This might also be done over the telephone when setting up the interview appointment. For example, if an employer is trying to hire a cocktail server, he should verify that the applicant is of legal age to serve alcohol based on state laws. A specific, nonnegotiable job qualification such as a minimum age for serving alcohol is often called a **knockout factor,** and these should be verified before conducting an interview. It is also a good idea to verify the applicant's needs with respect to pay, benefits, working days and hours, his desire for part-time or full-time status, and so forth at this stage of the interview process. If it is determined, at this point, that the applicant does not fit the position requirements and there is no flexibility, politely end the interview and move on to the next candidate.

CLOSED-ENDED AND OPEN-ENDED QUESTIONS

A crucial mistake that novice interviewers make time and time again is to talk too much and not listen enough to what the applicant has to say. Remember, your goal, as the employer, is to find out whether the applicant is a good fit for the open position. That means that the interviewer must retain control of the interview at all times. The interviewer should also focus his or her questions on one major area at a time. For example, thoroughly cover work history before moving on to education and so forth. Different questioning techniques should be used to best acquaint yourself with the applicant. **Closed-ended questions,** or *direct* questions, generally lead to short, yes-or-no-type answers and are good questions to ask at the beginning of the interview as you are getting a feel for the applicant's demeanor and skills. These types of questions are also useful in obtaining specific bits of information such as, "Did you report directly to the hotel's general manager or to some other person?" Other examples might be as follows:

INTERVIEWER: *I see you worked as a server for two years at the Casa Restaurant downtown. Is that correct?*

APPLICANT: *Yes.*

INTERVIEWER: *How many covers would you say the restaurant served during a typical lunch period?*

APPLICANT: *Between one hundred and one hundred and fifty.*

Closed-ended questions often begin with words such as *what, who, where, which, when,* and *how many.* A skilled interviewer will often follow a closed-ended question with an **open-ended question.** These types of questions are sometimes referred to as *indirect* questions and are designed to draw a lengthier and more detailed answer from the applicant. The majority of questions asked should be of the open-ended variety, as these will require the applicant to talk more. Consider the following example:

INTERVIEWER: *You state in your application that you did a lot of tableside preparation and service in your job at the Casa Restaurant. Tell me about the types of tableside prep and service you personally provided.*

APPLICANT: *Yes, it was mostly French-style service: steak Diane, Caesar salads, cherries jubilee, and dishes like that.*

INTERVIEWER: *Could you describe to me the steps you would take to prepare a Caesar salad, tableside?*

APPLICANT: *Sure. First I would assemble the ingredients in the cold prep area, and then I . . .*

Other open-ended questions may require the applicant to list items (What things did you like best/least about your current or previous job?) or to make comparisons (How did working for the general manager at hotel A compare with your previous job, working for the manager at hotel B?). Once the applicant begins to respond, it is important for the interviewer to listen actively. He or she should avoid the temptation to interrupt or to pick right up where the applicant leaves off. Note taking, while important, may also interfere with the active listening process. Sometimes a long, silent pause will be sufficient to encourage the applicant to continue talking. This technique allows skilled interviewers to learn a good deal about job applicants.

SITUATIONAL AND BEHAVIORAL QUESTIONS

Posing **situational questions** is another technique that some interviewers use. This type of question presents a hypothetical situation to the applicant, which enables the interviewer to evaluate the applicant's answer based on his or her approach and solution to the hypothetical situation. A good example of this style of questioning is as follows:

INTERVIEWER: *Imagine that it's a busy night in the restaurant and everyone is in the weeds. The restaurant is one server short, and one of your customers is very angry because he has been waiting for more than 40 minutes for his food. When you go into the kitchen to check on his order, the line cook tells you that the item ordered was eighty-sixed earlier in the evening and that they had forgotten to write it down. You know your customer is going to be irate when you go back out into the dining room to deliver the bad news. Tell me how you would handle this situation in such a way that the customer does not leave dissatisfied?*

Some interviewers like situational questions such as this because they believe they are useful in assessing an applicant's reasoning and analytical abilities under a modest amount of stress. Others argue that using hypothetical or "what if"-type questions may only lead the applicant to provide the answer that he thinks the interviewer wants to hear, and there is no way of knowing if a person would *actually* respond in the way stated.

When the interviewer poses **behavioral questions,** the applicant is asked to describe an *actual occurrence* that may have happened on the job, in an educational setting, or even during an activity that occurred during an outside-of-work activity. An example is "Tell me about your most recent experience in a dysfunctional group." Questions such as this are almost always followed up with more probing questions, which allow the interviewer to focus on key aspects of the answer. For instance, the interview may follow up with questions such as, "What was your role in turning the group around?" or "Was the group successful? Why or why not?" It is important to remember that any questions asked should help the manager decide if the applicant meets the behavioral dimensions being sought, such as friendly, service oriented, and so forth.

HOW LONG SHOULD THE INTERVIEW LAST?

Often, inexperienced managers and supervisors wonder how much time should be allotted to the interview process. There is no perfect answer here, but most experts agree that whatever amount of time is necessary in order to thoroughly cover an applicant's background is appropriate. This may range from 20 minutes to several hours, depending on the level of the job and the experience of the applicant.

QUESTIONS TO AVOID

It is important to keep in mind that certain areas of questioning are simply off-limits on both the job application form and during the job interview. Application forms and job interviews have traditionally been used as instruments for eliminating "unsuited" or "unqualified" candidates from consideration. Unfortunately, in some instances, organizations have been found to use them to restrict or deny employment opportunities to some ethnic groups, religious sects, and so forth, and lawsuits have resulted. Whether intentionally discriminatory, some of the questions asked on job applications and during interviews have the potential to leave a hospitality business vulnerable to legal charges of unlawful discrimination. The courts generally assume that the questions a particular employer poses will be used for the sole purpose of helping it to make informed hiring decisions. It is for this reason that all questions must be job related, and the hospitality organization should be prepared to defend itself in court if the questions are challenged as discriminatory. Figure 9.4 details the kinds of questions that should be avoided on both job applications and during a job interview.

As you have already learned in Chapter 2, Title VII of the Civil Rights Act of 1964 makes it illegal to discriminate in employment matters based on an individual's race, color, religion, sex, or national origin. Title I of the ADA makes it illegal for an employer to discriminate against an individual based on disability. The Age Discrimination in Employment Act (ADEA) prohibits employment discrimination against any person aged 40 and over. And, of course, there are also numerous state and local laws that either duplicate or expand upon these

MARITAL STATUS

Inappropriate: Are you married?
Is this your maiden or married name?
With whom do you live?

Appropriate: After hiring, marital status on tax and insurance forms is allowed.

PARENTAL STATUS

Inappropriate: How many kids do you have?
Do you plan to have children?
Are you pregnant?

Appropriate: After hiring, asking for dependent information on tax and insurance forms is allowed.

AGE

Inappropriate: How old are you?
What year were you born?
When did you graduate from high school?

Appropriate: Before hiring, asking if the applicant is over the legal minimum age for the hours or working conditions, in compliance with state or federal labor laws. After hiring, verifying legal minimum age with a birth certificate or other ID, and asking age on insurance forms.

NATIONAL ORIGIN

Inappropriate: Where were you born?
Where are your parents from?
What's your heritage?

Appropriate: Verifying legal U.S. residence or work visa status is allowed.

RACE OR SKIN COLOR

Inappropriate: What race are you?
Are you a member of a minority group?

Appropriate: Generally indicate equal opportunity employment. Asking about race only as required for affirmative-action programs.

RELIGION OR CREED

Inappropriate: What religion are you?
Which religious holidays will you be taking off from work?
Do you attend church regularly?

Appropriate: Contact religious or other organizations related to an applicant's beliefs, if applicant listed them as employers or references is allowed.

CRIMINAL RECORD

Inappropriate: Have you ever been arrested?
Have you ever spent a night in jail?

Appropriate: Questions about convictions by civil or military courts, if accompanied by a disclaimer that states it will not necessarily cause loss of job opportunity. Specific convictions, if related to fitness to perform the job, is allowed. Generally, employers can ask only about convictions and not arrests, except for law-enforcement and security-clearance agencies.

DISABILITY

Inappropriate: Do you have any disabilities?
What's your medical history?
How does your condition affect your abilities?

Appropriate: Ask if the applicant can perform specific duties of the job with or without accommodation. After hiring, ask about medical history on insurance forms.

Figure 9.4

Appropriate and inappropriate interview questions, according to Title VII of the 1964 Civil Rights Act. (*Source: U.S. Equal Employment Opportunity Commission.*)

federal laws. To stay on the right side of the law, the National Restaurant Association suggests that employers ask themselves these questions:[5]

1. Is the information being sought job related? Is it needed to judge the applicant's competence or qualifications for the job? Is it a valid predictor of successful job performance?

2. Will the answer to the question tend to eliminate minorities, people with disabilities, people over age 40, or members of one sex, either intentionally or unintentionally? Will the answer disqualify a significantly larger percentage of members of one particular group more than others?

THE JOB OFFER

The final hiring decision, or extending a job offer to a particular applicant, marks the end of the employee selection process, assuming the job applicant accepts the position being offered. In an effort to maintain good public relations, small hospitality operations should always notify applicants who have not been accepted, either in writing or by phone. A job applicant should never be hired on the spot, no matter how desperate the employer is to fill a position. Time must be allocated to evaluate all qualified applicants against one another and to conduct a proper background check. A conditional job offer may be made contingent upon the employee successfully passing a background and reference check, but management must make it clear that the job offer can and will be withdrawn if the employee doesn't successfully pass the background and/or reference check. This process may cause the applicant to cease his search for a job, raising the probability that he will be available to work for your organization.

THE ACT OF THE EMPLOYEE

Respondeat superior is a Latin phrase that means, "Let the master answer." It is a legal doctrine that means that the act of the employee is the act of the employer. This means that you, the employer, can be legally responsible for your employees' actions, so long as those actions are conducted within the scope of employment. The kind of conduct that is or is not considered "within the scope of employment" can be somewhat confusing even for the courts and the lawyers to sort out. Suffice it to say, you could find yourself on the wrong side of a lawsuit if your employee causes someone harm or injury during the workday at your establishment. A restaurant operator could be held liable if

ethical dilemma

Eric manages a small yet very successful family-owned restaurant. This afternoon he is interviewing applicants for the position of dining room hostess. He is stunned when he sees his three o'clock appointment arrive: She is a beautiful blonde with a stunning figure and a dazzling smile. He would love to ask this woman out for a date, and she isn't wearing a wedding band, but still, he can't be sure whether she is married or perhaps dating someone special. Even though he knows it's improper, he wonders if he should try to find out more information during the interview. He could actually ask her if she is married or if she has kids. He may even be able to work in her "dating" status if he's careful. The applicant doesn't seem all that old or sophisticated, so she will probably not even know the difference, if he takes his time and works his questions into the normal course of the interview. If Eric proceeds with his plan, which of the *10 Ethical Principles for Hospitality Managers* may be violated here? If Eric wants to make an ethical decision, what factors must he consider? Depending upon Eric's choice, what will be the consequences for him? For the applicant? For the restaurant?

a delivery driver employed by the restaurant causes an automobile accident. A lodging operator could be liable if a bellhop with access to a hotel passkey steals a guest's belongings from a hotel room or, even worse, enters a hotel room and somehow harms or injures someone. Whether the employee's actions are simply the result of an accident or are actually premeditated does not really matter. The law can be quite narrowly construed with respect to respondeat superior.

A Tennessee Waffle House restaurant was sued when a waitress, who got angry at a customer, threw a syrup bottle at the customer, hitting him squarely in the head and causing harm and injury. In a North Carolina case, a Taco Bell customer sued the restaurant chain when the customer discovered that a kitchen employee had spit on his food before serving it. The customer was a state trooper, and the guilty employee later claimed that he "just did not like cops." Sometimes employees just go a little nuts, and they do things that management would never foresee, actions that are certainly not "on their job descriptions." The point here, however, is to try eliminating these problems in advance, and while we'll see that there are never any guarantees, there are things we can do to head off such incidents at the pass.

BACKGROUND CHECKS

For many jobs, preemployment screening is required by either federal or state law. For example, most states require criminal background checks for anyone who works with children, the elderly, or disabled. The federal **National Child Protection Act** authorizes state officials to access the FBI's National Crime Information Center (NCIC) database for some positions. Many state and federal government jobs require a background check, and depending on the kind of job, may require an extensive investigation for a security clearance. Since the terrorist attacks of September 11, 2001, the current emphasis on security and safety has dramatically increased the number of employment background checks being conducted nationwide. While there are no laws at this time *requiring* hospitality industry employees to undergo background checks, many of the larger hotel and restaurant chains do conduct preemployment drug screening as well as criminal background checks on prospective employees. Many smaller operations are likely to find this process too time-consuming and expensive and have thus far managed to get by without having to dig too deeply into prospective employees' pasts. Most employers are becoming more cautious, however, so this could change as access to computer databases becomes more available and more affordable.

A background check can consist of something as simple as telephoning a former employer to check an applicant's job references, or it may be more in-depth and include an investigation of the potential employee's history and acquaintances. Figure 9.5 illustrates some of the potential information that might be covered in a background check. Note that many of these sources are public records created by government agencies.

WHY CONDUCT BACKGROUND CHECKS?

Employers check potential and current workers for several reasons. The things an employer wants to know about an applicant can vary with the kinds of jobs that the applicant might be seeking. Here are a few of the reasons for employment screening.

■ *Negligent hiring* lawsuits are on the rise. If an employee's actions hurt someone, the employer may be liable. The threat of liability gives employers reason to be cautious in checking an applicant's past. A bad decision can wreck havoc on a company's budget and reputation, as well as ruin the career of the hiring official. Employers no longer feel secure in relying on their instinct as a basis to hire. The concept of negligent hiring was thoroughly covered in Chapter 3.

INFORMATION THAT MAY BE OBTAINED	NOTES
Driving records	This is normally allowed if driving a vehicle is job related.
Social security number	Allowed for payroll records after the employee has been hired or, if needed, to conduct a criminal records check.
Bankruptcy	Records may be obtained if an applicant will handle large sums of cash.
Past employers	Past employers may be contacted in order to determine work history, salary history, reason for leaving, and so on. Many past employers give little information for fear of being sued.
Education records	Transcripts from schools may be requested if education is job related.
Military records	These may generally be obtained, but the information used must be job related.
Credit records	The applicant must give his or her written permission, and the information obtained must be job related. An example is an applicant will handle large sums of money.
Criminal records	These and other court records are generally public (with the exception of juveniles), and the information obtained, if used to deny employment, should be job related. Example: You would not have to offer a position of valet parking attendant to an individual convicted of grand theft auto.
Drug test records	Preemployment drug screening is allowed and the information obtained—if positive—is generally sufficient to deny employment.

Figure 9.5   Information that may be obtained when management conducts a routine background check on a job applicant.

- *Current events* have caused an increase in employment screening.

- *Child abuse and child abductions* in the news in recent years have resulted in new laws in almost every state that require criminal background checks for anyone who works with children. The move to protect children through criminal background checks now also includes volunteers who serve as coaches for youth sports activities and scout troop leaders.

- *Terrorist acts of September 11, 2001* have resulted in heightened security and identity-verification strategies by employers. Potential job candidates and long-time employees alike are being examined with a new eye following September 11, 2001.

- *Corporate executives, officers, and directors* now face a degree of scrutiny in both professional and private life that was foreign to them before the Enron debacle and other corporate scandals of 2002.

- *False or inflated information* supplied by job applicants is frequently in the news. Some estimates are that 30 to 40 percent of all job applications and résumés include some false or inflated facts. Such reports make employers wary of accepting anyone's word at face value.

- *The "information age"* itself may be a reason for the increase in employment screening—the availability of computer databases containing millions of records of personal data. As the cost of searching these sources drops, employers are finding it more feasible to conduct background checks.

It is important to remember that many states have enacted legislation that restricts, to a certain degree, the kind of information that an employer may access during a background check. In California, criminal histories or "rap sheets" compiled by law enforcement agencies are not public record. Only certain employers such as public utilities, law enforcement, security guard firms, and child care facilities have access to this information. This is not true in all states, however, so the prudent hospitality business manager will always consult legal counsel when setting up a system to prescreen job applicants.

At the federal level, the **Fair Credit Reporting Act (FCRA)** sets some guidelines that govern the type of information that can be collected during a background check, but this is mostly financial information that is found in most people's credit reports. Information such as bankruptcies, tax liens and judgments, civil suits and judgments, accounts in collection, and account or debt write-offs are examples of the types of information that is in some way restricted by the federal government.

OBTAINING THE APPLICANT'S PERMISSION

In some situations, management must first obtain the applicant's permission and often a signature before obtaining certain background records. Examples include the following:

- *Education records.* Under federal law, transcripts, recommendations, discipline records, and financial information are confidential. A school should not release student records without the authorization of the adult-age student or parent. However, a school may release "directory information," which can include name, address, dates of attendance, degrees earned, and activities, unless the student has given written notice otherwise.

- *Military service records.* Under the federal **Privacy Act,** service records are confidential and can only be released under limited circumstances. Inquiries not authorized by the subject of the records must be made under the **Freedom of Information Act.** Even without the applicant's consent, the military may release name, rank, salary, duty assignments, awards, and duty status.

■ *Medical records.* In many states, medical records are confidential. There are only a few instances when a medical record can be released without the applicant's knowledge or authorization. The FCRA also requires the applicant's specific permission for the release of medical records. If management, however, requires physical examinations after making a job offer, they will have access to the results. The ADA allows a potential employer to inquire only about the applicant's ability to perform specific job functions and specifically prohibits health questionnaires and physical examinations before an actual job offer is made.

If you hire an outside company to do a background check on a job applicant or current employee, the FCRA requires that you do each of the following:

■ Get written permission from the individual for the background check.

■ Get permission on a separate document.

■ Get special permission if medical information is requested.

■ Give notice of the individual's right to ask about the nature and scope of the report, if the report will include interviews with others.

■ Give notice and a copy of the report *before* an adverse employment decision is made.

■ Give notice of rights and procedures to dispute inaccurate or incomplete information.

You must also remember that some state laws are stricter than the federal law, in which case the employer should follow the stricter law.

MANY EMPLOYEES HAVE SKELETONS IN THEIR CLOSETS

InfoLink Screening Services, a California company that conducts background checks for employers, found that 8 percent of the people they investigated had criminal convictions. The crimes included forgery, robbery, possession of stolen goods, assault with a deadly weapon, welfare fraud, larceny, hit-and-run, dealing cocaine, grand theft auto, check fraud, aggravated battery, sexual assault, burglary, and attempted murder. InfoLink sorted out the data and found that some workers were more likely to have rap sheets than others:[6]

■ Food services, 12.4 percent

■ Automobile dealers, 12.1 percent

■ Retail, 11.7 percent

- Transportation, 10.7 percent
- Business services, 10.2 percent
- Manufacturing, 9.8 percent
- Hospitality, 8.6 percent
- Staffing, 8.5 percent
- Construction, 8.1 percent
- Finance, 6 percent
- Health care, 5.7 percent

WHO PERFORMS BACKGROUND CHECKS?

There are many companies that specialize in employment screening. The most important thing to keep in mind is that companies conducting background checks fall into several broad categories. These categories can range from individuals commonly known as "private investigators," to companies that do nothing but employment screening to online data brokers. Large hospitality operations that employ large numbers of people may have an established relationship with a third-party background-checking company or may even use an affiliated company for their employment screening. Other background-checking companies may work on a less formal basis with employers. With the information age upon us, it is easy for employers to gather background information themselves. Much of it is computerized, allowing employers to log on to public records and commercial databases directly through dial-up networks or via the Internet. Finding one of these online companies is as easy as using Internet search engines to find Web sites that specialize in "background checks." Employers should beware of companies advertising on the Internet that they can "find everything about anyone." They are not necessarily going to be in strict compliance with federal and state laws, especially the provisions that require accuracy of background check reports. A small business owner who establishes a relationship with a reputable screening company has much to gain. Figure 9.6 illustrates the type of criteria that should be considered when searching for a company to conduct background checks on prospective employees.

WHO SHOULD BE CHECKED?

Deciding who to check can be tricky, and it often depends upon the size of the company and the particular position for which the company is hiring. As stated earlier, many large hotel and restaurant organizations do routine preemploy-

The following is criteria to consider when contracting a background-check company:

- Follows the FCRA and applicable state and laws.
- Gives you guidance about your responsibilities as a user of consumer reports.
- Provides forms to obtain permission and gives the required notice to the applicant or employee.
- Provides forms and guidance if you are faced with an "adverse action" decision.
- Meets its obligations to provide the individual access to reports and to his or her file.
- Follows required procedures for investigating inaccurate information.

Figure 9.6   Criteria to consider when choosing an outside firm to process background checks on job applicants.

ment drug tests and criminal background checks on *all* applicants to whom they intend to offer a job. It would not make sense, financially, to prescreen every single applicant, but certainly those who the company intends to offer specific jobs to would be good candidates for screening. Where there may be fees involved, the employer almost always pays; otherwise, it could be deemed illegal discrimination to not hire those who are unable to afford the drug and criminal background screening fees.

While it is probably best for small operations to also screen all job candidates, this is often out of the reach, financially, for small lodging establishments and restaurants. Certainly any employee who will have access to either private company financial information or sensitive employee information would be a good candidate for screening. Employees who are responsible for large sums of money, such as bookkeepers, managers, and cashiers, may also be good candidates. Many operations require that such employees be bonded. This means that the organization has actually purchased an insurance policy on the employee, and the organization would be reimbursed by the insurance company if the employee steals or somehow misappropriates company funds.

Because of high instances of negligent hiring lawsuits, more and more hospitality operations are screening employees who are required to drive for a company business, as well as employees who have high levels of customer contact, such as hotel bellhops, maids, room service waitstaff, and delivery drivers, who may be required to enter a customer's home.

REFERENCE CHECKS

Reference checks may be as simple as a brief telephone call to an applicant's former employer to verify facts such as date of employment, salary, and job title. Reference checks limited to such factual information are generally relatively easy to accomplish. Perhaps you feel that the position you are hiring for requires that the applicant be a team player. Can you ask a former boss if the applicant fits the bill? You can ask almost anything you like, but questions such as these are designed to elicit an *opinion* rather than facts; you should know that most businesses—large or small—are going to be very reluctant to provide such information. Many companies fear a lawsuit based on libel or slander, so information about a previous employee's job performance, work ethic, attendance at work, attitude, and other job-related criteria that are important to you when you need to make a hiring decision are often extremely difficult to get.

Figure 9.7 illustrates the types of questions you may want to ask when calling a job applicant's previous employer(s) to check references. Just remember, you may or may not be successful in obtaining much valuable information.

SHOULD I GIVE REFERENCES ON A PREVIOUS EMPLOYEE?

As a manager or a supervisor in a hospitality operation, you too could be sued if you provide opinions about previous employees that are not factual and, perhaps more important, not defensible in court. Consider this scenario: You receive a call from a restaurant manager requesting an employee reference on John Smith. John Smith worked as a busboy at your restaurant for two months. You terminated this employee because one of your servers accused him of stealing her tip off of a table one busy Saturday night. There were no witnesses to this alleged crime, but you took the server's word over that of the busboy, and you didn't care much for the busboy's attitude anyway. When you fired the busboy, you simply told him that even though he was still on a 90-day probationary status, you did not feel he was going to work out. What will you tell the restaurant manager about this former employee?

1. That he stole a server's tip?
2. That he had a bad attitude?
3. That he didn't work out?

SAMPLE REFERENCE CHECK QUESTIONS

- When did (name) work for your company? Could you confirm starting and ending employment dates? When did he or she leave the company?
- Why did (name) leave the company?
- What was (names) starting and ending salary?
- What was (names) position? Can you describe the job responsibilities?
- Could I briefly review (name's) resume? Does the job title and job description match the position that (name) held?
- Did (name) miss a lot of work? Was he or she frequently late? Were there any issues you are aware of that impacted (names) performance?
- Did (name) get along well with management and coworkers?
- Was (name) promoted while with your company?
- Did (name) supervise other employees? How effectively? If I spoke to those employees, how do you think they would describe (name's) management style?
- How did (name) handle conflict? How about pressure? Stress?
- Did you evaluate (name's) performance? Can you speak about the strong and weak points? What was noted as needing improvement during this performance review?
- What was (name's) biggest accomplishment while working for your company?
- Would you rehire (name) if the opportunity arose?
- If I describe the position we are hiring for to you, could you describe how good a fit you think (name) would be for the position?
- Is there anything I haven't asked that you would like to share with me?

Figure 9.7　Sample questions that may be asked when checking a job applicant's previous employment references.

If you chose answer one, be prepared to go to court. This is an *opinion,* not a fact. Considering there were no witnesses and considering that you chose *not* to prosecute the busboy, it would be very difficult to provide evidence of reason one if you are sued and have to go to court. Perhaps you think that two is a safe response. Think again! How exactly does one *define* a bad attitude? Did the busboy curse at the customers and staff? Did he merely grumble on occasion about his schedule? Clearly, a *bad attitude* can mean different things to different people, and as a manager or a supervisor, it is best to avoid such generalizations when giving references for a former employee. How about response three?

This may seem to be the safest response of the three options, but even here you may be treading on thin ice. This type of reference gives a negative connotation and may indeed prevent the busboy from finding employment, in which case you could be sued for slander. One bit of good advice when giving references on former employees: only say what is factual, objective, and easily proven or defended in court.

SUMMARY

- When hospitality managers do a poor job of screening job applications and conducting job interviews, the result is often costly employee turnover.
- It is essential to match the right applicant with the right job in order to attract and retain a quality workforce.
- Most job application forms are standardized fact-finding forms on which applicants provide basic information such as personal data, employment status, education and skills, work history, and references.
- A signature line that the applicant must sign affirms that the applicant has provided true and accurate information.
- One-on-one job interviews are the most effective way of matching the right applicant with the right position.
- Antidiscrimination laws on the local, state, and federal level restrict certain lines of questioning both within the job application and during the job interview.
- Interviewers should put job applicants at ease and ask a variety of closed-ended, open-ended, and behavioral-style questions during the personal interview.
- Too much talking and not enough listening is one of the primary mistakes that novice interviewers make when conducting job interviews.
- Hospitality managers could be sued for negligent hiring if they fail to conduct a routine-background check on a newly hired employee and that employee later causes harm or injury to a guest or to another employee.
- Large hospitality enterprises have been conducting routine-preemployment drug screening and criminal background checks on prospective employees for many years, but smaller operations are often less likely to do so, primarily because of a lack of funds, time, or both.
- The kind of information that can be obtained legally when conducting a background check on a job applicant is largely regulated by both federal and state laws.
- The prudent hospitality operator will always seek qualified counsel when designing a policy so as to avoid any civil liability.

PRACTICE
QUIZ

1. In order to avoid charges of illegal discrimination, companies that require preemployment drug screening should pay the fee on behalf of those being screened.

   A. True   B. False

2. All hospitality organizations, large and small, should customize the job application forms because each business is specific and unique.

   A. True   B. False

3. A job applicant's educational background is always job related, so this area should be explored in detail on every job application, regardless of the position.

   A. True   B. False

4. Behavioral questions are normally hypothetical, or "what if" questions.

   A. True   B. False

5. Job applicants should sign and date the application form, affirming that the information they have provided is true and accurate.

   A. True   B. False

6. Which of the following questions on a job application would likely be considered discriminatory and, therefore, illegal?

   A. Are you of legal age to serve alcohol in this state?

   B. Are you pregnant or do you intend to become pregnant?

   C. Are there any specific days or hours of the day that you cannot work?

   D. Can you perform the essential functions of the job with or without accommodation?

7. When previewing a job application, which of the following questions should management consider when determining whether the applicant might make a suitable candidate?

   A. Is the application neat and clean, or messy with erasures and misspellings?

   B. Did the applicant follow instructions when filling out the application?

   C. Are there any gaps in employment or omissions on the application?

   D. All of the above.

8. Which federal law requires that schoolteachers and camp counselors undergo certain background checks before being hired?

   A. Americans with Disabilities Act

   B. Privacy Act

   C. National Child Protection Act

   D. Free Credit Reporting Act

9. Questions that normally elicit a short, uninvolved answer are called

   A. Open-ended questions

   B. Closed-ended questions

   C. Rhetorical questions

   D. Behavioral questions

10. The Age Discrimination in Employment Act prohibits employment discrimination against any person who is

   A. 25 years of age and over

   B. 30 years of age and over

   C. 35 years of age and over

   D. 40 years of age and over

REVIEW QUESTIONS

1. List and discuss some of the steps that managers should take when preparing to conduct job interviews. How do these steps facilitate the interview process and help management achieve its goals? Be specific and use examples from the lecture and the textbook to support your answers.

2. Give two or three examples of closed-ended and open-ended questions that could be used during a job interview. How does each of these questions allow management to learn more about the applicant? What are some advantages and disadvantages of each type of question? Be specific and use examples from the lecture and the textbook to support your answers.

3. Conduct an Internet search and identify two or three different companies that conduct background and reference checks on prospective employees. What kinds of services does each of the company's provide? Would some of the provided services be more suitable to the hospitality industry than others? Be prepared to share your findings with the rest of the class.

4. Assume you are a hotel front-office manager who is interviewing an applicant for the position of front-desk clerk. Write one or two behavioral questions, including two or three follow-up, probing questions for each. An example of a behavioral question might be this: "Tell me about a time when you helped an employee in understanding a difficult policy?" An example

of a follow-up, probing question might be this: "What did you do or say that helped?" Be prepared to present your questions to the rest of the class and to explain how such questioning techniques aid the manager when conducting a job interview.

5. Working with a classmate, telephone two or three large hospitality operations in your area and interview the human resources director. Specifically, you would like to know what kinds of information the facility is allowed to provide when a potential employer calls to check the references of a previous employee. Interview the owner or manager of two or three small, independent operations. What kinds of information do these individuals normally provide with respect to the preceding text. How do the larger operation and the smaller operation compare? What are the benefits of providing limited information on previous employees? Are there any drawbacks and, if so, to whom? Be prepared to share your findings with the rest of the class.

HANDS-ON HRM

Jake Albertson is an American who manages a small but luxurious inn on a Caribbean island off the coast of Puerto Rico. The inn's business is mostly seasonal, attracting high-end travelers from the United States beginning around Thanksgiving until late spring. Mr. Albertson employs a small, year-round staff that is mostly made up of island locals, but he boosts his hiring considerably during the busy season, and he prefers to hire American college students because of their superior English skills. In order to make the inn's hiring package attractive, American students are provided free round-trip airfare as well as basic accommodations located on site. They are paid a reasonable weekly salary, and the inn provides all employee meals that are free of charge.

Albertson has made most of his hiring decisions for the upcoming tourist season, but he still needs to hire a qualified bartender for the inn's busy outdoor bar and verandah. One afternoon, Mr. Albertson receives a phone call from Louise Guggenheim of Boston, the inn's wealthy owner. Mrs. Guggenheim informs Albertson that a friend's niece, Julie, would like to "come down" and "help out" for the season. When Mr. Albertson makes it clear that he is looking for someone who is properly qualified and has previous bartending experience, Mrs. Guggenheim states, "Anybody can bartend, Jake." "And besides," she adds, "a good-looking girl behind the bar should help increase revenues." She promises to fax Julie's résumé and transcripts right away.

Jake Albertson is less than impressed after reading Julie's résumé. Her major in college is fashion design, and not only are her grades below average, but also her work experience includes only six months as a retail store clerk in a large department store chain. A few days later, Albertson receives a very well-written cover letter and résumé from Bert Roberts, a 23 year old who has just graduated from a hospitality school in New England and has been working as a bartender in an upscale, New York City hotel for the past two years. He decides to e-mail Bert Roberts so that they can arrange a convenient time to conduct an initial telephone interview, and just as he logs on to the computer in his office, the phone rings and it is Mrs. Guggenheim. "My friend's niece is coming down on the first plane tomorrow. I told her you had a job for her."

QUESTIONS ▶

1. If the general manager decides to hire Bert Roberts, who is more qualified instead of Julie, how should he deal with Mrs. Guggenheim?
2. As the manager of a privately owned, family business, how should Jake Albertson balance the needs of the business with the needs of the owner when both sets of needs are in conflict with each other?
3. How would this situation be different if there was not a shortage of qualified labor on the Caribbean island?
4. Do Mrs. Guggenheim's perceptions of what qualifies an individual to work at the inn differ with those of Jake Albertson? If you answered yes, should Albertson attempt to change her perceptions? Why or why not?

KEY TERMS ▶

Job application A standardized form on which job applicants provide personal data, work preferences, work history, educational background, and references.

Job interview A face-to-face session in which an interviewer and applicant discuss job position, job expectations, background, and work history so that the interviewer can determine if the applicant is a good match for the position.

Turnover rate A comparison of the number of employees who have separated from an organization with the number of employees in the organization; usually expressed as a percent.

Comptroller A position in large hotels (may also be referred to as "controller") that oversees the hotel's accounts payable, accounts receivable, cash accounting, and payroll systems.

Conditional job offer A job offer made that is contingent upon the employee successfully passing a background and reference check, but management must make it clear that the job offer can and will be withdrawn if the employee doesn't successfully pass the background and/or reference check.

Knockout factor The lack of specific, nonnegotiable job qualifications that may deem a job candidate as unsuitable for a specific position. An example would be an underage applicant who has applied for a position to serve alcohol.

Closed-ended questions Questions that typically lead to short yes-or-no-type answers. They are effective for quickly covering ground at the beginning of the interview.

Open-ended questions Questions that often begin with "how" or "why" and that are intended to draw a more lengthy and detailed response from the applicant.

Situational questions Situational-type scenarios that are designed to gauge how an applicant would respond to certain situations that could occur in the workplace. These are often hypothetical or "what if" questions.

Behavioral questions Questions that require the job applicant to describe an actual occurrence, such as, "Tell me about your most recent experience with an irate customer."

Respondeat superior A Latin term that means, "Let the master answer." It refers to a legal doctrine stating that the act of the employee is the act of the employer.

National Child Protection Act A federal law that, among other things, requires teachers, day school workers, and others who are involved with children to undergo routine-background checks.

Fair Credit Reporting Act (FCRA) A consumer protection law that regulates the disclosure of consumer credit reports by consumer/credit reporting agencies and establishes procedures for correcting mistakes on one's credit record. The law also covers many areas of routine employee background checks.

Privacy Act A federal statute that forbids the disclosure of specific material held by federal agencies on the grounds that its release could invade the privacy of the subject of the report or document.

Freedom of Information Act A federal statute that allows any person the right to obtain federal agency records unless the records (or part of the records) are protected from disclosure by exemptions contained in the law.

NOTES ▶

1. Nicholas Nickolas, "No More Seedy Service" (Miami, FL: Restaurant Report, LLC) www.restaurantreport.com.

2. David Wheelhouse, *Managing Human Resources in the Hospitality Industry* (East Lansing, MI: Educational Institute of the American Hotel & Lodging Association, 2002), 68.

3. Ibid., 68.

4. *SlinkCity* Web site, 2005, www.slinkcity.com/funny-resumes.html.

5. *The Legal Problem Solver* (Washington, DC: National Restaurant Association, 2003), 67.

6. "Many Employees Have Skeletons in Their Closets," *Courier-Journal* (Louisville, KY) October 17, 2005, sec. 6D.

UNIT
3

ORIENTATION
AND TRAINING

CHAPTER 10

NEW-EMPLOYEE ORIENTATION

We will orient you to who we are—our heart, our soul, our goals, our vision, our dreams, so you can join us and not just work for us. You have the right to know our hopes, our dreams, and our goals.[1]

Horst Schultz, former president and COO, Ritz-Carlton Hotel Company

CHAPTER OBJECTIVES

After completing this chapter, you will be able to

- Describe the benefits of providing new-employee orientation.
- Identify areas that should be covered in new-employee orientation.
- Explain why orientation should precede job training.
- Recognize that a new-employee orientation program helps to improve employee retention.
- Identify the manager or supervisor's role in new-employee orientation.

HRM IN ACTION As a new hospitality manager or supervisor, you have worked very hard to recruit, interview, and select the perfect applicant to fill the job opening in your restaurant or lodging operation. You have made the all-important job offer, and the applicant has accepted! However, if industry statistics ring true, sometime within the next three to four months, your new employee will have moved on to another job in your competition's restaurant or hotel. Perhaps you did not do a good job of matching the right applicant with the right job opening. Or perhaps you failed to successfully familiarize your employee with the company's mission and policies or didn't train him adequately from the start. One of the primary reasons for conducting **workplace orientation** with brand-new employees is to ease their transition into your place of business and to make them feel good about their decision to come to work for you.

STARTING OFF ON THE RIGHT FOOT

If you have ever taken a brand-new job, then you know what it is like to show up on your first day of work, not knowing much of anything or anybody. Most new employees who are thrown into this kind of environment will feel a certain level of anxiety, and they certainly do not yet have the knowledge or experience to become a valuable and productive member of the team. An employee orientation program that is well-thought-out can work wonders when it comes to new employees socializing in the workplace. **Socialization** is the ongoing process through which new employees begin to understand and accept the values, norms, and beliefs held by others in the organization. Good orientation programs are designed to familiarize new employees with their roles, the organization, its policies, and other employees. Some organizations refer to this process as a "gentle brainwashing;" others simply see orientation as getting the new employee started on the right foot.

Large hospitality organizations such as hotel and restaurant chains may have rather extensive employee orientation programs. New food and beverage servers who are employed at Nashville's famous Opryland Hotel may spend as much as two and one-half days in new-employee orientation before they ever begin actual on-the-job training. Of course, this makes sense when you consider that the Tennessee hotel has nearly 3000 guest rooms and more than 16 different restaurants, lounges, and bars. In general, the larger the facility and the more extensive the operation, the lengthier and more in-depth the orientation program will need to be.

THE NEED FOR NEW-EMPLOYEE ORIENTATION

Many small hospitality business managers make the mistake of assuming that because their operation is small in scope, new-employee orientation is a waste of time and money. Nothing could be further from the truth! Even the smallest lodging or restaurant operation can benefit from offering a new-employee orientation program, and the good news is that it requires a lot less time and costs considerably less money than a larger corporation's orientation program.

TALES FROM THE FIELD

When I was getting my hotel-restaurant management degree, I was hired as a part-time desk clerk in one of the area's largest hotels. I was soon fully trained, and after about six months, the front-office manager called a meeting to determine why the front-desk staff was not selling the hotel rooms more aggressively to walk-ins. He was shocked to learn that several of us had never seen any of the hotel's guest rooms because we had never gone through orientation. How can you really sell something that you've never seen? Needless to say, we got a very thorough guided tour that day!

Jennifer, 23, Indianapolis, Indiana

Hospitality operations, large and small, devote a considerable amount of time and resources to hiring people. An employer has already made a considerable investment in a new employee by the time she starts the first day on the job. At the same time, the new worker has anxieties that may hinder the transition from recruit to productive employee. These first-day jitters normally manifest themselves with thoughts such as "Will I be able to do the job?" "Will I fit in around here?" or "Will the other employees like me?" These feelings are natural, but they do hinder both the employee's initial job satisfaction and his or her ability to learn the job. In the workplace, initial impressions are strong and lasting because new employees have little else on which to base judgments. Management must work to make those initial impressions favorable so that new employees become satisfied and productive members of the team. New-employee orientation helps to make newly hired employees feel more comfortable in their new surroundings and helps them to understand the key goals of the organization, important policies, and procedures. They feel valued as members of a team helping to achieve a common goal at the workplace.

BENEFITS OF ORIENTATION

The benefits of a well-conducted employee orientation program far outweigh any potential pitfalls that may occur. Employee orientation helps to reduce new-employee anxieties, so new workers are able to learn their duties and are more productive. Orientation also helps new employees to learn their duties faster so they quickly become valuable members of the team, which benefits both the employee and company.

The Benefits to the Company Overall

Almost all organizations will realize the overall benefits of providing orientation because it provides a consistent overview of the company. Other benefits to the organization may include the following:

- Helps new employees feel good about their decision to work for your company
- Introduces new employees to the owner and managers of the organization
- Improves employees' understanding of company goals and priorities
- Decreases employee turnover because employees are aware of the company's goals and policies from the start of their employment, which ensures that they work to achieve the company's goals and priorities

Another primary goal of an effective new-employee orientation program is to create a positive mind-set about the company and the job. In other words, you want the new employee to feel good about his or her decision to come to work for you. Remember, there is a lot of competition among hospitality businesses when it comes to recruiting and hiring the very best employees—when a qualified applicant chooses *your* place of business, that applicant has cast a vote of confidence for you and your business over all the others.

The Benefits to the Supervisor and to Management

Managers and supervisors will benefit from an orientation program because well-adjusted employees with positive attitudes toward the company learn their specific job-related tasks more quickly and effectively and are more likely to make it through the first 10 to 14 critical days, a period during which many newly hired employees make up their minds about whether they should stay in their new job or whether they should quit. Other benefits that orientation provides to the supervisor as well as management include the following:

- Having a well-trained staff
- Consistency in performance of all employees
- Aids in evaluating employee performance
- Supports the supervisor's role
- Lower rate of employee turnover

The Benefits to the Employee

Perhaps no other party benefits from a solid new-employee orientation program more than the actual new employee. Some benefits include the following:

- Builds an important foundation for employee motivation
- Builds higher levels of job satisfaction
- Properly sets the stage for the training that is to follow
- Builds self-esteem from the feeling of being part of a successful team

Setting the stage for new employees within the organization will make things easier as management and supervisors begin the training process. Employees will feel more positive, less anxious, and more receptive to the training program. A well-trained and self-motivated staff is the most valuable resource that a small restaurant or lodging operation can have, and this lends itself extremely well to the overall success of the operation. A short but thorough new-employee orientation program is essential to ensure that the operation's goals and priorities are clear to the new employees who are motivated to achieve the company's goals.

ORIENTATION PROGRAMS

Whether an orientation program is a two-day event or takes place in a mere one to two hours, most orientation programs will cover many of the same categories. In larger hospitality organizations, more formal orientation programs usually rely on the human resources department. In smaller operations, the general manager or even the owner assumes the lead role. Often, orientation is broken down into two broad areas: general topics of interest to almost all new employees and specific job-related issues that may only apply to the workers in a specific area or department. It is important to note that orientation should *not* be confused with training. Orientation always comes first because it lays the foundation for the training that follows. Figure 10.1 illustrates the general topics of interest that most new employees within a large organization tend to learn about during orientation. A representative of the human resources department would normally cover these areas.

ORGANIZATIONAL ISSUES

- History of the business or company
- Organization chart
- Names and titles of key personnel
- Employee's department and where it fits in
- Layout and tour of the physical facilities
- Overview of services and products provided
- Employee handbook covering policies and rules
- Safety and security procedures

EMPLOYEE BENEFITS

- Pay scales and paydays
- Vacations and holidays
- Rest breaks
- Training and education benefits
- Counseling
- Insurance and retirement benefits
- Rehab programs

Figure 10.1

A representative from the organization's human resources department may cover the topics on this list with new employees.

Clearly, many of the topics listed in Figure 10.1 would not be applicable to a smaller lodging or restaurant operation. But it is relatively easy to downsize the list to make it more appropriate for smaller operations. Consider the following list of general topics for a small restaurant and bar operation:

- Provide a short history of the business and the owner's philosophy.
- Introduce employees to the owner, executive chef, and general manager.
- Describe how the new employee's job fits into the overall operation.
- Explain layout of the dining room and kitchen areas.
- Provide a tour of the facility both inside and outside.
- Provide an overview of the menu and how it is used as a marketing tool.
- Review of the employee handbook.

At some stage in the orientation process, the new employee is typically "passed off" to his or her immediate supervisor. This is true even in larger operations where human resources personnel normally cover the broader organizational issues. The supervisor must resist the temptation to begin the training process at this point in time; training will follow, but this orientation period is necessary so that management can set the stage for eventual job-specific training. There are still a few department-specific items that should be covered to ensure a smooth transition to effective training. Figure 10.2 illustrates the topics that the new employee's immediate supervisor should cover during orientation.

INTRODUCTIONS

To the new employee's supervisor

To trainers

To coworkers

JOB DUTIES

Tour of the job location

Review the job description and job tasks

Review the job safety requirements

Provide a broad overview of the job

Review the job's objectives

Review the relationship to other jobs and departments

Figure 10.2

The new employee's supervisor would cover these department-specific topics during new-employee orientation.

Photo 10.1

New-employee orientation should cover simple things like showing a new employee where and how to clock in each day.

While each of the items on Figure 10.2 may not be applicable to the smallest of operations, the list is easily customized. Consider the following list, which would be more applicable to a very small hospitality business operation:

- Introduce new employee to coworkers
- Introduce employee to other supervisors
- Tour the job location, including storage and supply areas
- Review the job description and job tasks
- Explain parking, time clock, and uniform procedures

Most new-employee orientation sessions in a small hospitality business operation should take less than two hours to complete. As the new employee is exposed to orientation, coworkers, and, later, to training, the company's values, beliefs, and traditions are slowly absorbed.

ethical dilemma

Susan is the manager of a medium-sized restaurant and bar that is successful and privately owned. The restaurant's turnover is high, and Susan desperately needed to hire a new busperson. She hired Michael, but now she realizes that she made a mistake because he is just not a good fit for the position. During training, Michael painfully realizes that Susan and some of the other staff seem to be making fun of him. Susan realizes that she made a snap decision when she hired Michael, and now she will need to figure out how to get rid of him. If Susan follows through with her plan, which of the *10 Ethical Principles for Hospitality Managers* could she be in danger of violating? What would be the negative or positive consequences of her decision? Who else would be affected besides her and Michael? How could this ethical dilemma be avoided?

MAKE NEW-EMPLOYEE ORIENTATION FUN

New-employee orientation should be a positive event, and many hospitality organizations work hard to make it so. Isn't it interesting that companies will often throw a festive celebration to honor a long-time employee who has now decided to leave the organization, yet rarely do companies "celebrate" the hiring of a new employee? Consider some of the following activities that would go a long way in making new-employee orientation more welcoming and even more productive:

- Have a cake with candles on the new employee's desk or work area on her first day on the job.
- Make sure that the new employee's supervisor is present to welcome her on day one.
- Ensure that the new employee has someone to eat lunch or dinner with during the first few days on the job.
- Try to send the new employee home after the first day with some positive experience that he will likely share with family members or friends.

Remember, too, that individuals learn new things in different ways. Rather than subjecting the new employee to a constant stream of new faces during employee introductions, break up the learning process and perhaps institute "learning games." Examples might include the following:

- Have contests where new employees are shown photographs of key managers and supervisors and award prizes to those new employees who correctly match the most names with faces.
- Take the new employees on a tour of the property and ask them to obtain the signatures of the employees to whom they are introduced.

AVOID COMMON MISTAKES

There are some common pitfalls that occur during orientation that should be avoided at all costs. Hospitality managers and supervisors are responsible for ensuring that the new employee is not

- Overwhelmed with too much information in a short period of time.
- Overloaded with forms to complete.
- Given only menial tasks that discourage job interest and company loyalty.
- Pushed into the job with only a sketchy orientation.

It is important that hospitality managers and supervisors do not work under the mistaken impression that "trial by fire" is the best orientation.[2] Consider some of the "Tales from the Field" on page 201. You must ask yourself: "What were these organization's thinking?"

WORK WITH A CHECKLIST

One of the best ways to ensure that new-employee orientation is productive for both the employee and the organization is to create a checklist that managers and supervisors may consult. In larger hospitality operations, such a checklist may be provided by the human resources department. In smaller operations, the owner or the general manager may be responsible for preparing it. If different tasks on the checklist are going to be performed by different people, then the individual's name should be specified and appear next to the task. In general, the larger the hospitality business is, the larger the checklist. In the example that follows, the checklist has been broken into three broad categories: (1) Things to do before the new employee arrives, (2) things to do on the employee's first day at work, and (3) things to do by the end of the first week of employment.

Before the New Employee Arrives

In preparation of the new employee's arrival, you should do the following:

- Notify everyone in the new employee's department that a new person is starting and what the person's job will be.
- Ask other staff members to welcome the new employee and encourage support.
- If possible, identify an employee to act as a mentor to the new employee for the first week.
- Enroll the employee in new-employee orientation.
- Send the new employee a welcome letter and a schedule for the first week.

First Day on the Job

A new employee may be anxious about starting a new job. Try to create a comfortable environment and remember not to overwhelm the employee. On the first day you should do the following:

- Give a warm welcome and discuss the plan for the first day.
- Tour the employee's assigned work area.
- Explain where restrooms, refreshments, and break areas are located.
- Provide any required keys.
- Arrange to have lunch with the new employee.
- Tour the property and introduce the new employee to key personnel.
- Introduce the new employee to his or her mentor.
- Review the company's organizational chart and explain the department's relationship to the big picture.
- Review the employee handbook.

During the First Week

Be sure the following items are handled in the first week of employment:

- Review the employee work area to ensure that any needed equipment or supplies are in place.
- Ensure that the employee has received a proper uniform and name tag.
- Set up a brief meeting with the new employee and his or her mentor to review the first week's activities.
- Schedule a meeting with human resources to ensure that the new employee has completed all necessary paperwork.

When planning a new-employee orientation program and checklist, it is important to remember that many new hires in the hospitality industry question their decision to work for your company by the end of their first day. Their anx-

TALES FROM THE FIELD

1. A hotel front-desk clerk was forced to endure two days of orientation during which the human resources department makes presentation after presentation that are followed by hours of boring videotapes. The clerk had already worked for the hotel for nearly six months.

2. A new kitchen line cook was assigned as a mentor to the one employee with the worst attitude, negative company outlook, and the least amount of interpersonal skills.

3. A new hotel bellhop was asked to sit in a noisy lobby for an hour to read and sign-off on the 100-page employee handbook.

4. A new dining room host's first week of work was scheduled to coincide with his supervisor's vacation.

5. A new hotel reservationist was left to sit at her workstation to figure things out on her own while everyone else paired off to go to lunch.

6. A new maintenance supervisor had not been assigned a work area, so he was asked to sit in the hallway for the first four days and then asked to share a desk with another employee after that.

7. A new accounting clerk, after standing at the front desk for more than 20 minutes while front-desk personnel figured out what to do with her, was accidentally sent to the restaurant, where she was given an apron and instructed to "get started on the dishes."

8. A new part-time pastry chef was not introduced to coworkers, and another pastry chef, thinking his job had been taken away from him, stormed out of the restaurant and quit. The new employee was hired as a part-time assistant to the full-time pastry chef.

9. A new front-desk clerk hired to work the 3- to-11 shift was asked to straighten a lobby brochure rack—for eight hours—because the front desk had heavy arrivals and no one had time to train him.

10. A new administrative assistant began her job in a hotel sales office when the entire staff was under intense pressure to complete the hotel's marketing plan in 48 hours.

ieties are fueled by mistakes that companies often make during that first-day orientation program. Hospitality managers and supervisors who are planning a new-employee orientation program should ask themselves: "What do we want to achieve during orientation? What first impression do we want to make?" There is no doubt that a hospitality company's positive first impressions can "cement the deal" for a newly recruited employee.

SUMMARY

- Employees who are brand-new to an organization often have feelings of anxiety and wonder if they will fit in or if they will be able to do the job.
- It is important to help the new employee fit in, especially in the critical first 10 to 14 days on the job.
- Orientation programs set up for new employees provide both a broad overview of the company's goals and its philosophy as well as a more targeted view of the specific job itself.
- When new employees feel good about their decision to work for your company, morale increases, retention increases, and employee turnover can be diminished.
- Within the first 30 days of employment, many hospitality industry employees have already made up their minds about whether they plan to stay or leave their new job.
- While feelings of anxiety for a new employee are normal, they do hinder the learning process, which can be an obstacle to effective training.

PRACTICE QUIZ

1. Employee orientation should only be conducted after a new employee has been fully trained.

    A. True   B. False

2. In large hospitality organizations, the human resources department is responsible for conducting the entire new-employee orientation program.

    A. True   B. False

3. Most new-employee orientation sessions in small hospitality operations take less than two hours to complete.

    A. True   B. False

4. The most successful orientation programs can best be characterized as "trial by fire."

    A. True   B. False

5. New-employee orientation benefits the company, management, and the new employee.

    A. True   B. False

6. Which of the following topics should *not* be covered during new-employee orientation?

    A. An overview of the company and its philosophy

    B. Meeting managers, supervisors, and coworkers

    C. Specific job-related training

    D. Physical tour of the facility inside and out

7. In smaller hospitality operations, who should assume the role of conducting new-employee orientation?

    A. The human resources department

    B. The general manager or the owner

    C. The employee's immediate supervisor

    D. B and C only

8. Which is *not* a benefit to employee orientation?

    A. Helps new employees see how they "fit" into the organization overall

    B. Could possibly reduce employee turnover

    C. Provides time for new employees to complete paperwork, no matter how many forms there may be to complete

    D. Helps new employees feel good about their decision to work for that company

9. The critical period between the time a new employee begins a new job and the time that the employee makes up his or her mind about staying or quitting is usually

    A. 90 or more days

    B. 60 to 90 days

    C. 30 to 60 days

    D. 10 to 14 days

10. When a new employee has feelings of anxiety, the result could be which of the following?

    A. Learning could be hindered.

    B. Such feelings could be an obstacle to effective training.

    C. New workers may decide to quit and go somewhere else.

    D. All of the above.

REVIEW QUESTIONS

1. Explain in your own words the process of socialization, and give examples from your own work experiences in which you may have undergone this process. If you have no specific work experiences to draw upon, use the example of starting classes in a new school. Did the process affect you in a negative way or in a positive way? How exactly? Use examples and be specific.

2. Assume you own or manage a small food service or lodging operation. Prepare an outline that details each of the topics you will cover during new-employee orientation. Also, determine who among your staff will be responsible for delivering each topic in your orientation program. Explain

your choices, and be specific, using examples from both the lecture and your textbook.

3. Prepare some ideas for two or three learning games that could be implemented during new-employee orientation. Try to match the "game" with one of the learning objectives in the orientation plan you wrote for question 2. For example, you might play the "name game" as described earlier in this chapter as a fun way to help a new employee remember the names and faces of key personnel. Be prepared to share your ideas with the rest of the class.

4. Write an orientation checklist that would be appropriate for either a large hospitality operation or a smaller operation. Locate a student in your class who has written a checklist that is different from your own. Compare and contrast the two checklists, and be prepared to discuss any similarities and differences between the two lists with the rest of the class. Which elements of the orientation checklist do you feel are most important and why? If you had to delete an element or two as being less important, what is your rationale for doing so? Explain in full.

5. Because it is important to send a new employee home after his first day of work with some positive experience, come up with two or three ways that this could be done in a typical hospitality setting. What would you do on the employee's first day that would be so positive that the new employee would likely go home and tell his family members or friends about it? Be specific and give examples.

HANDS-ON HRM ▶

Alma and Louise first met when they both enrolled in a culinary arts degree program at the local community college. Both women were career changers: Alma was leaving a legal secretary's position that she had held for nearly 12 years, and Louise, who had worked at an auto assembly plant, was recently laid off when the factory closed and moved its operations overseas. Both women were divorced and were struggling to balance school, work, and the challenges of raising young children in a single-parent household. As their friendship developed, they decided that they would pool their resources and open the restaurant of their dreams as soon as they graduated from culinary school.

Alma felt that she had a "better head for business" than Louise, so before opening the new restaurant, they agreed that Alma would spend three weeks training their newly hired staff. The costs were quickly piling up, and Louise was worried. "We haven't even served our first guest yet," she said to Alma, "and our preopening budget is already shot." Alma explained that many restaurants fail "right off the bat" because of poor training, and while she agreed that the costs were high, she convinced Louise that the efforts would pay off down the road in the form of lower-employee turnover and enhanced customer service.

Eight months after opening, the restaurant really began to take off. Even though the turnover rate was about 60 percent, far below the industry average, Alma and Louise found that they were hiring and training new employees almost every week. As business continued to grow, the owners had their hands full with the daily operation of the restaurant. Louise, as executive chef, was primarily responsible for all aspects of the kitchen, and Alma focused her efforts on standardizing procedures and setting up systems to control food, beverage, and labor costs.

The new owners were pleased that they were able to make a small profit after their first year of operation, but they were concerned that employee turnover rates had escalated to just over 100 percent. While still below industry averages, they realized that if they did not somehow stop the "revolving door of employees," their business would run the risk of failure. Alma understood that as her responsibilities had grown, she no longer was able to devote her full attention to new-employee orientation. She decided to turn this task over to a small team of loyal employees who had been with the restaurant from the start. She reasoned that if anyone "knows how things work around here," these employees do.

Less than three months into the second year of operation, turnover had increased to nearly 200 percent. Alma and Louise both felt that they were hiring quality applicants, and they agreed that the problem lay somewhere within the orientation and training program. One night, after a particularly grueling day, the two sat down over a bottle of wine to discuss the problem and explore their options.

QUESTIONS ▶

1. What should the owners' first step be to control the escalating turnover rates? What areas of the operation should they focus on to uncover the apparent flaws in the orientation and training program?

2. How might Alma have better prepared her "loyal team" for taking over orientation and training responsibilities? Which aspects of orientation and training should a restaurant's owner or manager be responsible for, and which aspects should be turned over to other employees?

3. If the restaurant were franchised and part of a large chain, how might a chain's system of orientation and training differ from that which Alma and Louise have put into place? What similarities might there be?

4. Are the challenges Alma and Louise are facing unique to such independent restaurant owners and operators or are they commonplace? Explain your answer in detail.

KEY TERMS ▶

Workplace orientation An introduction of new employees to the workplace so that they can learn what is important to the organization, to management, and to fellow employees.

Socialization A process through which new employees begin to understand and accept the values, norms, and beliefs held by others in the organization.

NOTES ▶

1. Sandra Sucher and Stacy McManus, "The Ritz-Carlton Hotel Company," *Harvard Business Review* (March 2001).
2. William Werther, *Human Resources and Personnel Management* (New York: McGraw-Hill, 1983), 280.

CHAPTER 11

TRAINING TO PERFORMANCE STANDARDS

If you go to a good hotel and ask for something, you get it. If you go to a great hotel, you don't even have to ask.[1]

John Collins, human resources director, the Ritz-Carlton, Boston Common

CHAPTER OBJECTIVES

After completing this chapter, you will be able to

- Distinguish between training and development.
- Identify how training benefits employees, management, and the company.
- Recognize that an effective training program should include performance standards and needs assessment.
- Describe the performance management cycle.
- Determine the essential tasks associated with a particular job and develop performance standards for each task.
- Define needs assessment and describe approaches to conducting an effective needs assessment.
- List and describe the five learning principles.
- Identify factors to consider when selecting a particular training method.
- Distinguish between on-the-job and off-the-job training methods.
- Describe key training methods and the major learning principles associated with each method.
- Develop an evaluation process to assess the results of training and development.

 **HRM IN ACTION** Hospitality managers and supervisors must invest a substantial amount of time and money into the **training and development** of their employees, if they hope to create a positive work environment where workers are motivated to consistently produce quality products and deliver exceptional service. In hospitality operations, both large and small, the lack of proper training and development is one of the leading causes of employee turnover. When employees do not know what is expected of them in terms of their job responsibilities, they get frustrated, and frustrated employees are the employees most likely to make a mental decision to look for another job. Sadly, in many operations, employees tend to become frustrated at the workplace within the first 30 to 60 days of employment if their manager never clarifies their job responsibilities. Assuming that the manager has made the proper hiring decision during the employee selection process, the manager owes it to himself, as well as to the new employee, to provide the employee with ongoing effective training and development to ensure job satisfaction as well as professional development.

TRAINING NOW AND DEVELOPMENT LATER

When management effectively qualifies a new employee and ensures that the right applicant has been hired for the right position, and then provides the new employee with a proper orientation, the employee will still not be able to perform her job duties in a satisfactory manner. New employees and even experienced workers need proper training to ensure that their job performance matches company standards. Some hospitality managers attempt to take short cuts by hiring only workers who have previous hospitality industry experience.

Requiring previous hospitality industry experience for upper-level employees in positions such as sales and marketing or food and beverage management may be logical, but the practice makes little sense when selecting entry-level workers, especially if management's goal is to make an end run around the training process. Figure 11.1 provides some reasons given by hospitality managers for why they provide little to no training.

Training is the process that provides employees with the knowledge and the skills required to operate within the systems and standards set by management. While training can be extremely in-depth and enormously demanding, it is essential to ensure employee job satisfaction and productivity. Lack of training or training that is poor contributes to high employee turnover and the delivery of substandard products and services.

Training helps employees do their current jobs more effectively. While the benefits of training may contribute to the quality and effectiveness of an employee's performance in her current position, **development** helps the employee

The following are reasons some hospitality managers have given for providing little or no training:

1. "It's too demanding when we get busy, so we overlook it or just cancel it altogether."
2. "We don't have anyone here who knows how to train."
3. "We don't train new employees; they don't stick around long enough."
4. "It's too expensive to do it right, so we just rely on the 'shadow system.'"
5. "We can't afford the downtime; all new employees need to be productive from day one."
6. "No one here speaks Spanish well enough to be a trainer."
7. "We tried that once, but we lost the training manuals, so we just never restarted it."
8. "Everyone here already knows how we do things."
9. "I hate it, but when times are lean, training is always the first thing cut from my budget."
10. "Our purveyors provide most of our training for us."

Figure 11.1   Reasons some hospitality managers give for providing little to no training.

to gain knowledge and skills to help prepare her to handle future responsibilities, with less emphasis on her present job duties. The ultimate goal of training is to focus on an employee's present job, while development focuses on the employee's potential future advancement within the company.

BENEFITS OF TRAINING AND DEVELOPMENT

As the hospitality industry becomes more and more competitive, having competent, well-trained employees is essential at all levels of employment. Not only does an effective training program teach new employees important skills and knowledge about their positions within the company, but it also helps to encourage employees to have a positive attitude toward customer service. Training is expensive, both in a monetary sense and also with regard to productivity because workers who are learning their job responsibilities are not yet fully productive. As a result, if a company encounters tough times and costs are reduced, training and development budgets are often the first to disappear. This is a mistake. Hospitality managers must treat training and development as investments in their organizations' futures, not just as a line-item expense. A hospitality

Training Benefits the Employee

1. Increases job satisfaction and recognition
2. Moves employee closer to personal goals
3. Encourages self-development and self-confidence
4. Helps the employee become an effective problem solver
5. Allows employee to become productive more quickly
6. Sustains a positive attitude toward customer service

Training Benefits Management

1. Improves communication between managers and employees
2. Improves morale and builds cohesiveness between managers and employees
3. Aids in evaluating employee performance
4. Makes policies and procedures viable
5. Aids in sustaining systems and standards
6. Helps to identify employees for promotions or transfers

Training Benefits the Organization

1. Leads to improved profitability
2. Reduces accidents and safety violations
3. Helps create a positive corporate image
4. Aids in organizational development
5. Assists in developing employees for internal promotions
6. Helps employees adjust to change
7. Reduces costly employee turnover

Figure 11.2   The benefits of employee training.

organization's commitment to the training and development of its employees not only benefits the employees but also management and the company. Figure 11.2 highlights some of these key benefits.

Hospitality organizations that devote themselves to training and development enhance their employees' capabilities and strengthen their own competitive advantage over other competing operations. Effective training also furthers the employees' personal and professional goals and enhances their abilities, increasing their value to the overall success of the organization. Another important stakeholder who benefits from employee training is the organization's valued guests and customers. These individuals benefit because they receive quality products and services and, as a result, become repeat customers.

TALES FROM THE FIELD

As the new general manager of a nice, privately owned restaurant, I had a lot of respect for the lovely couple who owned the business because they actually let me do the job that they hired me to do: manage the restaurant. These owners put aside nearly 2 percent of the restaurant's annual sales for marketing and advertising. In some years, this could amount to nearly $50,000. Our efforts were pretty successful because we almost always attracted huge crowds and lots of new business anytime we launched a promotion. Unfortunately, our staff was not always that well trained, so more often than not, we ended up losing business in the long run. This loss of business was not only a result of having to comp free meals when we got overrun and just messed things up, but it was also due to the negative word of mouth we were getting because our staff just couldn't execute to meet our customer's needs. I talked to the owners and got them to agree to reduce the advertising budget by 50 percent and to increase the training and development budget by 50 percent, so over half the money that used to go to advertising was now being devoted to training instead. The results were remarkable; we still attracted large crowds, but now our staff could actually execute with superb food and service. Now, almost the entire budget originally intended for advertising goes to training and development. We learned that satisfied customers were our very best form of advertisement.

Greg, 31, Akron, Ohio

PERFORMANCE STANDARDS AND NEEDS ASSESSMENT

Training is not a magic wand that will provide a universal solution to every company need. The jobs within the company also need to be properly designed with clear and objective **performance standards,** which provide benchmarks against which employee performance is measured. And managers must also work diligently to match the right applicant with the right position; the best training in the world is of no use whatsoever if the employees who are being trained are not well suited for the positions they've been hired to fill. Managers must also assess the needs, objectives, content, and **learning principles** associated with the training. This **needs assessment** is an important step when determining the training necessary because it assesses the needs of the organization in order to identify the goals that should be achieved as a result of the training.

UNDERSTANDING PERFORMANCE MANAGEMENT

We will first focus our attention on an effective performance management program, because this is essential to the training process. Managing employee performance is one of the most important functions of a hospitality manager. **Performance management** is an ongoing, continuous process of communicating and clarifying job responsibilities, priorities, and performance expectations in order to ensure mutual understanding between supervisor and employee. Performance management occurs on a continuous cycle and enables a manager to encourage employee development by providing frequent feedback and fostering teamwork among his staff. This particular function of management emphasizes communication between management and employees and focuses on adding value to the hospitality organization by promoting improved job performance and encouraging employees to develop their skills and knowledge. Figure 11.3 details a performance management cycle.

As Figure 11.3 illustrates, the performance management process requires that a manager clarifies job responsibilities; defines performance standards; trains employees to performance standards; and documents, evaluates, and discusses performances with employees.

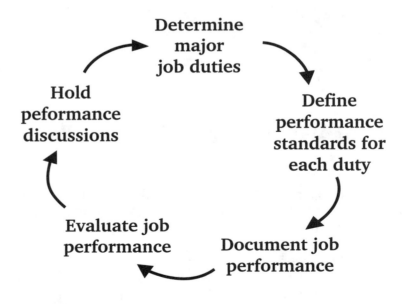

Figure 11.3   The performance management cycle.

ethical dilemma

Jeremy was recently hired as a bartender at a posh, downtown hotel, and he has been on the job for a little more than four months. He is beginning to really like his coworkers, and his work schedule fits perfectly with his class schedule at the local university. The hotel has just adopted a policy that imposes sanctions on those employees found to be working under the influence of alcohol or illegal drugs, and Jeremy is worried about his supervisor, Alex, who is the hotel's beverage manager. Alex is responsible for training Jeremy, and frequently during training, Jeremy thought he detected alcohol on Alex's breath when they were beginning work in the afternoons and sometimes after work breaks later in the evening. But until the new policy was announced, it never occurred to Jeremy that he should say anything to Alex, let alone tell anyone else about it. Alex has been really nice to Jeremy, and Jeremy is not the kind of person who feels comfortable discussing such matters with others.

Two days before the announcement of the new alcohol and drug policy, Alex tells Jeremy that he is being considered for the position of food and beverage director for the entire hotel. Although pleased at the prospect of Alex's promotion, Jeremy wonders if Alex's drinking will get in the way of meeting his responsibilities. Jeremy worries that, with additional job pressures, Alex's drinking problem will worsen. Should Jeremy talk to Alex about his drinking, or should he keep quiet and mind his own business, leaving the problem up to Alex and those who have the responsibility to select someone for the job? If Jeremy decides to keep quiet, will he be in violation of any of the *10 Ethical Principles for Hospitality Managers,* and, if so, which ones? How will Jeremy's decision affect his relationship with hotel management? With Alex? What would you do? Why?

IMPORTANCE OF PERFORMANCE STANDARDS

Developing effective performance standards is an important part of the performance management cycle. Effective job performance standards serve two important functions. First, they become targets for employee efforts, and second, they are criteria against which job success is measured. For hospitality managers and supervisors, they are indispensable. You first encountered this concept in Chapter 6 where you learned that some organizations' job descriptions break down each task into a performance standard, or the *what, how,* and *to what standard* each task within the job description is to be accomplished. This concept will be repeated in Chapter 12, where you will learn the important role that objective performance standards play in the overall effectiveness of the hospitality organization's performance appraisal system. Unclear performance expectations and poor employee feedback are two of the primary reasons for poor employee job performance.

In order to be effective, performance standards should be

- Attainable
- Specific
- Observable
- Meaningful
- Measurable
- Stated in terms of quality, quantity, timeliness, or cost

Employee involvement in the development of performance standards is also important. It is often said that if you want to know how to best complete a task, ask the employee who does it every day. It is important that the *established standards describe the conditions that will be met when performance is satisfactory.* For example, how well, how much, and at what speed is the standard expected to be performed? Measurable standards should also provide for ranges of acceptable performance. There should be several levels of performance so that excellent performers can be differentiated from satisfactory performers, poor performers, and so forth.

PERFORMANCE STANDARDS AND TRAINING

Performance standards are not only the basis for performance evaluation, but they are also essential to effective training because they clearly state how you and the employee will recognize when expectations have been met, exceeded, or not met. When an employee's performance meets or exceeds standards, it is safe to assume that training to that standard has been effective. Additional training and coaching is necessary when an employee's performance does not meet established standards.

HOW TO SET PERFORMANCE STANDARDS

Some hospitality operations break down each job into its essential tasks. These tasks or job duties are normally listed within the position's job description. Here are some essential tasks or job duties that may be listed in a job description for the position of hotel switchboard operator:

■ *Answer* incoming calls.

■ *Take* messages for guests when they do not answer their room phones.

■ *Record* guest messages in the appropriate logbook.

■ *Provide* guests dialing instructions for local and long-distance calls.

■ *Enter* wake-up call requests into the wake-up call system.

■ *Balance* call accounting data at end of shift.

Notice that the first word in each of the above six tasks is in capital letters and that each of these words is an action verb. These tasks tell the employee *what* to do. This list does not, however, provide information regarding *to what extent* each task should be performed. This information will be provided in the task's performance standards. The example below provides performance standards for task number one: Answer incoming calls.

TASK: *ANSWER incoming calls*

Performance standard: Performance will be satisfactory when the following occurs:

■ Telephone is answered in three or fewer rings; employee has a smile on his or her face, and employee uses appropriate address such as "sir" and "ma'am."

■ Employee does not leave callers on hold for longer than 30 seconds without acknowledging they are still waiting.

■ Information provided to callers is correct and complete.

■ Customer complaints do not exceed two-per-annual rating period.

In some cases, once developed and communicated, the standards may need to be modified as a result of feedback from the employees who work in the position. This is especially true in the case of a newly created position. In other instances, performance standards may need to be revised for particular positions as the focus of the hospitality organization changes. Some organizations may choose to set a range of behaviors as follows:

■ *Excellent performance.* Answered in one ring or less

■ *Good performance.* Answered in one to two rings

■ *Satisfactory performance.* Answered in two to three rings

■ *Marginal performance.* Answered in four to five rings

■ *Poor performance.* Answered in five or more rings

Performance standards may also measure a task by more than one standard. An example from a hotel housekeeping department follows:

TASK: *Meet daily room-cleaning quota*

■ *Quantity standard.* Clean no less than 18 rooms per day.

■ *Quality standard.* No more than 1 percent of the rooms cleaned are found to have deficiencies by the housekeeping inspector.

■ *Effective use of resources standard.* Work is completed with no more than an average of 5 percent overtime in a one-week pay period.

In all instances, the performance standards should accurately reflect the skills, behaviors, and goals that the organization values.

DETERMINING TRAINING NEEDS

Large, chain-affiliated hospitality organizations allocate great sums of money to training and development. Hard Rock Cafe, for example, spent as much as $4.5 million per year educating and training workers prior to September 11, 2001.[2] They have since reduced their training budget somewhat, but the organization still devotes considerable financial resources to training and developing the employees who staff and manage its 115 restaurants located in 44 different countries.

For a large chain such as McDonald's, it takes qualified and talented managers and employees to sustain such a global food service retailer. Hamburger University, McDonald's worldwide management training center, is a 130,000-square-foot facility on an 80-acre campus located at the corporation's headquarters in Oak Brook, Illinois. The facility includes 17 teaching rooms, a 300-seat auditorium, and four special team rooms for interactive education. Hamburger University translators can provide simultaneous translation of more than 27 different languages. Twenty-two full-time international resident professors teach students from more than 199 countries. Hamburger University has graduated more than 70,000 McDonald's restaurant managers.[3]

In these examples, some money goes to train workers for new jobs, and other expenditures update the knowledge and skills of current workers. Still other expenditures prepare managers and workers for future challenges. If these large hospitality organizations are to get maximum benefit from these staggering expenditures, their training and development efforts must concentrate on the people and the situations that will benefit most. To best determine what training and development is needed, human resources professionals in these organizations perform a needs assessment by assessing both company and individual needs.

While smaller hospitality operations can only dream of the megabuck training budgets enjoyed by their larger counterparts, the small amounts of financial resources they *can* devote to training are just as valuable. To ensure their smaller budget is properly targeted, these smaller operations must conduct needs assessments to ensure their training and development investments produce the desired results. Conducting a needs assessment helps to diagnose current prob-

Photo 11.1   Large operations have the financial resources to provide state-of-the-art corporate training centers for their managers.

lems within the organization and future challenges that the organization might face, and then it helps to determine ways to meet those challenges with the help of training and development. Challenges can be external or internal. An example of an **external challenge** occurred in 1990 when Congress passed the ADA. You learned about this important federal law in Chapter 2. As a result of this law being passed, managers and supervisors who interviewed job applicants needed updated training to ensure that they would not ask the kinds of questions that might violate this new federal law. Sometimes changes within an organization's strategy can create a need for additional training. This kind of **internal challenge** occurred in the early 1980s when the Holiday Inn hotel chain rolled out a fully computerized reservation system for use in each of the chain's one thousand hotels worldwide. All Holiday Inn employees had to be trained so they could successfully navigate through the reservation system when dealing with their guests.

APPROACHES TO NEEDS ASSESSMENT

One approach to assessing the training needs of a hospitality business is simple **observation.** Supervisors see their employees on a daily basis; therefore, day-to-day observation is perhaps the best source of recommendation for employee training. A more refined approach is **task identification.** This occurs when management evaluates a particular job description to identify the essential tasks that the job requires. Then, specific plans are developed to provide the training necessary for employees to perform these essential tasks.

Another approach involves **employee surveys.** Management surveys potential trainees in an attempt to identify specific areas about which they want to learn more. When surveys are conducted, one benefit is that the trainees are more likely to be receptive to the training because they have helped to determine its focus and find it to be more relevant to their day-to-day jobs. **Exit interviews** are another valid source for assessing training and development needs. Exit interviews occur when an employee separates from the organization for any reason. A human resources employee normally speaks with the departing employee in an attempt to determine exactly *why* the employee is leaving the organization. In smaller operations where no human resources department exists, it may be necessary to have the exit interview of a departing employee conducted by someone other than the employee's immediate supervisor.

Needs assessment is not only a valid diagnostic tool that helps a company to identify training needs, it also helps to reveal shortcomings that can be traced to other management activities like job placement, iorientation programs, or ineffective recruiting. By uncovering repeated shortcomings, managers and supervisors can modify these activities to ensure a better fit between job applicant and job performance.

DETERMINING TRAINING OBJECTIVES

After specific challenges are identified and training needs are diagnosed, the hospitality manager must develop **training objectives.** Training objectives should always conform to performance standards. In other words, objectives should state the desired behavior and the conditions under which it should occur. Training objectives, like performance standards, will serve as the standard against which individual performance and training programs will be measured. Consider the following performance standards that may be associated with a typical task listed in the job description for a hotel reservations clerk:

TASK: *Process call-in hotel reservation requests*

Performance standard: Performance will be satisfactory when the following occurs:

- Hotel availability information is provided to call-in customers within 30 to 60 seconds.

- A one-party room reservation is completed within one to three minutes after all information is obtained from caller.

- Confirmation information provided to callers is correct and complete.

Objectives such as these give both the employee and the trainer specific goals that can be used to evaluate their success. If the objectives are not met, management can use this information to assess the effectiveness of the training program, the quality of the trainer, and the ability of the trainee.

LEARNING PRINCIPLES

As a manager, you should recognize that people learn differently. **Learning principles** represent the ways in which people learn most effectively. The more these principles are reflected in training, the more effective training is likely to be. The five primary learning principles are repetition, participation, relevance, transference, and feedback. Although the rate at which people learn varies from person to person, incorporating the following learning techniques will help speed up the learning process for all those involved in a particular training session. Consider the examples provided, which relate to each of the techniques that follows:

Repetition. Perhaps you learn things best by repetition and memorization. If this is the case, when you study for a big exam, you may repeat key ideas to yourself so that you can remember them during the test.

Participation. Some individuals find learning to be easier when they are actively involved in the learning process. Consider how long it may have taken you to learn how to ride a bicycle, if you did not actively participate in the process.

Relevance. Most adult learners need relevance. In other words, it is easier for them to learn if they consider the material to be meaningful and important to their current situation. For example, some culinary students attending a large university were not thrilled to learn that a new curriculum change would require them to take Spanish until they discovered that the course would focus on words and phrases that would be useful in a kitchen or back-of-house hotel setting. Many realized that after a day or so of instruction, they would be able to go to their jobs that evening and actually converse with their Spanish-speaking coworkers.

Transference. Some learners need transference, or a close match between the training conditions and the real world. Airline pilots are often trained in flight simulators because the simulators closely resemble the actual cockpit and flight characteristics of the plane. Culinary students receive instruction in labs that closely resemble real-world kitchens. The closer the demands of the training program match the demands of the actual job itself, the faster the person will learn.

Feedback. Feedback from a trainer provides learners with information regarding their progress. Without feedback, learners may become discouraged. Proper feedback encourages learners to adjust their behavior so that training goals are met and training is considered effective. When you receive an exam grade, you have received feedback on your academic performance from your instructor. Your grade may or may not be an accurate reflection of what you *know,* but it is usually an accurate reflection of your study habits. A good grade will encourage you to continue the same study habits, and a poor grade will indicate that you have to adjust your study habits to achieve a more acceptable grade on a future exam.

CONSIDERATIONS WHEN SELECTING TRAINING TECHNIQUES

There are a number of training delivery techniques the hospitality industry may use for the training and development of employees. No single technique is always best; in fact, the best method will often depend upon the following circumstances:

- *Cost-effectiveness.* Hospitality managers must judge the cost of the training technique in relation to the expected outcome.

- *Desired training content.* The information that is to be delivered will sometimes determine the best training technique to utilize.

- *Facility.* Whether the hospitality operation has space dedicated to training will often dictate the technique that will work best.

- *Trainee and trainer preferences.* The preferences and the capabilities of both the trainee and the trainer need to be considered.

- *Learning principles.* Not all training techniques incorporate all the learning principles, but some techniques do come close.

A particular hospitality operation's circumstances will help to determine the importance of each of these five factors. For example, cost-effectiveness may be a minor factor when kitchen staff is being trained on how to react during emergency fire procedures.

TRAINING METHODS

On-the-job-training, or **OJT,** is probably one of the most commonly used training techniques for hospitality industry front-line employee. Sometimes this method is called **job instruction training,** or **JIT.** This type of training is delivered directly to the employee while on the job. It is effective when used to teach employees the tasks they need to perform in order to effectively do their jobs. In this case a trainer, a supervisor, or even a coworker serves as the instructor. When this training method is properly planned and executed, it is very effective because it is one of the few training techniques that incorporates each of the five learning principles. Unfortunately, this method is often botched to the extent that it is rendered completely useless. We will discuss the reasons for this in a moment.

In order to be effective, proper OJT should consist of the steps that follow. Note that when one of the five learning principles is incorporated, that principle appears in italics.

Photo 11.2 On-the-job training (OJT) is common in the hospitality industry.

STEPS TO TAKE WHEN CONDUCTING OJT

1. *Tell* by providing the employee with an overview of the task, its purpose, and its desired outcomes. Emphasize the relevance of the training.
2. *Show* or demonstrate the task so that the employee has a model to copy.
3. *Do* the task; trainer and employee demonstrate, practice, and repeat the process until the employee has mastered the task.
4. *Review* with the employee by providing feedback.

Figure 11.4   Steps in the OJT method.

1. The trainer gives the employee an overview of the task, its purpose, and its desired outcomes, with emphasis on the *relevance* of the training.
2. The trainer demonstrates the task to provide the employee with a model to copy. Because the employee is shown the actual actions that the job requires, the training is *transferable* to the job.
3. The employee is allowed to do the task. The trainer demonstrates the task and the employee *participates* by repeating the task until she actually masters the task. Repeated demonstrations by the trainer and practice by the employee provide the *repetition* and *feedback* for the trainee.

Sometimes this training method is called *Tell, Show, Do,* and *Review.* Figure 11.4 illustrates each of the steps that should be taken when providing OJT.

Problems Associated with OJT

As noted earlier, this training method is quite effective when properly planned and executed. Problems can occur, however, when managers try to take short cuts. Some of these problems are as follows:

- *Poor choice of trainer.* Whether a manager, supervisor, or coworker is delivering OJT, it is important to choose the individual wisely. The person selected to conduct the training should be patient, have adequate job knowledge, be a good communicator, and have an outgoing personality. Be sure the individual you have selected wants to train others; you'd be surprised how many do not.
- *Lack of trainer preparation.* Allow the trainer time to prepare a timetable for instruction and to assemble and set up any needed materials or supplies. No responsible trainer wants to hear: "Hi, this is our new employee, Lisa. You'll be training her tonight during dinner rush."
- *Poor choice of place and time.* OJT means on the job, so it is normal to attempt to conduct training during regular business hours. This presents a

challenge to hospitality business managers because regular business hours usually mean customers and guests need to be served at the same time the OJT is taking place. *Management should ensure adequate labor is scheduled so that the trainer and trainee can have their training session without constant interruptions.*

Job rotation or **cross-training** is another effective training method that is widely used in hospitality operations. To cross-train employees in a variety of jobs, supervisors will often move the trainee from job to job. Each move is normally preceded by OJT. This method of training is effective because it gives workers the ability to perform a variety of jobs at the workplace and sometimes helps to eliminate the potential for boredom. Housekeeping employees can be cross-trained in laundry, hotel bell-staff may be cross-trained as lifeguards or as front-desk agents, restaurant food servers can be cross-trained to work the cashier/greeter station, and kitchen grill workers can be cross-trained to work in the pantry. Each of these examples helps to provide employees with exposure to a variety of jobs and provides management with greater flexibility when assigning tasks. Cross-training also enables management to run a smooth operation when employees are on vacation or absent, because cross-trained employees can step in and perform the tasks of the absent employee. Cross-training employees also helps employees to develop skills and acquire knowledge that may lend themselves well to potential career advancements.

Problems with Job Rotation and Cross-training

Perhaps the greatest problem associated with cross- training is that employees sometimes see the process as nothing more than job loading. pIf this is the chosen training method, it should benefit *both* the employee as well as management. Another problem occurs if the hospitality business is operating under a union's collective bargaining agreement, or contract. We discussed the union contract in Chapter 5, so you will recall that these contracts may have provisions that prohibit cross-training.

TRAIN THE TRAINER PROGRAMS

Training the trainer means that the hospitality organization identifies an existing employee—or several employees—who has the desire and some talent for teaching others, and then teach this person to train other staff members. By training one key person to train others in the organization, you distribute the knowledge and create a repository of knowledge within the organization. A train the trainer program could involve sending one staff member to an outside training class to learn about training techniques, or an experienced manager could train the trainer in-house. An effective train the trainer program will teach inexperienced trainers such skills as how to facilitate a training session, how to deal with employees who are having trouble learning, and how to utilize different training techniques based on learning objectives or outcomes desired. Given the budget constraints that many smaller hospitality operations experience, it is not always possible to send many staff members to outside training. Developing an internal training program can be empowering, and it allows smaller organizations to become more self-sufficient.

OFF-THE-JOB TRAINING METHODS

Job rotation and OJT are **on-the-job training methods** in which instruction is delivered directly to the employee while on the job. **Off-the-job training methods** do not necessarily occur entirely away from the workplace, but this sort of training is usually provided in a traditional classroom setting or similar venue. Off-the-job training includes lectures, video presentations, computer-based training, role playing, case studies, simulation exercises, and **self-study.**

Lecture and **video presentations** tend to rely more heavily on communications than on the modeling approach presented in OJT and job rotation. Providing employees with a lecture is cost-effective when a large amount of information needs to be delivered to a sizeable group of trainees. Often, lectures occur during new-employee orientation when management wishes to cover the information contained in the employee handbook with new hires. Video presentations are similar to lectures and are an effective way to deliver information. Many chain restaurants utilize CD-ROMs and videotapes to deliver basic information about corporate culture as well as more specific, job-related training. These video presentations are usually available in Spanish and other languages, which is quite beneficial considering the cultural diversity of today's hospitality industry employees.

INCREASED USE OF TECHNOLOGY

Advances in technology have brought about substantial changes regarding the delivery of training within many organizations. **Computer-based training** can be delivered via CD-ROM or over the Internet, using **E-learning** techniques such as traditional, computer-based instruction, videoconferencing, and even satellite communications. The Educational Institute of the American Hotel & Lodging Association provides subscribers access to **streaming videos** via the Internet. The program, called Cyber Cinema, consists of an online library that contains hundreds of training videos produced by the organization. Subscribers need only log on to the Internet, enter a username and password, and choose

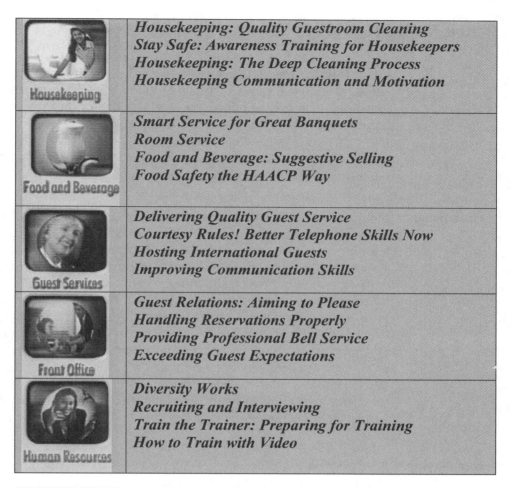

Housekeeping	*Housekeeping: Quality Guestroom Cleaning* *Stay Safe: Awareness Training for Housekeepers* *Housekeeping: The Deep Cleaning Process* *Housekeeping Communication and Motivation*
Food and Beverage	*Smart Service for Great Banquets* *Room Service* *Food and Beverage: Suggestive Selling* *Food Safety the HAACP Way*
Guest Services	*Delivering Quality Guest Service* *Courtesy Rules! Better Telephone Skills Now* *Hosting International Guests* *Improving Communication Skills*
Front Office	*Guest Relations: Aiming to Please* *Handling Reservations Properly* *Providing Professional Bell Service* *Exceeding Guest Expectations*
Human Resources	*Diversity Works* *Recruiting and Interviewing* *Train the Trainer: Preparing for Training* *How to Train with Video*

Figure 11.5   Partial list of AH&LA Cyber Cinema training videos. *(Courtesy of American Hotel & Lodging Association Educational Institute.)*

the video that they want to view.[4] Figure 11.5 lists some training video titles available through Cyber Cinema.

Many hospitality organizations have discovered that when training is delivered via the Internet or a company **Intranet,** it is more cost-effective than the more traditional, on-the-job training methods. Other benefits of utilizing technology for training include the following:

- Employees can take control of their own learning.
- Training is delivered at the convenience of the trainee.
- Training results can be tracked and monitored.
- More people can be trained in less time.
- It saves money on training expenses.

OTHER TRAINING METHODS

Other training methods available to the hospitality manager include internships, role playing, case studies, and self-study, sometimes called **programmed learning.** The overall effectiveness of any one of these methods will depend largely upon who is being trained, the level of the trainee within the organization, what the expected outcomes are, and whether there are appropriate materials available and/or skilled trainers to support the training method chosen. We'll look at each method in a bit more detail.

Internships   Many college students who are preparing for future careers in the hospitality industry are probably already familiar with this term. An internship involves learning from a more experienced employee or employees within the industry. This approach to training can be very effective because it requires high levels of participation from the trainee and provides the trainee with high transferability to the job. Often, employees who have been selected for future advancement are put into formal management training programs in which, ideally, the trainee will be introduced to a wide variety of jobs in the organization. A trainee in a hotel organization's management training program may spend a month or so in the housekeeping department and the front office, a month or so in food and beverage operations, and perhaps another month or so in accounting or in sales and marketing so he or she is exposed to the various job opportunities within the organization.

Role Playing   **Role playing** is a process that forces trainees to assume different identities. It is a training method that is sometimes used to change employee attitudes. For example, a male worker may assume the role of a female supervisor, and the supervisor may assume the role of a male worker. Both trainees would be given a typical work situation and told to respond as they would expect the other to do. This training technique involves participation and feedback. Hospitality sales and marketing professionals sometimes utilize this training method to help fine-tune their sales presentations before presenting to an actual client. One trainee would play the role of the sales manager, and another individual would play the role of the prospective client.

Case Study   When trainees study case situations related to the workplace, they learn about real or hypothetical situations or circumstances and the actions others have taken when faced with these situations. Aside from learning about the content of the case, a **case study** helps trainees to develop decision-making skills. In most cases, this approach to training provides some transference as well as participation through discussion and feedback.

METHODS	Repetition	Participation	Relevance	Transference	Feedback
On-the-job					
OJT	Yes	Yes	Yes	Yes	Sometimes
Cross-training	Sometimes	Yes	Yes	Sometimes	No
Internships	Sometimes	Yes	Yes	Sometimes	Sometimes
Off-the-job					
Lecture	No	No	No	Sometimes	No
Video	No	No	No	Yes	No
E-learning	Yes	Sometimes	Yes	Sometimes	Sometimes
Role playing	Sometimes	Yes	Sometimes	No	Sometimes
Case Study	Sometimes	Yes	Sometimes	Sometimes	Sometimes
Self-study	Yes	Yes	Sometimes	Sometimes	Sometimes

Figure 11.6   Training approaches and associated learning principles.

Self-Study   The self-study training method is also called programmed learning. This is a useful training method when employees are scattered geographically or when learning requires little interaction. Carefully planned instructional materials can be delivered either online via the Internet or company intranet, or in books and manuals, or even via CD-ROMs. Well-designed materials will provide learner participation, repetition, relevance, and feedback. Transference, however, tends to be low. Figure 11.6 lists all of the training methods discussed in this section and the learning principles associated with each one.

As Figure 11.6 reveals, some techniques make more effective use of the training approaches than others. However, even those techniques that use fewer learning principles, such as lecture, can be effective depending upon the hospitality operation's circumstances.

EVALUATING TRAINING

The purpose of training and development is to teach untrained employees new skills or to prepare current employees for future responsibilities. In order to determine whether the hospitality manager's efforts have been successful, training and development activities need to be systematically evaluated. Managers and those involved in delivering the training often assume that the training has value because to them the content seems important. The question most often ignored is "Did the training achieve the objectives?" In other words, the criteria used to evaluate training effectiveness should focus on outcomes. The hospitality manager can normally rely on a number of guidelines to determine the effectiveness of training. These include the following:

- *The reactions of the trainees to both the content delivered and the method used to deliver it.* Sometimes this information is obtained by asking trainees to fill out an evaluation form once the training is complete.

- *The knowledge or the learning acquired through the training experience.* A pre- and post-test can be given to determine what the trainees have learned and retained.

- *Changes in employee behavior as a result of the training.* Because behavioral changes are sometimes the best indicator of success, the evaluation criteria should be stated in behavioral terms whenever necessary.

- *Measurable results or improvements in the individuals or the hospitality business overall.* Examples might include things like lowered turnover, fewer guest complaints, or fewer accidents.

SUMMARY

- The lack of proper training and development of new and existing employees is one of the leading causes of hospitality industry turnover. In order to ensure consistent quality in products and services, managers must provide effective and ongoing training and development.
- Training is of little use if management has made an improper hiring decision; managers must work hard to ensure that they are matching the right person with the right job.
- New and even experienced employees need proper training to ensure that their job performance matches company standards; hospitality managers should not take improper training shortcuts by hiring only those with previous hospitality industry experience, if the goal is to make an end run around proper training.
- Training helps employees perform their current jobs, and development helps employees handle future responsibilities, with less emphasis on present job duties.
- A hospitality manager's commitment to training and development pays dividends to the employees, to management, to the company, and to the guests and customers.
- In order for training to be effective, jobs must be properly designed with clear and objective performance standards.
- Before offering training, management should conduct a needs assessment to diagnose the problems or challenges that the training should address. Once a needs assessment is conducted, management should determine training objectives.

- Performance management is an ongoing, continuous process of communicating and clarifying job responsibilities, priorities, and performance expectations in order to ensure a mutual understanding between the supervisor and employee.
- A needs assessment may be performed through observation, task identification, and employee surveys.
- People learn differently, so it is important to choose a training method that reflects as many of the five learning principles as possible. These learning principles include repetition, participation, relevance, transference, and feedback.
- Training methods include OJT, cross-training, lecture, video presentation, computer-based training, internships, role playing, case studies, and self-study. OJT is the most popular method of training line-level employees in the hospitality industry.
- In order to determine training effectiveness, outcomes should be systematically evaluated by hospitality managers to ensure that designated knowledge was acquired and that changes in behavior occurred as a result of the training.

PRACTICE QUIZ

1. Training focuses on employees' current positions, and development helps employees handle future positions.

   A. True   B. False

2. The employee selection process and new-employee orientation process have no real impact on training effectiveness.

   A. True   B. False

3. Because training is costly, when times are tough, some hospitality operations reduce their training budgets in order to save costs.

   A. True   B. False

4. Developing performance standards is the process of diagnosing present and future challenges which the hospitality operation may face so as to ensure that training objectives meet desired outcomes.

   A. True   B. False

5. Transference is a learning principle best achieved when employees are allowed to repeat tasks over and over until they are able to accomplish those tasks according to company standards.

   A. True   B. False

6. When properly planned and executed, which training method best achieves all of the five learning principles:

   A. Case study

   B. Video presentations

   C. On-the-job training (OJT)

   D. Lecture

7. Training effectiveness should be evaluated according to all of the following guidelines except:

A. Knowledge and skills acquired by the trainee

B. How the training fits into the performance management plan

C. Changes in employee behavior as a result of training

D. Measurable results or improvements in the hospitality operation overall

8. Which of the following is not an approach for conducting a needs assessment?

A. Observation

B. Case study

C. Task identification

D. Employee surveys

9. Which of the following represents an external challenge that a hospitality business may choose to address through training?

A. A new dishwasher hired in the hotel food and beverage division has difficulty keeping up with workflow when the restaurant is busy.

B. The on-the-job injury rate of housekeeping employees has exceeded company standards.

C. A local ordinance that bans smoking in all bars and restaurants will go into effect three months from now.

D. The restaurant's general manager and its executive chef have created an entirely new wine list that has considerably more breadth and depth than the previous wine list.

10. Which of the following conditions would not enhance cross-training or job rotation as a training technique?

A. The employee to be trained has hopes for a future job advancement.

B. Management wishes to groom the employee for future job advancement as well as achieve flexibility in scheduling.

C. The employee scheduled for training is bored with his current job duties.

D. Management needs to be able to call on this employee at any time, because the operation has high turnover and high absenteeism.

REVIEW QUESTIONS

1. Which training technique would you recommend for a new dining room cashier? Which technique would you recommend for an inexperienced kitchen supervisor? Explain your reasons in detail.

2. Discuss the personal qualities and characteristics that may make one trainer selected to conduct OJT more effective than another trainer. Be specific and use examples.

3. A hotel front-desk agent's job description contains the following task: *Greet arriving guests in a friendly, courteous, and efficient manner.* Rewrite this task so that it contains objective and measurable performance standards.

4. Your restaurant has traditionally allowed patrons to smoke at the bar as well as in a small, designated smoking area located in the main dining room. A new city ordinance that bans smoking in all restaurants and bars will go into effect in three months. The ordinance requires the physical removal of all ashtrays as well as posting required signage at the restaurant's entrance. Do you feel that this situation requires training? If so, why? If not, why not? What kind of training, exactly, would you implement if you chose to do so? Why? Which restaurant employees would need the training? Why?

5. You manage a small hotel or restaurant, and the local hospitality college has contacted you about their desire to place interns in your facility so they can each secure a 400-hour internship that is required for graduation. Devise a written plan that would identify the skills, knowledge, and behaviors you would want the interns to achieve while working in your facility. What kind of training and development plan would you implement in order to ensure a successful internship program? Would you pay the student interns or would you insist that their compensation would be the experience they gain from the internship itself? Why or why not? Be specific.

HANDS-ON HRM ▶

Merry has just been hired to work the 3-to-11 shift at the front desk of a large, 450-room downtown hotel. She is thrilled to have been offered the position, even though it meant leaving her previous job where she had worked as a bellhop at a luxury hotel on the other side of town. She held that position for nearly two years, and her employee evaluations and her customer comment cards were excellent. Every time a front-desk position became available at her previous job, she would eagerly apply for it, but for some reason, management always seemed to select another candidate. When Merry saw the advertisement for the current position, she jumped on it, and she landed an immediate interview with the hotel's front-office manager, Alice.

When Alice offered Merry the position, she explained that the hotel does not have a "formal training program." She said that Merry would be "shadowing" Mark, her strongest 3-to-11 clerk, and that after a week or so, she would be ready to work shifts by herself. Alice also explained that the hotel had a rather busy period coming up soon, so Merry's training would be swift. "After this busy period and when you're through training," Alice said to Merry, "we'll get you set up for orientation."

When Merry arrived the next afternoon to begin training with Mark, none of the other front-desk clerks knew who she was. After a few moments, Alice came out of her office. "Hey guys," she said, "this is Merry." "Mark is training her tonight on the 3-to-11 shift." "Be sure to introduce

Mark to Merry when he gets here; I have to run to the bank, and I won't be coming back on [the] property tonight."

Mark came into the back office as the last 7 to 3 clerk had just clocked out and was leaving. "Hey Mark, gotta run," she called out. "Your new trainee is out front, her name is Sherry." "Trainee?" Mark exploded. "Alice didn't say anything about a trainee." "She seems nice," the clerk said, "but I hope she catches on fast; you've got 184 arrivals tonight."

As Mark came behind the front desk, he introduced himself. "I'm Mark," he said. "You must be Sherry." "Actually, it's Merry," Merry replied. She offered her hand. "Well, whatever," he said, ignoring her hand and going directly to the cash drawer to begin counting his bank. "I hope you've got some experience," he said, as he counted money. "We're going to be really busy tonight, and it's just me and you." "Oh yes," Merry said eagerly. "I was with the Fountain Court Hotel for nearly two years." "Well, we'll see," said Mark. "That's a much smaller hotel; I doubt they ever got as busy as this place gets." Merry explained that even though the Fountain Court was smaller, the level of service and demanding guests kept everyone on their toes. "As a bellhop," she began, but Mark cut her off. "Bellhop!?" he yelled. "That's it?" How in the hell does Alice expect me to train a former bellhop all by myself when we have nearly 200 arrivals tonight? What a joke!"

QUESTIONS ▶

1. Depending upon how things go during this first night of training as Merry "shadows" Mark, do you think that Merry will continue to feel good about her choice to work for this hotel, or will she begin looking for another job? Explain you answer. Should Merry decide to leave within her first 90 days of employment, what are the direct and indirect costs that the hotel will incur?

2. What mistakes has Alice made with respect to setting up Merry's training program with Mark? What specific changes should Alice make to the overall front-desk training program?

3. Do you empathize with Mark, or do you feel that he simply has a bad attitude and has no business training new employees. Explain your answer in detail.

4. If Mark is indeed the proper person to be conducting the training for new 3-to-11 desk clerks, what things could Alice do to ensure that Mark is able to approach his training duties with a more positive attitude? Explain.

KEY TERMS ▶

Training The process that teaches employees the knowledge and the skills they need in order to operate within the systems and performance standards set by management. Training puts more emphasis on an employee's present job duties.

Development Programs designed to help employees develop skills and knowledge necessary to handle future responsibilities.

Performance standards Benchmarks against which performance is measured.

Learning principles Guidelines that provide information concerning how people learn most effectively.

Needs assessment An evaluation conducted to diagnose an organization's current problems and future challenges and determine ways to meet those challenges through employee training and development.

Performance management An ongoing, continuous process of communicating and clarifying job responsibilities, priorities, and performance expectations of employees.

External challenge Challenges the organization faces that come from outside the organization such as new government rules, laws, or regulations.

Internal challenge Challenges the organization faces that come from inside the organization such as a change in company strategy.

Observation approach An approach to conducting a needs assessment in which supervisors observe employee performance and make training recommendations based upon observations.

Task identification An approach to conducting a needs assessment in which managers evaluate the job description to identify the essential tasks that the job requires.

Employee surveys An approach to conducting a needs assessment in which employees are surveyed in an attempt to determine training needs.

Exit interview A conversation held with a departing employee in an attempt to learn their views of the organization.

Training objectives The outcomes desired from the training and development process; objectives should state the desired behavior and the conditions under which it should occur.

Learning principles Guidelines that indicate how people learn most effectively.

Repetition learning principle Repeating or memorizing information as a method for learning.

Participation learning principle An active, hands-on approach to learning.

Relevance learning principle Information that the trainee deems relevant and meaningful to his or her current situation.

Transference learning principle A close match between the training conditions and the real world.

Feedback learning principle Learners are provided with information on their progress.

On-the-job training (OJT) Training that is delivered directly on the job.

Job-instruction-training (JIT) *See* on-the-job-training (OJT).

Job rotation Moving employees from job to job; each move is normally preceded by OJT.

Cross-training *See* job rotation.

On-the-job-training methods Training methods in which the instruction is delivered directly on the job.

Off-the-job-training methods Training methods in which instruction is delivered away from the actual job, perhaps in a classroom setting either onsite or offsite.

Self-study A training method in which employees guide their own training, individually, without the presence of other trainees or a trainer.

Lecture presentation A training method in which the trainer, or lecturer, delivers a large amount of information to either a single trainee or a group of trainees.

Video presentation The use of a videocassette or DVD to deliver training content.

Computer-based training The use of a computer to deliver training content either via CD-ROM, Internet, or corporate intranet.

E-learning Computer-based training in which content is delivered via the Internet or corporate intranet.

Streaming videos Media is sent in a continuous stream and is played as it arrives so a Web user does not have to wait to download a large file before seeing the video or hearing the sound.

Intranet A private, computer network that is intended for internal use only within an organization.

Programmed learning *See* self-study.

Role-playing A training method in which individuals assume different identities, or roles.

Case study A situation or circumstance relating to the workplace described in writing in which the trainee is asked to read and respond either verbally or in writing.

NOTES ▶

1. Paul Hemp, "My Week as a Room Service Waiter at the Ritz," *Harvard Business Review* (June, 2002).
2. Donna Hood Crecca, "School of Rock," *Chain Leader* (November 2004).
3. Paul DeVeaux, "Life at Corporate U.," *E-Learning Magazine* (February 2001), 28.
4. For additional information on the AH&LA, visit their Web site at www.ei-ahla.org.

UNIT
4

COMMUNICATION
AND MOTIVATION

CHAPTER 12

PERFORMANCE APPRAISALS THAT WORK

Every exchange with your guest must emphasize that you will care for them, attend to their needs and that their business and concerns are valued. All your staff will need to reflect this behavior, understanding that Guest Satisfaction is the only performance yardstick.[1]

John Hendrie, CEO, Hospitality Performance, Inc.

CHAPTER OBJECTIVES

After completing this chapter, you will be able to

- Explain the importance of an effective performance appraisal system.
- Identify the uses of performance appraisals.
- Differentiate between informal and formal appraisal systems.
- List rater biases that can distort employee performance appraisals.
- Describe commonly used appraisal methods.
- Discuss the role of employee counseling in the appraisal process.
- Identify key legal concerns regarding performance appraisals.

HRM IN ACTION Conducting employee **performance appraisals** is one of the hospitality manager's most important tasks, but most will admit freely that this process is one that gives them difficulty. It is not easy to sit in judgment of an employee's performance, and it is often even more difficult to convey that judgment to the employee in a constructive and painless manner. Employees often see this process as nothing more than a yearly listing of their shortcomings, and managers who have a distaste for conflict and disagreements often prefer to avoid—or at least delay for as long as possible—the appraisal process altogether. How has such an important management function gotten such a bad rap? The answer can usually be found in poorly designed appraisal instruments, inadequately trained managers and supervisors, and/or a lack of clearly stated performance objectives for the employee.

EVERYONE BENEFITS FROM EFFECTIVE PERFORMANCE APPRAISALS

Conducting a performance appraisal is the process by which hospitality managers and supervisors evaluate an employee's job performance. When an effective performance appraisal system is implemented and properly managed, everyone wins: the employee, the organization's management, and even the operation's guests and customers. Most employees want to do a good job, and they will seek feedback as a guide to future behavior. Performance evaluations help identify the employee's positive accomplishments as well as areas of performance that need improvement. Pointing out an employee's strengths by highlighting past accomplishments boosts employee morale and instills positive self-esteem. When deficiencies are found, the manager can help the employee draft a plan to correct the situation. When management focuses on past accomplishments as well as future goals for improvement, employees are less likely to be defensive, and the process itself is more likely to motivate employees to improve any performance deficiencies.

The hospitality manager benefits from administering performance appraisals to his or her employees because a properly administered employee evaluation system will encourage positive manager/employee relations and will lead to improved employee performance over time. The organization's goals and performance standards are clearly stated, and employees are not left in the dark with respect to their role in their own success as well as in the overall success of the organization. Managers also benefit because detailed and specific employee performance feedback enables them to make informed decisions about pay increases, promotions, bonuses, and other employee-related decisions. Figure 12.1 describes some other uses of performance appraisals.

USES OF PERFORMANCE APPRAISALS

- *Improve performance.* Allows the manager and the employee to agree upon a plan of action for improving performance deficiencies.

- *Pay adjustments.* Allows management to determine who should receive pay raises.

- *Placement decisions.* Promotions and transfers are often based upon past or anticipated performance.

- *Training needs.* Poor performance may indicate the need for additional training. Good performance may indicate untapped potential that should be developed.

- *Career planning.* Feedback guides career decisions and highlights specific career paths that should be investigated.

- *Job design errors.* Poor performance could be a symptom of ill-conceived job designs. Appraisals may help identify these errors.

- *Equal employment opportunity.* Accurate appraisals that reflect true job-related performance ensure that placement decisions are not discriminatory.

- *Feedback to management.* Good or bad performance throughout the organization may be an indicator of how well management is performing.

Figure 12.1   Uses for performance appraisals.

Perhaps the group that benefits most of all when an effective performance appraisal system is in place is the organization's valued guests and customers. When the hospitality manager regularly reminds employees of the organization's commitment to high standards of guest service and of the importance of providing a quality product, employees react with greater commitment, and often exceed the customers' expectations. Satisfied customers are return customers, and their positive word-of-mouth advertising is an important element to the organization's overall success.

INFORMAL AND FORMAL APPRAISALS

When hospitality managers and supervisors provide their employees with daily feedback, this is an example of **informal performance appraisal.** Providing informal appraisals is the continual process of giving employees specific information about how well they are performing their job duties. Informal appraisals are best conducted on a day-to-day basis because the process encourages desirable behavior and it discourages undesirable performance before it becomes ingrained. For example, the front-office manager of a hotel spontaneously mentions that a heavy check-in of arrivals was handled well or poorly, or a restaurant server stops by the dining room manager's office to find out how her wine sales are faring for the month. Because there is a close connection between the behavior and the feedback, overall employee performance is more likely to improve. In addition, when open and honest informal feedback occurs, there will likely be fewer surprises when the time comes to conduct a more formal evaluation.

Formal performance evaluations should be conducted at least once or twice per year, and they should always be in written form so they are documented. A **formal performance appraisal** serves four major purposes: (1) to let employees know formally how their current performance is being rated, (2) to identify employees who deserve **merit raises,** (3) to identify employees who require additional training, and (4) to identify employees who are candidates for promotion. It is important that hospitality managers and supervisors be able to differentiate between an employee's current performance and his potential performance. Managers sometimes fail to make this distinction when they assume that an employee with the skills and abilities to perform well in one job will automatically perform well in a different or more responsible job. If you have ever seen a coworker promoted to a position in which he cannot perform adequately, this is probably the reason why. It is also important to note that the formal evaluation should not be used by management as an opportunity to sit the employee down and tell him everything that he has been doing wrong for the past year. Remember, when management provides continual, day-to-day feedback, the formal evaluation should be less threatening and there should be no big surprises.

COMMON PERFORMANCE APPRAISAL PROBLEMS

A well-designed performance appraisal system should provide an accurate picture of an employee's typical day-to-day job performance. Appraisals should not simply highlight poor performance; they should also identify acceptable and good performance. In order for the system to work effectively, appraisal criteria should be job-related and practical, have standards, and use dependable measures. Job-related criteria are defined as critical behaviors that constitute an employee's successful job performance. Consider evaluating a restaurant dishwasher on his "outgoing personality" when performing his appraisal. Such criteria doesn't really make sense considering this specific behavior has little effect on a dishwasher's successful job performance. Evaluating the same dishwasher's "attention to detail," however, would be a job-related evaluation and would, therefore, constitute a valid and reliable rating criterion. Performance appraisal methods are practical when both managers and employees easily understand them. A system that is too complicated may cause resentment, confusion, and nonuse.

Whatever performance appraisal method is used, there must be a written record of the standards. Effective hospitality managers should encourage employees to participate in developing performance standards based upon the crit-

TALES FROM THE FIELD

I somehow thought that when I got out of school, 'report cards' would be a thing of the past. Unfortunately, this is not the case. I graduated from culinary school and took a job as a sous chef in a large hotel located in the Southeast. I was supposed to receive my first evaluation after 90 days, but it never came. After about a year and two months, I was due for a raise, so I asked my chef about conducting my annual evaluation. I could tell right away that he wasn't very interested in doing this, but he probably felt that he had no choice since it was company policy. On the day that we were scheduled to meet, I got that same feeling in the pit of my stomach as I did when it came time for my old college to mail out my report card. I thought I deserved a good evaluation from my chef, but I still had that moment of doubt. My evaluation was somewhere between "low" and "average," and I couldn't believe my eyes as I looked at all the '2s' and '3s' he'd given me. I know I'm not perfect, but he didn't even offer me any advice or instruction on how to improve things. He also didn't offer me much of a raise either, and this was after I'd literally worked my tail off for the past year. I thought this over and when I calmed down, I spoke to human resources. They suggested I document my achievements over the past year and to come in to their office for a meeting, so I did. After about an hour of hearing my side of things, they increased the amount of the raise that the chef had offered and they assured me that chef would get more training on how to do employee evaluations.

Kelly, 32, Birmingham, Alabama

ical elements of the jobs to be appraised. Information about performance standards is typically gathered by conducting a job analysis, which was discussed in Chapter 11. It is important to note that standards should not be set arbitrarily by the hospitality manager or supervisor. Rather, the process should be a participative one, in which employees help to shape the performance standards for their positions. If this approach is taken, employee buy-in is more likely. Employees should also be advised of these established standards before the evaluation occurs, not afterward. Imagine reporting to the first day of class and your teacher hands you the textbook and says, "See you at the end of the semester when you will take your final exam." Not providing students with a syllabus or grading criteria is tantamount to providing no performance standards. Most students would be fearful of this scenario, and for good reason, because there is no clear direction or list of objectives provided!

A performance appraisal system that incorporates dependable measures is one that would allow others using the same measures and standards to reach the same conclusions about performance.[2] This is most easily accomplished when rating criteria are objective, or measurable. For example, two housekeeping supervisors who monitor a room attendant's daily performance utilizing **objective performance standards** would rate performance based on criteria like the number of rooms cleaned in a given amount of time and the level of quality of their cleaning standards. The results are objective and verifiable, and as a result, each supervisor would likely come to the same conclusion concerning the room attendant's performance rating. **Subjective performance standards** are based on the personal standards or opinions of those who are doing the evaluation and are generally not verifiable by others. For example, judging a hotel switchboard operator's performance on subjective criteria such as "politeness" and "courtesy" would lead to an inaccurate evaluation because most people have differing opinions about what defines "politeness" or "courtesy," and these differing opinions may lead to confrontations during the appraisal conference. Such standards tend to be inaccurate and should be avoided when identifying standards for performance assessment, if at all possible.

UNDERSTANDING RATER BIASES

Perhaps one of the biggest problems associated with subjective performance standards is the opportunity for rater **bias.** Rater bias occurs when supervisors and managers fail to remain emotionally detached while they evaluate employee performance. When bias occurs, an employee's performance evaluation will be inaccurate and distorted. The most common rater biases include the following:

- The halo-or-horns effect
- The error of central tendency
- The leniency and strictness biases
- Cross-cultural biases
- Personal prejudice
- The recency effect
- Similar-to-me bias

The Halo-or-Horns Effect

The **halo-or-horns effect** occurs when the supervisor's personal opinion of the employee sways her measurement of his performance. When you like an employee, you may favor that individual in such a way that your personal opinion distorts your evaluation of the employee's performance (halo effect). Or, you may dislike an employee and allow your negativity toward the employee to interfere with your rating of her performance (horns effect). This bias tends to represent all-or-nothing thinking and is most severe when supervisors evaluate personality traits instead of behaviors.

The Error of Central Tendency

Some supervisors prefer to avoid extremes when evaluating their staff, so employee evaluations are distorted to make each employee appear average. On some rating forms, evaluators may avoid checking *very poor* or *excellent,* opting instead to place their marks somewhere near the center of the rating scale. This sort of bias is known as the **error of central tendency.** Managers sometimes make this mistake because they believe that it will allow them to avoid confrontation with the employee being evaluated. This approach is unfair to the employee because it fails to honestly point out areas of performance that either need improvement or exceed expectations.

The Leniency and Strictness Biases

These biases occur when raters tend to be either too lenient or too strict in their evaluations, relative to employees' true or actual performance. The **leniency bias** occurs when raters tend to be easy in evaluating employee performance. Such managers see all employee performance as good and rate it favorably. This sometimes occurs because the rater wants the employee to view him in a positive light, but it is counterproductive. And, usually, the only one being fooled is the rater, not the employee. With the **strictness bias,** the opposite is true. This occurs when raters are too harsh in their employee evaluations. Sometimes these supervisors want their employees to see them as "tough" and "demanding." Both of these biases tend to occur more frequently when performance standards are vague and subjective, rather than objective and measurable.

Cross-Cultural Biases

Our culture tends to drive our perceptions of human behavior. When managers are expected to evaluate individuals from different cultures, they may apply their own cultural expectations to someone who has a different set of beliefs. With constantly increasing levels of cultural diversity among hospitality industry employees, this potential bias is more likely to occur. Managers can prevent this type of bias from occurring by becoming well informed about the cultural differences represented in the organization's workplace. Once the manager is aware, it is easier to recognize this bias and to prevent it.

Personal Prejudice

When supervisors form general opinions about certain groups, this may distort the ratings that those people receive. Sometimes, male supervisors give undeservedly low ratings to women who hold traditionally male jobs. When supervisors and managers are unaware of their prejudices, this makes such biases even more difficult to overcome. Each employee should be regarded as an individual, not just a member of a group.

The Recency Effect   The **recency effect** occurs when an employee's recent actions—either good or bad—distort her overall performance evaluation. Managers tend to recall recent actions more easily and, therefore, place greater importance on job behaviors that occur as the end of the performance-measuring period approaches. This can be overcome when management keeps good notes on employee performance and behavior throughout the appraisal period and then refers to those notes when completing the evaluation.

Similar-to-Me Bias   This type of rater bias occurs when the evaluator judges those employees who hold the same values and judgments as the evaluator as "superior". This error sends the message that those who emulate the boss will receive a favorable evaluation, and those who do not will be disregarded.

OVERCOMING OBSTACLES AND REDUCING ERRORS

Because most of the biases previously mentioned occur when subjective performance measures are used, it is best to avoid measurement criteria that are subjective in an effort to reduce such errors. Remember to evaluate employee performance against objective, measurable performance standards whenever possible. Training supervisors to make sound performance evaluations, providing feedback, and selecting the proper performance appraisal methods are also crucial to ensuring effective employee evaluations. When training supervisors and managers to conduct employee performance appraisals, it is important to alert them to the potential for biases to occur and to help them learn how to avoid these errors. Some managers are not even aware that such biases exist and are, therefore, more easily susceptible to them. In addition, managers and supervisors must understand the importance of impartiality and objectivity as they evaluate their employees' performance.

PERFORMANCE APPRAISAL METHODS

There are many methods used to evaluate employee performance. Most of these methods take a past-oriented approach, meaning that they focus on performance that has already occurred and that can, to some degree, be measured. While it is true that past performance cannot be changed, providing the employee with specific feedback and an action plan for improving performance going forward may lead to renewed efforts of improvement on the employee's

ethical dilemma

Sue has just taken a job as a restaurant executive chef in a small regional chain. She is responsible for conducting annual employee performance appraisals for her entire kitchen staff. The restaurant chain has quotas for ratings: Employees are rated on a scale from 1 to 10, but there can only be a certain number of 10s, 9s, and so forth. When Sue presents her finished appraisals to the regional manager for review and approval, he asks her to change the ratings of one of her best employees from a 9 to a 7 because there are too many 9s. Sue argues against it, but the regional manager insists that she make the change. Sue knows that this hard-working employee will be devastated, and she does not agree with the regional manager's decision, but she is given no choice. When Sue conducts the evaluation interview, she is tempted to tell the employee what happened. Would Sue be violating any of the *10 Ethical Principles for Hospitality Managers* if she tells the employee what happened? If so, which rule(s)? Would she violate any of the 10 principles if she does not tell the employee what happened? If so, which ones? Aside from changing corporate policy with respect to the quota system, could this dilemma have been avoided? How? If not, why not?

part. The most effective approach to performance appraisals must identify performance-related standards, measure those criteria, and then provide useful feedback to both employees and management. The goal, of course, is to improve employee performance. Since every hospitality operation is different, no single appraisal technique is a one-size-fits-all solution. The most widely used appraisal techniques include the following:

- Rating scales
- Checklists
- Forced choice method
- Critical incident method
- Behaviorally anchored rating scales
- Self-appraisals
- Management by objectives method

Rating Scales   You may be familiar with this form of employee evaluation, because rating scales tend to be widely used in the hospitality industry and have been around for many years. The **rating scale** method requires the supervisor to provide a subjective evaluation of an employee's performance based on a scale of low to

Instructions: For the following performance factors, please indicate on the rating scale your evaluation of the named employee.

Employee: _____ Department: _____

Supervisor: _____ Date: _____

	Excellent 5	Good 4	Acceptable 3	Fair 2	Poor 1
1. Dependability	____	____	____	____	____
2. Attitude	____	____	____	____	____
3. Cooperation	____	____	____	____	____
4. Attendance	____	____	____	____	____
5. Quality of work	____	____	____	____	____
Results	____	____	____	____	____
Totals	____ +	____ +	____ +	____ +	____

Total Score = _____

Signature of supervisor: _____

Signature of employee: _____

Figure 12.2   Sample rating scale employee evaluation form.

high, or poor to excellent. An example of a rating scale performance evaluation is provided in Figure 12.2.

As you can see, rating scales tend to be subjective in nature and the supervisor's ratings tend to be based more on personal opinion than on objective, measurable criteria. Some organizations that use such scales might total the points obtained, and then use this information to determine salary increases and promotions. The rating scale form can be relatively easy to design, and supervisors need little training or time to complete the form. Keep in mind, there are numerous disadvantages for using this method. Because the form is subjective in nature, rater biases are more likely to be reflected in the employee ratings. Also, because these forms are often used for a variety of jobs and positions, some of the rating criteria that are specific to one position may have little bearing on another.

Checklists   The checklist method provides a list of behavioral descriptions and requires the supervisor to check off behaviors that apply to the employee. When management assigns weights to different items on the checklist, according to each item's importance, the result is called a **weighted checklist.** The weights allow the rating to be quantified so that total scores can be determined. Figure 12.3 illustrates a portion of a weighted checklist.

Instructions: Check each of the following items that apply to the named employee's performance.

Employee: _____ Department: _____

Supervisor: _____ Date: _____

Weights   Check Here

(7.5)   1. Employee keeps work area neat and clean.   _____

(5.0)   2. Employee works overtime when asked.   _____

(4.0)   3. Employee cooperates and assists others when needed. _____

(3.5)   4. Employee secures work area when finished.   _____

Total of all weights: _____

Supervisor signature: _____

Employee signature: _____

Figure 12.3   Sample weighted checklist employee evaluation form.

The weights for each item are in parentheses but are usually omitted from the form the supervisor uses. This method is somewhat practical and standardized, but using such general statements reduces the form's job relatedness and does not allow for different levels of performance as a rating scale evaluation does. Another drawback occurs when a hospitality organization has a large number of job categories and, therefore, checklist items must be developed for each category. Other disadvantages include rater biases and the use of personality criteria instead of performance criteria.

Forced Choice Method

The **forced choice method** uses a scale or continuum that best describes the employee, using performance factors such as job knowledge, work quality and quantity, attendance, and initiative. This method requires the supervisor to select the one best statement that most accurately describes how the employee performs the job tasks that are considered most important for successful job performance. This method is sometimes called an **adjective rating scale.** Figure 12.4 shows a sample forced choice form.

Forced Choice Performance Evaluation Form	**Employee:** _____ **Department:** _____ **Supervisor:** _____ **Date:** _____				
Performance Factors	*Performance Rating*				
	Low	**Below Average**	**Average**	**Above Average**	**High**
Understands department functions	Poorly informed about department functions	Has fair knowledge of the department functions	Can answer most questions about the department	Understands all phases of the department.	Has complete mastery of all phases of the department.
Follows directions and company policy without supervision	Requires constant supervision	Requires occasional follow-up	Can usually be counted on	Requires very little supervision	Requires absolute minimum supervision
Accuracy, skill, completeness, and quality of work performed	Seldom meets the requirements and is almost always unsatisfactory	Work is often unsatisfactory and often does not meet requirements	Work is consistently satisfactory and usually meets requirements	Work is sometimes superior and rarely contains mistakes	Work is consistently superior and never contains mistakes

Figure 12.4   Sample forced choice or adjective rating scale evaluation form.

Employee: _____	Department: _____
Supervisor: _____	Date: _____
Evaluation period: _____ to: _____	

Control Safety Hazards in Kitchen DATE: *Positive Employee Behavior*	**Control Safety Hazards in Kitchen** DATE: *Negative Employee Behavior*
10/12: *Employee reported a broken rung on the kitchen utility ladder and flagged the ladder as unsafe.* 10/15: *Employee put out small trash can fire promptly.*	11/3: *Employee used kitchen grease mop to clean main dining room floor.* 11/24: *Employee was caught smoking a cigarette in the kitchen.*
Protects Company Assets DATE: *Positive Employee Behavior*	**Protects Company Assets** DATE: *Negative Employee Behavior*
10/3: *Sorted through damaged shipment of glassware to salvage usable wine glasses.*	11/3: *Used hotel guest room bath towel to clean kitchen countertops, resulting in ruined towel.* 11/19: *Left empty sauté pan on range and ruined pan.*

Figure 12.5   Sample critical incidents employee evaluation form.

Critical Incidents Method

The **critical incidents method** of employee performance evaluation focuses the manager's attention on employee behaviors that play a key role in executing a job effectively or ineffectively. This approach requires supervisors to maintain a log or a diary in which they write down examples of incidents that exhibit both acceptable and unacceptable job performance. A sample form is shown in Figure 12.5.

It is important that the supervisor records these critical incidents during the entire evaluation period for each employee. This method is extremely useful in that it gives employees specific job-related feedback. It also reduces recency bias if supervisors faithfully record incidents throughout the rating period. However, this particular system is time-consuming, and if supervisors fail to keep the diaries up-to-date, the critical incidents method of evaluation becomes ineffective.

When properly utilized, this method provides supervisors with a detailed list of behaviors that they can discuss with employees, explaining which behaviors are desirable and which require improvement on the employee's part. However, this method, when improperly utilized, ignores a large number of behaviors that tend to fall somewhere between the extremes of poor and excellent.

<table>
<tr><td>**Photo 12.1**</td><td>The critical incidents approach to performance evaluation requires the supervisor to keep a diary of positive and negative behaviors exhibited by each employee.</td></tr>
</table>

Behaviorally Anchored Rating Scales

Behaviorally anchored rating scales, sometimes referred to as **BARS,** is an evaluation approach that combines elements from both the forced choice and critical incidents methods of evaluating employee performance. When using the BARS method, supervisors rate their employees along a continuum just as they do with the forced choice and critical incidents methods, but they use specific, named behaviors as benchmarks, rather than general descriptions or traits. Figure 12.6 provides an example of a BARS for a hotel manager being rated on achieving hotel sales goals as a result of teamwork and collaboration. Note that in this example, specific job behaviors are listed. Keep in mind also that Figure 12.6 represents one page of what would most likely be a multiple page form, with each separate page representing a different behavioral dimension.

Another form of a BARS is a **behavioral frequency scale.** Rather than rating specific, named behaviors, this form requires the supervisor to indicate the frequency of the identified behavioral anchors, usually along a five-point scale from "almost never" to "almost always." Figure 12.7 illustrates an example of a behavioral frequency scale for a restaurant manager being rated on the ability to supervise staff.

BARS are somewhat complex to develop and administer because they address specific, job-related behaviors. Their validity tends to be superior to methods that are based on subjective personality traits, but because they must be created for each job, they can be costly to develop and maintain, especially for larger hospitality operations with an array of jobs.

Employee: _____	Department: _____
Supervisor: _____	Date: _____

Performance Category: Uses Collaborative Methods in Meeting Hotel Sales Goals

Rating	Behavior Anchor
5 [ ] **Very Good**	Develops workable plans for collaboration, including timelines and budgets; and works regularly with department heads to achieve goals; and gives credit to others for their contributions and provides supportive written materials of their work; and always follows up on agreements.
4 [ ] **Good**	Plans for collaboration usually carried out, helps all members of the team make meaningful contributions, and experiences some difficulties in full collaboration among identified team members.
3 [ ] **Below Average**	Has a plan for collaboration but experiences delays and frustrations with the nature of collaboration.
2 [ ] **Poor**	Has no effective plan for collaboration but expresses interest.
1 [ ] **Unacceptable**	Shows no interest in working with others. Does not seek direction on how to improve.

Figure 12.6   Sample BARS employee evaluation form.

Employee: _____	Department: _____
Supervisor: _____	Date: _____

Behavioral Anchor: Dining Room Staff Supervision

Behavior	Frequency			
	Always	**Frequently**	**Occasionally**	**Seldom**
Engages in synergistic relationships between supervisor and staff members				
Is actively involved with and constantly nurtures staff members				
Focuses on restaurant and individual needs				
Provides a stable and supportive learning and working environment				

Figure 12.7   Sample behavioral frequency scale employee evaluation form.

Self-Appraisals   **Self-appraisals** tend to be an effective method of performance evaluation when the goal is to further self-development. This system works well when evaluating supervisors and managers. When employees evaluate themselves, defensive behavior is less likely to occur and there is a motive for self-improvement. There is always the risk that the employee will either be too lenient or critical when evaluating her own performance, but if used properly, this method can be effective and can help employees set personal and professional goals for the future. The employee's involvement and commitment to the improvement process is critical for this method to be truly effective.

The **management by objective approach** to performance appraisal is often referred to simply as **MBO**. This approach requires the supervisor to be directly involved in determining performance standards for his employees. Ideally, the supervisor and the employee should jointly review the employee's job responsibilities, identify the processes and results needed, and then determine performance standards that will define how well the results are accomplished. In the best-case scenario, these goals are mutually agreed upon and objectively measurable. If both of these conditions are met, the employees are apt to be more motivated to achieve their goals, because they have actively participated in setting them. When assisting employees with goal setting, management should remember that four to six goals per rating period are usually sufficient, and the goals should be changed or adjusted as needed during subsequent evaluations.

One drawback to MBO is that objectives are sometimes either too ambitious or too narrow. This may result in frustration for employees or overlooked areas of performance. The MBO method of performance appraisal tends to be most effective when applied to supervisors and managers.

360-DEGREE PERFORMANCE APPRAISAL

A **360-degree performance appraisal** is a relatively new evaluation method that provides each employee the opportunity to receive performance feedback from his supervisor, three to four coworkers, and even customers. Most 360-degree performance appraisals are also responded to by the individual employee being evaluated in the form of a self-assessment. These types of appraisals are a powerful developmental method and quite different from traditional manager-employee appraisals. As such, a 360-degree process does not replace the traditional one-to-one process—it augments it and can be used as a stand-alone development method. One reason that this method has gained in popularity is that when used properly, it tends to reduce the instances of rater bias. In other words, as the number of evaluators increases, so does the probability of attaining more accurate information.

EVALUATION INTERVIEWS AND EMPLOYEE COUNSELING

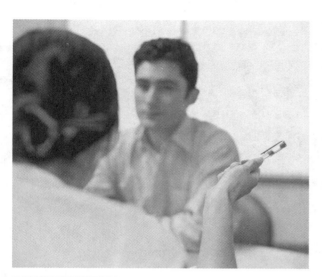

Photo 12.2   It is the manager's responsibility to conduct employee evaluations in person with each employee individually in a private area free from interruptions.

An **evaluation interview** occurs when the supervisor and the employee meet one-on-one to discuss the formal employee performance appraisal. The goal is to give the employee feedback about past performance and to devise an action plan when certain elements of job performance require improvement. Because employee evaluations are such a critical activity of effective hospitality management, the supervisor or manager must be prepared. Such preparation might include reviewing the employee's previous appraisals, identifying specific behaviors to be reinforced during the interview, and planning methods for providing feedback.

A manager's approach to providing feedback may differ depending upon the situation. One study identifies three effective approaches: **tell-and-sell, tell-and-listen,** and **problem solving.**[3] The tell-and-sell approach reviews the employee's performance and tries to convince the employee to perform better. It is most effective with new employees. The tell-and-listen method provides an opportunity for the employee to defend himself by providing explanations and/or excuses for a particular performance. The tell-and-listen method attempts to overcome the employee's defensive reactions by counseling him on how to perform better. The problem-solving approach identifies problems that might be interfering with the quality of an employee's performance. Sometimes such problems are outside of the employee's control and can best be addressed through additional training, coaching, or counseling.

The most effective performance review sessions create good employee-employer relations by ensuring that the interview is done in a positive way so as to ensure performance improvement. When managers stress the positive aspects of employee performance, the manager is giving the employee renewed confidence in her ability to perform satisfactorily. This positive aspect also allows the employee to keep desirable and undesirable performance issues in perspective because it prevents the employee from feeling that performance review sessions are entirely negative. Figure 12.8 provides additional guidelines for conducting effective performance evaluation interviews.

The review session should end with a mutual determination of the actions an employee should take to improve areas of poor performance going forward. During this concluding discussion, the supervisor usually offers to provide whatever assistance the employee may need to overcome the deficiencies discussed.

GUIDELINES FOR CONDUCTING EFFECTIVE PERFORMANCE APPRAISAL INTERVIEWS

1. Focus on positive aspects of employee performance.
2. Make sure the employee understands that the purpose of the interview is to improve performance, not to discipline.
3. Conduct a formal review at least annually and more frequently for new employees or those who are performing poorly.
4. Conduct the interview in private with minimum interruptions.
5. Be sure that criticisms are specific and nonpersonal; not vague and personal.
6. Focus on performance, not on personality characteristics.
7. Remain calm and do not argue with the employee being evaluated.
8. Assist the employee in identifying specific actions that he or she can take to improve performance.
9. Emphasize your own willingness to assist the employee's efforts.
10. End the interview by stressing positive aspects of the employee's performance.

Figure 12.8   Guidelines for conducting effective performance appraisal interviews.

LEGAL CONSTRAINTS IN PERFORMANCE APPRAISALS

Performance appraisals must be free from discrimination. The appraisal criteria, methods, and documentation must be designed to ensure that they are all job-related. Otherwise, there is a possibility that an employee may challenge decisions made by management based upon a flawed appraisal system in court because these decisions violate **equal employment** or other laws. Several lawsuits have arisen because managers and supervisors have said or done something that has adversely affected their employees. One of the more common lawsuits occurs when an employee who has consistently received favorable performance evaluations is suddenly fired for "poor performance." Managers make this sort of mistake when they go looking for a reason to let an employee go in an effort to scale down the staff, or for some other reason. If an employee's job performance is, in fact, substandard, then management should document that fact. This will protect the organization if a terminated employee later sues for **wrongful termination.**

SUMMARY

■ Conducting employee performance appraisals is the process of evaluating an employee's job performance. In order for this process to be effective, it is important that the process be properly implemented and managed.

■ Many hospitality managers and supervisors readily admit that conducting employee performance appraisals is difficult because it is difficult to judge an employee's performance in a constructive and painless manner.

■ Performance evaluations may be either formal or informal, and they should identify the employee's positive accomplishments as well as pinpoint areas that need improvement.

■ Managers, employees, and guests benefit when the operation conducts effective appraisals of its employees' job performance.

■ Informal evaluations are conducted on a day-to-day basis, and formal evaluations are presented in writing so they are documented and are normally conducted once or twice per year.

■ Performance appraisal systems are often flawed due to inadequate training of managers and supervisors and included forms that use language that is not job related, or if the organization uses a one-size-fits-all format that is not effective in evaluating employee performance in all jobs.

■ Bias occurs when managers and supervisors fail to remain emotionally detached while they evaluate employee performance. Types of biases include the halo-or-horns effect, the error of central tendency, the leniency and strictness bias, cross-cultural biases, personal prejudice, and the recency effect.

■ Various methods or forms exist for conducting formal employee performance appraisals, and each has its own advantages and disadvantages. Examples of the various methods commonly used in the hospitality industry include rating scales, weighted checklists, the forced choice method, critical incident method, behaviorally anchored rating scales (BARS), self-appraisals, and management by objectives (MBO).

■ When conducting an annual or semiannual performance appraisal, the supervisor schedules an evaluation interview in which she meets one-on-one with the employee being evaluated to discuss past performance and to devise an action plan to improve areas of job performance that are deficient.

■ Supervisors may take different approaches to conducting the evaluation interview; some approaches include tell-and-sell, tell-and-listen, and the problem-solving approach.

■ The most effective review sessions create positive employee-employer relations by ensuring that the interview is done in a positive way to encourage improved performance.

■ Performance appraisal systems and forms may not discriminate in any way so as not to violate equal employment laws or other laws.

PRACTICE QUIZ

1. Formal employee performance appraisals are normally conducted once or twice per year.

   A. True   B. False

2. Using subjective performance standards is best when designing a rating scale performance appraisal form.

   A. True   B. False

3. Managers and employees benefit from a well-designed and implemented-employee appraisal system, but guests and customers will generally see no impact at all.

   A. True   B. False

4. Informal employee appraisals should occur on a daily basis, but management should only discuss an employee's poor job performance during an annual or semiannual employee performance appraisal.

   A. True   B. False

5. Even when employee performance appraisals are improperly handled, employees are rarely allowed to sue the employer for wrongful termination.

   A. True   B. False

6. In order for an employee performance appraisal system to work effectively, which of the following appraisal criteria should not be present?

   A. Criteria should be job related.

   B. Criteria should be as subjective as possible.

   C. Criteria should be practical.

   D. Criteria should have standards.

7. Rating criteria such as "politeness" and "courtesy" are examples of:

   A. Objective performance standards

   B. Behaviorally anchored performance standards

   C. Subjective performance standards

   D. Rating scale performance standards

8. Supervisors who tend to avoid extremes such as "excellent" and "poor" when rating an employee's performance might be exhibiting which type of rater bias?

   A. Halo and leniency bias

   B. Strictness and horns bias

   C. Error of central tendency bias

   D. Recency effect bias

9. Keeping a diary or a log in which the supervisor notes examples of an employee's positive as well as negative job performance is an example of which type of appraisal method?

   A. Behaviorally anchored frequency scale

   B. Weighted checklist

   C. Forced choice method

   D. Critical incidents method

10. When conducting an evaluation interview with a new employee who needs to improve his or her job performance in a number of areas, the best approach would be which of the followung:

   A. Tell-and-listen approach

   B. Tell-and-sell approach

   C. Tell-show-do-review approach

   D. Problem-solving approach

REVIEW QUESTIONS

1. Develop five or six performance standards for a line-level, hourly position in a typical lodging or restaurant operation. Using the BARS method, create a form with a 1 through 5 continuum (1 is poor, 5 is excellent, and so forth, and identify specific behaviors that represent poor, average, excellent, and so forth. Be prepared to share your work with the rest of the class.

2. Cross-cultural biases occur when managers are required to evaluate employees from different cultural backgrounds other than their own. For example, in many Eastern cultures, the elderly are treated with greater respect and are held in higher esteem than in many Western cultures. If a young supervisor is asked to rate an older employee, this cultural value of "respect and esteem" could bias the rating. Likewise, in some Arabic cultures, women are expected to play a very subservient role, especially in public. Assertive women may receive biased ratings because of these cross-cultural differences. Do your own research and find three or four different examples of how this potential source of bias might present itself in today's culturally diverse hospitality industry. Be prepared to share your findings with the rest of the class.

3. Why must hospitality supervisors and managers be able to differentiate between an employee's current performance and his or her potential performance? Provide examples from your own experience in which managers have handled this task well and poorly.

4. Give examples of both objective and subjective performance standards for a typical hourly position in a hospitality business. What are the primary reasons for determining standards objectively? Explain in detail.

5. How does a properly administered employee performance appraisal system foster positive employee-employer relations? How can the appraisal system create the opposite effect and foster negative relations? Be specific and explain your answer in detail.

HANDS-ON HRM

Leslie Wilcox is the general manager of a restaurant that belongs to a large, national chain. Unit managers are required to conduct a performance appraisal on every employee during the month of March, in time to recommend employee pay raises that are awarded at the end of the restaurant's fiscal year in May. Leslie and her district manager, Nate Harper, will discuss each employee's review, and then, Leslie will be required to sit down with each employee, individually, to go over his employee performance appraisal. Leslie is expected to have these one-on-one appraisal feedback meetings in April. The goal of these meetings is to provide each employee with specific feedback about performance and to also address areas of performance that need improvement.

All employees at the unit level are evaluated using a standard form required by the national chain. The form includes the following evaluation criteria: skills and job knowledge; quality and quantity of work; neatness and punctuality; adhering to company rules and procedures; attitude, teamwork, and cooperation with coworkers; and initiative and resourcefulness.

Leslie does not really care for this aspect of her job in management because she dislikes the confrontation that sometimes occurs when an employee disagrees with the evaluation. Also, she feels it is hard to be objective. After last year's evaluations, the district manager questioned Leslie and said, "Your restaurant gets a lot of average to mediocre customer comment cards each year, yet you rate each employee very high in practically every area when you evaluate them. We may need to take a look at your evaluation process." Leslie knows that she needs to do a better job of evaluating her employees or her own job could be on the line.

QUESTIONS ▶

1. What could Leslie do to change the performance appraisal system in her restaurant in order to make it more effective? How could the employees benefit if changes are made?

2. What problems might Leslie encounter if she does decide to change the methods and rating system she uses when evaluating her employees?

3. Are the employees benefiting or not benefiting from the system that is currently in place? Please explain your answer and give specific reasons for your opinion.

4. Are there any legal issues that may present a problem for the restaurant based on the current system? Please explain in detail.

KEY TERMS ▶

Performance appraisal A process used to evaluate an employee's job performance.

Informal performance appraisal The process of giving employees day-to-day, specific verbal feedback on how well they are performing their job duties.

Formal performance appraisal A formalized, written approach to providing employees specific feedback on how well they are performing their job duties. The process normally occurs once or twice per year.

Merit raise An increase in salary given to an employee who has met or exceeded expectations.

Objective performance standards Job performance standards that are concrete, observable, verifiable, and measurable.

Subjective performance standards Job performance standards that are vague and that are not objective; they are usually based on opinions rather than facts and are not verifiable by others.

Bias A failure to remain impartial, which prevents objective consideration of an issue or an event.

Halo-or-horns effect A type of rater bias that occurs when the rater allows a positive attribute (halo) or a negative attribute (horns) to cloud the objectivity of the overall employee performance appraisal.

Error of central tendency A type of rater bias that occurs when the rater avoids extremeness such as excellent or poor, preferring to rate an employee's performance more toward the middle of the rating scale.

Leniency bias This bias occurs when the rater is not as critical of the employee.

Strictness bias This bias occurs when the rater is too critical of the employee.

Recency effect A type of rater bias that occurs when the rater allows a recent event—either negative or positive—to cloud the overall objectivity of the employee performance appraisal.

Rating scale A form or method used to conduct a formal performance evaluation; the rater normally rates the employee's performance on a scale of 1 to 5, with 1 being poor and 5 being excellent.

Weighted checklist A form or method used to conduct a formal performance evaluation in which the rater is required to check off behaviors that apply to the employee being evaluated.

Forced choice method A form or method used to conduct a formal performance evaluation in which the rater is required to select a statement or words that most accurately describe an employee's job performance. May be used interchangeably with adjective rating scale.

Adjective rating scale *See* forced choice.

Critical incidents method A form or method used to conduct a formal performance evaluation in which the rater is required to maintain a log of positive and negative employee performance.

Behaviorally anchored rating scales (BARS) A form or method used to conduct a formal performance evaluation in which the rater is required to rate the employee along a continuum using specifically determined job behaviors.

Behavioral frequency scale A form or method used to conduct a formal performance evaluation in which the rater is required to rate the frequency of identified job behaviors.

Self-appraisal A form or method used to conduct a formal performance appraisal in which the employee evaluates his or her own job performance in writing.

Management by objective (MBO) A form or method used to conduct a formal performance appraisal where the supervisor and the employee jointly review the job responsibilities, identify the processes and results needed, and then determine performance standards that will define how well the results are accomplished.

360-degree performance appraisal A performance appraisal method in which an employee's performance feedback is provided by the supervisor, coworkers, customers, and even employees—in the form of a self-evaluation.

Evaluation interview When the supervisor and the employee meet one-on-one to discuss the employee's formal performance appraisal.

Tell-and-sell An approach to conducting an evaluation interview in which the supervisor reviews the employee's performance appraisal and attempts to convince the employee to do better.

Tell-and-listen An approach to conducting an evaluation interview in which the supervisor reviews the employee's performance appraisal but allows the employee to provide explanations and defend his or her performance.

Problem solving An approach to conducting an evaluation interview in which the supervisor reviews the employee's performance appraisal, identifies problems that might be interfering with employee performance, and then assists the employee in devising an action plan to improve performance.

Equal employment laws Federal, state, and local laws that prohibit job discrimination based on factors such as age, race, sex, religion, national origin, marital or pregnancy status, or sexual orientation.

Wrongful termination A type of lawsuit that occurs when an employee is discharged without a proven cause; the employee has the right to sue the employer for damages such as loss of wage and fringe benefits, and, under certain circumstances, for punitive damages.

NOTES

1. John Hendrie, "Remarkable Hospitality: The Road Map to Excellence," *Restaurant Report*, www.restaurantreport.com.
2. William B. Werther, Jr., and Keith Davis, *Human Resources and Personnel Management*, 4th ed. (New York: McGraw-Hill, Inc., 1993), 341.
3. Norman R. F. Maier, *The Appraisal Interview: Three Basic Approaches.* (La Jolla, CA: University Associates, 1976).

CHAPTER 13

EFFECTIVE COMMUNICATION AND FEEDBACK

If employees are tickled to see the boss, I know that he or she is a great hands-on manager.[1]

J. W. Marriott, Jr.

CHAPTER OBJECTIVES

After completing this chapter, you will be able to

- Define communication and explain its importance as a management tool.

- Contrast formal and informal methods of communication.

- Discuss the common forms of upward and downward communication used by supervisors and managers in the hospitality industry.

- Outline circumstances that call for verbal, written, and electronic communication methods.

- List common barriers to effective communication and describe techniques for overcoming such barriers.

- Explain the difference between active and passive listening.

- Identify guidelines for providing positive and negative employee feedback.

 Excellent interpersonal or human relations skills are absolutely required if you hope to eventually become a successful supervisor, manager, or owner of a profitable hospitality enterprise. This is especially true for both lower-level managers and owners who have daily contact with both employees and valued guests and customers. Because the communication process contributes significantly to our overall interpersonal skills, our ability to communicate effectively will undoubtedly play a huge role in the success or failure of the operation.

THE COMMUNICATION PROCESS

The **communication process** is simply the sending and receiving of information, which is a powerful thing. Information enables managers and supervisors to make sound business decisions. Without it, important decisions about the organization, its environment, its products and services, and its employees and customers are made in a vacuum; nothing could be more dangerous for a hospitality business. Information is also an important key to employee satisfaction. For employees, a lack of sufficient information will often lead to high-stress levels and low morale among workers, two significant causes of turnover in the hospitality industry.

If information is the engine that drives the business, then the **communication systems** that management puts into place are what fuel the engine. Communication systems may be written or verbal and can be a combination of both formal and informal methods for circulating information throughout the organization.

AN EXAMPLE FROM MARRIOTT

When J. W. Marriott Jr. tours one of his hotels, he likes to stroll the entire property with the general manager at his side. Marriott is not only interested in the hotel's "numbers," but he also pays attention to the way the general manager interacts with the hotel's staff. Speaking of one such stroll, Marriott said that he and the hotel's general manager were "greeted by smiles, teasing, and hellos from just about every Marriott associate we passed. What's the big deal? Why was I so pleased? At Marriott, the reaction of staff to the GM is the ultimate litmus test of how well a hotel is run."[2]

This hands-on, **management-by-walking-around (MBWA)** approach has been an important part of Marriott's corporate culture for more than 75 years. It also illustrates an effective **informal communication method.** Other exam-

TALES FROM THE FIELD

I took a job in the kitchen of a really nice restaurant in Chicago when I graduated from culinary school. The restaurant was privately owned, and every evening—just before service—the owner would come in and give everyone a pep talk. He was an excellent communicator, and everyone really liked him a lot. You just knew that he cared about his employees, his business, and his customers. One afternoon I had just gotten to work, and when I walked into the kitchen, I saw one of the sous chefs screaming at the dishwasher. He was really talking down to him, and I was shocked because that was just not the way things were done in this restaurant. Just then the owner walked into the kitchen and saw what was going on. He walked up to the dishwasher and he said, "Hand me your apron." The dishwasher lowered his eyes and did as he was told, and then the owner took his wallet out of his pocket and peeled off two $100 bills. He handed them to the dishwasher and said, "Take the evening off and have a great time on me; I'll see you back here tomorrow night." He then handed the apron to the sous chef and said, "Put this on; you're washing dishes tonight."

Ashley, 24, Merrillville, Indiana

ples of informal communication may include an open-door policy and even the **employee grapevine. Formal communication methods** may consist of such things as memos, reports, employee suggestion boxes, and employee newsletters or bulletin boards.

WHICH COMMUNICATION METHOD IS BEST?

The extent to which management needs to convey or receive information, as well as the type of information that needs conveying, will best determine the optimal form of communication. Clearly, matters affecting policy, procedures, and other issues of importance will require more formal methods of delivery. The intended audience, or those who will receive the information, will also determine whether a more formal or informal approach is necessary. Formal communication often addresses task-related issues and tends to span the organization's chain of command. Examples include the following:

- A supervisor gives directions to an employee about how to greet a guest.
- An employee offers advice to a work team in her department.

■ An employee suggests a way to improve productivity to his supervisor.

■ A supervisor interacts with other supervisors at a weekly staff meeting.

■ An employee responds in writing to a request made by his supervisor.

Informal communication may or may not follow the chain of command; it may move in any direction, and it is as likely to satisfy social needs as it is to facilitate the functions of business. Informal communication methods such as MBWA, which was illustrated in the Marriott example, encourage effective two-way communication among staff as well as between managers and subordinates. The traditional **open-door policy,** in which employees are free to walk into any manager's office with their problems, is another way to foster informal communication. Most workers are reluctant to take a problem to their boss, or even to their boss's boss, so the best open-door policy is the one in which the manager gets up from her desk and walks out of her office to talk to employees in their space.

THE EMPLOYEE GRAPEVINE

Perhaps the least understood method of informal communication is the employee grapevine and the rumors and gossip it provides. When two employees chat in the break room about their trouble with a supervisor, this is grapevine communication. Some managers see this as a positive source of informal communication, and they have an interest in the grapevine because it provides useful, off-the-record feedback from employees—if managers are prepared to listen, understand, and interpret the information. The types of information that management finds useful with regard to the employee grapevine are illustrated in Figure 13.1.

- Information about problems or anxieties that employees may have
- Incorrect feedback that is evidence of breakdowns in communication systems
- Insights into goals and motivations of employees
- Identification of job problems that have high-emotional content
- Information about the quality of supervision
- Information about areas of job dissatisfaction
- Information about acceptance of new policies and procedures

Figure 13.1   Types of feedback "heard through the grapevine" that should be of interest to managers.

Managers who keep their employees in the dark about company concerns have the potential to breed anxiety and fuel gossip and rumors, a generally less-positive form of grapevine communication. A recent study conducted by ISR, a global employee research and consulting firm headquartered in Chicago, found that the majority of employees view the employee grapevine as more informative than what they hear from their boss when it comes to work issues, and 63 percent of workers said that rumors are usually how they first hear about important business matters.[3] Good leaders are good communicators, and this research shows that some managers have a lot to learn when it comes to communicating with their employees. One thing is certain: The employee grapevine will never go away, so wise managers will learn to tap into the grapevine's value as a way of identifying key issues of importance to employees.

DOWNWARD AND UPWARD COMMUNICATION

The most effective hospitality managers and supervisors make use of extensive communication systems to keep people informed. Although the goal is to facilitate an open, two-way flow of information, most messages are of the top-down variety. **Downward communication** is information that begins at some point in the organizational structure and cascades down the chain of command to inform or influence others. Downward communication is necessary to execute decisions and to give employees information about the organization. Successful hospitality operations should use a variety of downward communication methods because the diversity of multiple-communication channels is more likely to overcome barriers and reach the intended receivers.[4] Examples of downward communication include company and department newsletters and bulletin boards, e-mail and recorded messages, reports, booklets, and meetings held to inform employees about company issues.

Upward communication originates within the organization's lower levels and filters to its higher levels. This sort of communication is initiated by employees who seek to inform or influence those who are higher up in the organization's hierarchy. In many hospitality businesses, there is probably no area of communication that is more in need of improvement than upward communication. When supervisors have a good relationship with their line employees, and when two-way communication between these groups flows freely, upward communication is very powerful in that it allows employees to participate in the day-to-day decision making that goes on in the organization. Some hospitality businesses encourage this form of communication by using **employee suggestion boxes.** Workers are encouraged to write down their ideas or concerns and drop them in a special box, sometimes anonymously, where

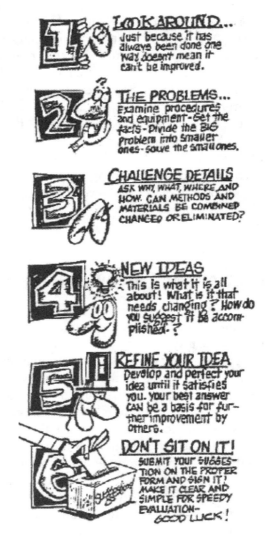

Figure 13.2

Indiana State Government Employees' suggestion box tips.

upper management will later retrieve them and, hopefully, act on them. In some instances, organizations will reward an employee who has come up with a cost-saving idea or with an idea to increase business and revenue. The state of Indiana encourages state government employees to utilize its employee suggestion program. Figure 13.2 illustrates Indiana's simple, yet user-friendly, six-step approach, which encourages government workers to participate in the program.

When information does not flow freely and upward communication is blocked, it may result in chaos and may even create dangerous conditions. Consider the following "Tales from the Field":

TALES FROM THE FIELD

I worked as a part-time night auditor in a good-sized hotel in my hometown during my summer breaks. Management never listened to anything employees had to say, but I didn't mind so much since I knew the job was only temporary. Usually during my work shift, the only employees on the property would be a part-time security guard and me. Part of my normal routine would be to go to the hotel restaurant and 'Z' out their cash register and bring the journal tapes back to the front desk. I usually cut through the kitchen when I did this. One morning at about 2 A.M., I headed into the kitchen, and I immediately smelled smoke. I flipped on the lights, but I couldn't see anything, but I could sure smell it. I followed my nose, which took me behind the line where I began to open warming drawers, and as soon as I opened this one drawer, flames shot out higher than my head. Someone had left greasy rags in there but hadn't turned off the drawer, so apparently when the air hit the rags, boom! Anyway, the flames had then gotten so bad that the grill and the hood started to flame up. I had no choice but to reach over and pull the ring that set off the emergency fire suppression system. Well, that put out the fire, but what a mess. It also set off the hotel's fire alarm, so the fire department showed up, and guests were now calling the front desk pretty concerned. The fire department got things under control very quickly, the guests went back to bed, and I immediately phoned the food and beverage director to let her know what had happened as well as the hotel's GM. The F&B director was great; she immediately called staff in to start cleaning up the mess of powder that was sprayed all over by the fire system so that the restaurant could open for breakfast, but when the GM came in, he was irate. He fired me the next day, saying that I overreacted and that I should have used a handheld fire extinguisher to put out the fire. I couldn't believe it! I later heard from some coworkers that corporate came in and fired the GM after a bunch of employees called the home office to complain about how this manager reacted. I was later offered my job back, but I declined. I'd pretty much had enough by then.

Lee, 28, Cincinnati, Ohio

VERBAL AND WRITTEN COMMUNICATION

Managers and supervisors must constantly rely on their verbal communication skills. Meeting with an employee, training a new hire, instructing staff members, as well as soothing the ruffled feathers of a disgruntled guest are all superb examples of instances in which excellent communication skills are

Photo 13.1   The benefits of verbal communication include the ease and speed with which large amounts of information can be conveyed.

essential in order for managers and supervisors to work effectively with their employees, as well as their guests.

There are many benefits to delivering information to others orally. Certainly, the ease and speed with which large amounts of information can be conveyed is one benefit. One's facial expressions, body language, and tone of voice used will also add depth to the information being delivered. Many would argue that due to the evolution of e-mail and other electronic means of communication, verbal communication provides a more personal interaction and fosters feelings of trust and goodwill.

If the message you need to send is somewhat complex and official, or is intended for a more formal audience, then written communication is generally the method that should be used. Forms of written communication include memos, reports, presentations, and so forth. Generally, the lengthier and more involved the message, the greater the need for presenting the information in written form. This method also provides an official record or other such documentation, which may be important in the future for substantiating facts and information. Providing communication in writing also helps to eliminate confusion and ambiguity over the message that is being sent.

ethical dilemma

Willie worked as a front-office manager for a large, national hotel chain. His hotel shared a region with 11 other properties, and all of the front-office managers knew each other well, because they often attended regional meetings and training seminars together. None cared very much for Stan, the regional director; in fact, most of them thought he was an arrogant jerk, and they rarely skipped an opportunity to tell a joke about him or share some gossip about Stan's most recent tirades.

Business was slow one evening at Willie's hotel, so he wrote a rather derogatory poem about Stan and he set it to the music of a popular song. He was proud of his creativity, so he e-mailed his song to his good friend Mark, who worked as the front-office manager at a property across town. Mark was so impressed with Willie's talent that he forwarded the song to Julie, who worked 500 miles away. Julie loved it and forwarded it on to two or three other front-office managers in the region, and before long, everyone had received an e-mailed copy of Willie's clever song—even the regional director, Stan, who was not one bit impressed. Stan told Willie's general manager to fire Willie the next day, and even though the general manager thought the song was pretty clever, she followed orders and terminated Willie for improper use of the hotel computer system. Did Willie violate any of the *10 Ethical Principles for Hospitality Managers,* and, if so, which ones? Was Stan being ethical when he directed the GM to terminate Willie? Why or why not? Did any of the other front-office managers in the region violate any of the 10 principles? Explain.

THE INFORMATION SUPERHIGHWAY

E-mail, voice mail, cell phones, pagers, the Internet, and even corporate intranets have forever changed the way in which individuals communicate with one another. Hospitality businesses, large and small, increasingly rely upon these electronic means of sending and receiving information. Today's technology enables key staff members to be in constant contact with management—and vice versa—no matter where in the world each person is located. Of all of these electronic methods of communication now available, e-mail is probably the most popular Internet application because it extends and enhances our ability to communicate with others regardless of physical geography. E-mail encourages informal communication. The ease of quickly typing a reply to a message and zapping it off within minutes of receiving the initial message is a powerful and efficient way to communicate. However, such ease and informality may create problems for those using e-mail, so it is necessary to use judgment, restraint, and thoughtfulness when communicating by e-mail. Figures 13.3 and 13.4 illustrate some common e-mail dos and don'ts.

PROPER E-MAIL ETIQUETTE

- Do check and review your organization's e-mail policy. Many companies have rules about the types of messages that can be sent.
- Do try to think about the message content before you send it out.
- Do make sure that the content is relevant to the recipients. Nobody likes to receive junk mail.
- Do be polite. Terse messages can be misinterpreted.
- Do try to use humor and irony sparingly. You can use smiles such as :) or :(to indicate facial expressions, but make sure that the recipient understands what they mean.
- Do ensure that you have a relevant "Subject" line.
- Do be patient, especially with inexperienced e-mail users. Give people the benefit of the doubt—just because you are familiar with e-mail etiquette, it doesn't mean that they are.
- Do include a brief signature on your e-mail messages to help the recipient identify you, especially if you are dealing with someone you do not know very well.
- Do be careful when replying to mailing list messages or messages sent to many recipients. Are you sure you want to reply to the whole list?
- Do remember to delete anything that isn't needed or that is trivial.

Figure 13.3   Examples of proper e-mail etiquette at the workplace.

IMPROPER E-MAIL ETIQUETTE

- Don't reply to an e-mail message when angry; you may regret it later.
- Don't keep mail on your server longer than necessary, especially large attachments.
- Don't type in capitals, as this is considered to be shouting. This is one of the rudest things you can do.
- Don't overuse punctuation such as exclamation marks! In particular, avoid more than one exclamation mark (!!), especially if your e-mail is quite formal. Also, overuse of ellipses (e.g., " ....") can make a message difficult to read.
- Don't send large attachments without checking with the recipient first.
- Don't send excessive multiple postings to people who have no interest. This is known as "spamming" and is considered to be ignorant, and may lead to serious trouble with your Internet service provider (ISP) or IT department.
- Don't send chain letters or "make money fast" messages. These are annoying to most recipients.
- Don't criticize people's spelling; it is considered petty. Many people have no way of running a spell-check on their messages and will make typos.
- Don't "flame" people by sending them abusive e-mail messages.
- Don't make personal remarks about third parties. E-mail messages can come back to haunt you.

Figure 13.4   Examples of improper e-mail etiquette at the workplace.

In business, the formality of e-mail messages tends to vary, between the semi-formal approach, previously the domain of the interoffice memo, and the chatty exchanges that you might have with someone over the telephone or while sitting in the break room. The approach you take when e-mailing will depend upon your intended audience. And remember that because e-mail messages are surprisingly permanent and are technically online written messages, a good rule of thumb is to think before you zap the "Send" button.

CORPORATE WEB-SURFING POLICIES

A large percentage of companies are monitoring Internet use by workers, hospitality operations included. While some organizations still allow some personal use of the Web, many companies will ask employees to limit the amount of time they spend at online shopping sites, and some companies will block employee access to some Web locations altogether. Companies are taking advantage of new Web-filtering software programs that allow management to retain and review employees' e-mail messages, and most companies have some kind of policy regarding personal e-mail use. Other types of monitoring software allow organizations to monitor and track e-mail content, keystrokes, and the time an employee spends at the keyboard. Plenty of workers have been fired for misusing the Internet. A good rule of thumb for hospitality managers and employees is to apply good judgment when accessing the Internet and to keep focused on the task at hand.

COMMON OBSTACLES TO EFFECTIVE COMMUNICATION

The messages that we send are not always the messages that are received. It is easy for our communications to be rendered ineffective if the sender and/or the receiver interpret the message in a way that distorts or obscures the intended meaning. For example, if your new friend Cameron phones you and says, "Hey, I thought I'd come over and knock you up!" this message may be deemed as either extremely offensive or, at the very least, quite confusing. Once you realize that Cameron is from New Zealand and in the vernacular of that country, to "knock someone up" means to go knock on their door and pay them a visit—the message is no longer unclear.

Obstacles, or barriers, to effective communication can take many forms. Examples include cultural differences, which can affect attitudes, opinions, and values; differences in background, which include education, past experiences, and intelligence; our prejudices and perceptions; our assumptions and expectations; and our emotions.

Photo 13.2   Providing managers and supervisors with basic Spanish language skills can eliminate communication barriers in some instances and may even make the hospitality operation's job openings more appealing to Hispanic job applicants.

Cultural Differences

When individuals have different cultural backgrounds, effective communication can be challenging because differences in backgrounds will affect our attitudes, opinions, and values. Two individuals may even share the same cultural backgrounds but still differ in the way they think about things and look at certain issues. The old adage that one can talk about anything but religion and politics has a ring of truth to it, as people have strong feelings about these issues. Even some family members cannot agree on these matters. It is best for hospitality managers and supervisors to err on the side of caution here, especially with respect to such activities as telling off-color jokes, ethnic-based jokes, and so forth. Not only does this behavior put you at risk of losing the respect of your coworkers and subordinates, but it could get you into legal trouble as well.

Differences in Background

People sometimes struggle with the communication process when they do not share similar backgrounds. Someone's background might include the level of education attained, the past experiences encountered, and the person's overall level of intelligence. These inherent differences do not suggest that the individual with more education is *better* than the individual with less, or that the person who has had a wider variety of unique experiences is better than the person who has had less.

Obviously, it is important to be aware of such differences and adjust your approach to the communication process appropriately. Kitchen jargon can be dif-

The Lingo	And the Translation:
1. Adam's ale, hold the hail	1. Water, no ice
2. Blowout patches	2. Pancakes
3. C.J.White	3. Cream cheese and jelly sandwich on white bread
4. Drag one through Georgia	4. Coca-Cola with chocolate syrup
5. Flop two	5. Two fried eggs, over
6. Sinkers and suds	6. Doughnuts and coffee
7. Jack Tommy	7. Cheese and tomato sandwich
8. Put out the lights and cry	8. Liver and onions
9. Sweep the kitchen	9. Hash
10. Burn one, take it through the garden and pin a rose on it	10. Hamburger with lettuce, tomato, and onion
11. Paint a bow-wow red	11. Hot dog with ketchup
12. Burn the British and draw one in the dark	12. English muffin, toasted, with black coffee
13. Adam and Eve on a raft and wreck 'em	13. Eggs on toast, scrambled
14. A spot with a twist	14. Tea with lemon
15. Whisky down	15. Rye toast

Figure 13.5   Diner slang popularized in the 1930s and 1940s.

ficult for newcomers to grasp, and, often, modern slang falls on deaf ears if the receiver of the message is significantly older than the sender. The reverse is true when older slang is directed at a younger audience. Consider the plight of the 15 year old who worked the counter at his parent's diner after school: A customer walked in, plopped down on a lunch counter stool, and said, "Gimme some Joe." "My name's Luke," said the kid, somewhat perplexed. "No," the guy said, "Joe, you know, coffee." Diner slang is colorful jargon used by waitresses and countermen in the 1930s and 1940s. More examples can be found in Figure 13.5.

Prejudices and Perceptions   Aside from differences in age, education, and culture, prejudices and perceptions can also distort communication. In the hospitality industry, workers are often drawn from diverse backgrounds, which will, of course, influence the language they use and the meanings that they give to words. We often think of prejudice as biases certain individuals have against people of a specific race, gender, sexual orientation, and so forth. Prejudice may also include biases against certain religions, against people who are overweight, against people whose political opinions differ from our own, and even against people who grew up in different parts of the United States. It is important not to form wide-sweeping opinions about members of a certain group. Words should be chosen carefully so as not to offend; otherwise, the message you are sending will simply stir up anger and cause your message to be rejected.

An individual's perceptions can be a barrier to effective communications. People tend to see and sense things differently. Using words that have no real, concrete meaning will often lead to confusion and chaos. Here are some examples that could lead to problems in the kitchen:

- "Just season it to taste, please."
- "I only need the coffee warm, not too hot."
- "Could you dice some carrots; I need a lot."
- "The music playing in the dining room should be soft, not loud."

When giving direction and instructions to your staff, it is best to use language that is measurable, concrete, and not open to interpretation.

Assumptions and Expectations

When you assume listeners know what you are talking about, you are simply asking for trouble. If, in fact, the listener is oblivious, the entire message may be lost. It is best to know for certain that the listener is on the same page as you so that you avoid anger and confusion when your message is not properly acted upon. This is especially true in operations that may have employees who do not speak English as a first language. People who come from certain cultural backgrounds may be reluctant to tell you that they do not understand something. Misguided assumptions may also lead to jumping to inaccurate conclusions, which prevents effective communication. Where expectations are concerned, we often get exactly what we expect to get. In other words, if you expect very little from your employees because you think that they are basically lazy and stupid, then that is exactly what you are likely to get. We communicate our expectations all the time, whether we realize it or not. Communicating high expectations will often result in high achievement on the part of your employees.

Emotions

Emotions are a powerful force, but they have no real place in effective communication at work. In fact, emotions may be one of the most difficult obstacles to overcome, particularly the emotion of anger. Things said in anger tend to bury the message entirely, leaving the listener only with feelings of anger, fear, or anxiety. A good rule of thumb is to regain your composure before speaking.

OVERCOMING BARRIERS TO EFFECTIVE COMMUNICATION

Some of the barriers and obstacles may never be completely overcome. People are different, and that is unlikely to change anytime soon. The hospitality industry draws employees from diverse backgrounds that, in some cases, only tend to complicate the communication process further. Being aware of these obstacles is the first step to overcoming them. There are some other actions that effective managers and supervisors can take to overcome the barriers to effective communication. These actions include the following:

Think about what you are going to say. If the message you intend to deliver is not entirely clear to you, then it certainly will not be clearly conveyed or received by the listener. If your message is to be delivered in writing, jot down some notes and reread what you have written, ensuring clarity of message.

Keep your emotions under control. No one will be rational 100 percent of the time, but it is a good practice to maintain rationality *most* of the time. Remember that extreme emotions will cloud your message and misconstrue meaning. When in doubt, chill out first.

Be a good listener. Most people are not very good listeners. We hear things, but that is not necessarily the same as listening. Active listening is the key to being a good listener, and we will examine active and passive listening techniques in the next section of this chapter.

Actions speak louder than words. Be sure that your actions and your body language match your message. Nonverbal cues carry a lot of weight, so the effective manager must be tuned in to body language, both his own and that of the listener.

Provide and ask for feedback. It is important to provide employees with feedback, whether it is positive or negative. It is also important to ask for feedback to ensure that messages sent have been properly received. We will look at feedback techniques in the final section of this chapter.

ACTIVE AND PASSIVE LISTENING

Much of the information presented in this chapter thus far has focused on communication methods that involve sending or delivering information. While these skills are certainly necessary in order to achieve effective communication, they only paint half of the picture. The other half of the picture is, of course, your ability to listen effectively. **Passive listening** is simply hearing; in other words, you are not really processing the entire message. You may get bits and pieces, but more likely than not, you will not process the information that was sent. **Active listening,** on the other hand, requires effort and concentration because you want to fully understand what the speaker is saying. There are generally four requirements for active listening:

1. *Listen with intensity.* Because it is easy for the mind to wander, active listening requires concentration and focus. Instead of thinking about what you will make for dinner or what you will wear to next week's party, you are an active listener if your thought process involves summarizing and integrating what is being said.

2. *Listen with empathy.* Your ability to put yourself in the speaker's shoes means that you must put your own thoughts and assumptions on hold and try to understand what the speaker wants to communicate, rather than what you want to understand.

3. *Listen with acceptance.* This means that you are objective about the message being sent and that you do not prejudge the speaker or the content of the information being delivered. Distractions occur when you disagree and begin to compose some objection or retort in your mind. It is more effective to concentrate on the entire message as it is delivered and to withhold objections until the speaker is finished.

4. *Take responsibility for the message.* In other words, now may be the time to ask for clarification, to disagree with a point made, to agree, or simply to respond in some meaningful manner. Active listeners take responsibility to ensure that they have received the speaker's full, intended meaning.

PROVIDING EFFECTIVE FEEDBACK

Some inexperienced hospitality managers and supervisors believe that *managing* means strolling out of the office once or twice a day and trying to catch an employee doing something wrong. That way, the manager can *manage* things, by telling the employee what he has done wrong. This action is usually followed by the manager making a hasty retreat back to the office, leaving the employee in the dust with a bewildered look on his face. Effective managers realize that there will be times when they will need to correct employee behavior so that standards of performance are being met, but these managers also spend a great deal of time trying to catch employees doing things right. When this occurs, and it *will* occur often if the manager is truly doing his job, it presents an opportunity to provide some **positive feedback** and, thus, reinforce positive behavior. Believe it or not, **negative feedback** can also change behavior when properly directed.

The Role of Positive Feedback   Telling your employees that they are doing a good job and then pointing out specific examples is providing positive feedback. When the executive housekeeper says to the room attendant, "Great job! This room is perfect. I can see that you take a lot of pride in your work," the manager has left the room attendant with a feeling of pride for a job well done, and the manager has also reinforced the importance of properly cleaning the hotel's guest rooms. Such feedback only takes a moment to deliver, but its effects can last a very long time.

Positive feedback is easy to deliver, so it's unclear why many managers and supervisors fail miserably in this area. Employees in some hospitality operations get so little feedback from management that they begin to wonder whether the work that they do even matters. These are the employees who quickly get frustrated and leave the company for greener pastures—not in the sense that they leave for more money, but that they prefer to work for an organization where what they do is important to the overall success of the operation, that what they do matters. Delivering positive feedback usually feels good, both to the deliverer and to the receiver. Positive feedback is almost always well received because it reinforces what people want to hear or what they already believe to be true about themselves.

The Role of Negative Feedback   Strolling out of the office and barking at the employee who has done something wrong is not negative feedback. It certainly is *negative,* but the missing element would be the *feedback.* Managers often avoid negative feedback because they know that it will be met with resistance by their employees. Most people only want to hear the good things, not the bad. Negative feedback should not be avoided, however, but simply reworked in such a way that it becomes an effective management tool. The ultimate goal of negative feedback is to change incorrect behavior or performance, so it is best used when you are dealing with absolutes such as hard numbers, data, and other specifics. Telling an employee that she has a bad attitude is really not telling that employee anything at all. What does *bad* mean exactly? Did she come to work somewhat grouchy and a few minutes late, or did she get into a screaming match with a customer?

GUIDELINES FOR PROVIDING FEEDBACK THAT WORKS

The goal of feedback is either to enforce behavior (positive feedback) or change behavior (negative feedback). In order for feedback to be effective, you should remember the following points:

- *Be specific.* This is most important when the feedback is meant to correct behavior or actions that do not meet performance standards. Even when you are providing positive feedback, specifics are important so that the employee knows exactly which behavior to repeat.

- *It's not personal.* Don't attack the person; attack the behavior. Rather than saying, "You're doing a bad job," choose wording that focuses on the behavior, *not* on the employee's personality. Focusing on the person rather than the behavior will rarely be met with anything but a negative reaction and is hardly productive.

- *Be in the moment.* Feedback that is either negative or positive must be delivered in a timely manner. It does no good to delay negative feedback because much information can be lost over time. It's best to correct inappropriate behavior at the moment it occurs. This principle also applies to positive feedback.

- *Keep the goal in mind.* Negative feedback should only be offered when doing so can change behavior. What is your goal in delivering negative feedback? Do you just need to dump on someone, or can you pinpoint specific behavior that needs improving and offer reasons for why it should be improved.

One final thing to keep in mind when offering negative feedback is that the feedback should be directed at something over which the employee has control. Negative feedback also presents management with a good opportunity to offer suggestions on how the employee can change behavior for the better.

SUMMARY

- Effective managers and supervisors need excellent interpersonal or human relations skills in order to communicate with employees and provide the kind of work environment where talented employees can self-motivate.

- The communication process—sending and receiving information—contributes significantly to one's human relations skills.

- When employees lack sufficient information, the result can be stress and low morale, which leads to high employee turnover rates.

- Communications systems drive the communication process; these systems may be written, verbal, formal, and informal.

- The extent to which management needs to convey or receive information, as well as the type of information that needs to be conveyed, will determine whether formal or informal methods should be used.

- Formal communication may be written or verbal, and it usually follows the chain of command. Informal communication may also be written or verbal, but it may not follow the chain of command; it may move in any direction.

- The employee grapevine is an example of informal communication, but managers should have an interest in the grapevine because it can provide useful, off-the-record feedback from employees.

- Downward communication begins at some point higher in the chain of command and flows downward, whereas upward communication passes from the organization's lower-level employees to its higher-level employees and management.

- Verbal communication is effective because of the speed with which large amounts of information can be conveyed. Written communication is effective when the message is complex and/or an official record needs to be created.

- The use of e-mail is probably the most popular Internet communication method, and special care should be taken to ensure that users within a particular organization follow e-mail etiquette.

- Obstacles to effective communication include cultural differences, differences in background, prejudices and perceptions, assumptions and expectations, and emotions.

- Managers can overcome common barriers to effective communication by thinking about what they are going to say or write, keeping their emotions under control, being good listeners, matching their actions with their words, and providing feedback to employees and asking for feedback from them as well.

- Passive listening is simply hearing, not processing, the information being sent. Active listening requires concentration and listening with intensity, listening with empathy, listening with acceptance, and taking responsibility for the message.

- The purpose of positive feedback is to boost morale as well as to reinforce positive actions or behavior. The purpose of negative feedback is to change behavior.

- When providing either positive or negative feedback, managers should be specific and should focus on the behavior and not on the employee personally. They should also be sure that the feedback is timely, and they should keep the end goal in mind.

PRACTICE QUIZ

1. Management-by-walking-around (MBWA) is a formal, written communication system that has been in place at the Marriott Hotel Corporation for more than 75 years.

   A. True   B. False

2. Formal communication systems are always preferred to informal communication systems because otherwise, employees will not pay attention to the information being sent.

   A. True   B. False

3. In organizations with open door policies, employees are sometimes reluctant to take a problem to their boss or to their boss's boss.

   A. True   B. False

4. Keeping employees in the dark about company concerns will often fuel gossip and rumors, but that is okay because most managers find this information useful.

   A. True   B. False

5. Downward communication is normally initiated by employees who are lower in the organization's hierarchy.

   A. True   B. False

6. Which of the following is *not* a key benefit of verbal communication?

   A. It works well when the message is complex.

   B. It works well because it can deliver large amounts of information with speed and ease.

   C. It works well because of the added benefit of tone of voice.

   D. It works well because of the added benefit of body language.

7. Differences in background is a common obstacle to effective communication because of all of the following except:

   A. Individuals may not share the same education levels.

   B. Individuals may not share the same emotions.

   C. Individuals may not share the same past experiences.

   D. Individuals may not share the same level of intelligence.

8. Active listening techniques involve all the following except:

   A. Empathy

   B. Acceptance

   C. Intensity

   D. Emotion

9. Positive feedback seeks to accomplish which of the following?

   A. Ignore employee morale

   B. Reinforce negative stereotypes

   C. Reinforce positive behavior or actions

   D. All of the above

10. Which of the following is *not* a guideline for providing effective feedback?

    A. Always wait a few days before delivering negative feedback so as to keep your emotions in check.

    B. Focus on specific behavior whether your feedback is positive or negative.

    C. Feedback should either seek to change or reinforce actions and behavior.

    D. Negative feedback regarding something over which the employee has no control should not be given.

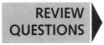
REVIEW QUESTIONS

1. Provide some examples of how information has flowed through the employee grapevine where you work now or where you have worked in the past. Was the information gathered from the employee grapevine accurate

or inaccurate? How do you know this? If you have not had work experience, use the student grapevine as your source for this assignment. Be prepared to share your findings with the class.

2. Do your own Web research on Internet etiquette, or *netiquette*. Give examples of the types of communication shortcuts that can be used when sending or replying to e-mail. How do these shortcuts impede the communication process, or do they? Be specific and be prepared to share your work with the class.

3. In your own words, explain the difference between active and passive listening. At what times might passive listening be preferred to active listening and vice versa? Provide examples of a conversation you have had with a friend or a coworker when it was clear to you that the person to whom you were speaking was passively listening. How did this make you feel? Why?

4. Construct three separate e-mail messages that would properly address each of the following scenarios: (1) a message to your boss explaining why last month's food cost percent in the restaurant was 11 percentage points over budget, (2) a message to all eight of your front-office employees requiring them to attend a mandatory meeting at which you plan on discussing methods to raise the hotel's average daily rate, and (3) a reply e-mail message to a travel agent who has e-mailed you requesting a travel agent discount for a night on which the hotel will likely be sold out. Compare your messages with those of at least one other student. How are they similar? How are they different? Be specific and provide examples to the rest of the class.

5. Following is a list of industry jargon (words, phrases, abbreviations) that is common in the hospitality and tourism industry. Review the list and write the meaning of those items on the list with which you are familiar. If you are unfamiliar with some words or phrases, conduct a general Internet search to learn their meanings. Compare your list with that of a fellow classmate. How do your lists differ? In what ways are they the same? Is the use of industry jargon beneficial in some way or is it problematic? Explain your answer.

ASAE	Bureau	FAM	IATA number
ASTA	CVB	MPI	No-show
B&B	Citywide	Rack rate	RFP
Blitz	Cover	SMERF	Site visit
DMC	Eighty-six	Walk	WTO

HANDS-ON HRM

Erica Stiles used to love her job as a line cook at the Third Street Bar & Grill. The money was good, the chef was great about working around Erica's school schedule, and she had a lot of fun working with the other employees at the restaurant. Things could not have been better for Erica, but all that changed when the chef called everyone together early one afternoon for a very important meeting.

"Guys," said Chef Todd, "you know we've only been open a year, and already, business is booming. The owners are so pleased," he continued, "that they've decided to open another location downtown." Chef Todd explained that the restaurant's owners had requested that he immediately transfer to the new location so that he could take charge of all of the preopening activities. "Wow, that's great," said a few of the kitchen employees. "But what about us?" asked Erica. "I mean, who will we report to now?"

"Well, that's one of the reasons I called all of you in," said Chef Todd. "We have decided to promote Keith here to the position of sous chef, so you guys will now report to him, and he'll continue to report to me."

The kitchen suddenly became very quiet as each of the employees looked at one other, somewhat astonished. Keith Berryman was a decent line cook, but that was about it. Most of the employees felt that he had a holier-than-thou attitude, since he and Chef Todd had worked together at a couple of other restaurants before coming to the Third Street Bar & Grill. "I'll expect each of you to follow Keith's lead in all matters," said Chef Todd. "I know he'll make a good boss, and besides, I'm not leaving; I just won't be around everyday like before."

Although she had concerns about the decision to promote Keith, Erica put on her best smile, walked up to Keith, extended her hand, and said, "Congratulations, Keith. I know I'll learn a lot by working for you." Slowly, the other employees too came up and offered Keith their congratulations.

As Chef Todd gathered his briefcase and left the kitchen, Keith announced, "Listen up, everybody. We're going to make a few changes around here, starting with the schedule. In the morning," he said, "you'll find your new work schedules posted on my office bulletin board. And I don't want to hear any whining about day care issues, school schedules, or hot Saturday night dates. We've got a restaurant to run."

With that, Keith went into the chef's office, closed the door, propped his feet on the desk, and thought to himself, "I've finally arrived."

"This is terrible," said Jason, one of the other line cooks. "If his new scheduling system messes up my day care arrangements, I could lose custody of my kids." "Tell me about it," added Jennifer, one of the restaurant's two pastry chefs. "My boyfriend and I only have one car, and he makes a lot more money than I do, so I have to rely on him for transportation." Erica had already thought about these things when she added, "I can't adjust my school schedule at all, and this is my last semester." "I can't even quit," she said, "because this job is my final internship, and I could flunk out of school if I don't get through this."

As the evening wore on, the restaurant got busier and busier, but Keith remained in the chef's office, only coming out once or twice for a few moments to scrutinize the plates being picked up by the servers. Near the end of the evening, he came out again, grabbed a salad plate off of a server's tray, and took it to Erica who was at the garde manger station that evening.

"Hey, culinary student," he said to Erica, loudly enough for everyone else to hear. "Don't they teach you anything about portion control at that school of yours? This salad is way too big." He slid the salad plate toward Erica and said, "Remake it, and do it right this time. In the real world, we call this controlling food cost." As Erica stood with an embarrassed look on her face, he wheeled around, went back into the chef's office, and slammed the door behind him.

Everyone in the kitchen watched as Erica methodically remade the salad. "I can't believe what a jerk he's being, Erica," said Jason. "That salad looked perfect to me." "No kidding," added Jennifer. "This promotion has already gone to his head; I can see we're all in for some real hell." Erica, laughing, said, "Oh, he's just practicing 'seagull management,' that's all." "What?" asked Jason, as the other line cooks looked at Erica. "Just something one of my professors told us in class last week," she said. "You know, like a seagull, the manager flies in, makes a lot of noise, dumps on everybody, then flies off again."

QUESTIONS ▶

1. Could Chef Todd have approached this meeting with his kitchen staff in a better, more organized fashion? What were some problems with the way he chose to communicate the restaurant's news to the employees?

2. What feedback errors and communication blunders has Keith made during his first evening as sous chef of the restaurant? How can he overcome these errors and reestablish good employee morale?

3. Should the rest of the kitchen staff go to Chef Todd with their concerns? What might be the result if they do? If you were in Chef Todd's shoes, how might you counsel the newly promoted sous chef?

4. Should things get worse for Erica, should she quit and, thus, terminate her internship, which may delay her graduation, or should she stick it out? Explain the reasons for you response.

KEY TERMS ▶

Communication process The method by which information is delivered from a sender to a receiver.

Communication systems Provides formal and informal methods for moving information throughout an organization.

Management-by-walking-around (MBWA) Managers exhibit this method of management when they leave their offices and engage employees one-on-one at their workstations.

Informal communication methods May be written or verbal; examples include open door policies, the employee grapevine, and MBWA.

Employee grapevine Informal communication that arises spontaneously from the social interaction of people in the organization.

Formal communication methods May be written or verbal; examples include memos, reports, employee suggestion boxes, newsletters, and meetings.

Open-door policy A company policy whereby the manager's door is always open to employees who may wish to voice a complaint or state an issue.

Downward communication Information that flows down the chain of command to set policy, to provide information, and to influence others.

Upward communication Information that flows from the lower levels of the organization to the higher levels. This often represents information initiated by employees who seek to inform or influence those who are higher in the corporate hierarchy.

Employee suggestion box A common tool used to seek employee input where employees write suggestions or cost-saving ideas and drop them in a box. Management will later retrieve the suggestions submitted by employees and review them.

Passive listening Hearing but not processing the information being sent.

Active listening A concentrated effort to focus and to fully understand the message that is being sent.

Positive feedback Employee feedback that seeks to boost morale and reinforce positive behavior or actions.

Negative feedback Employee feedback that serves to correct behavior that is unacceptable and that does not conform to performance standards. It is essential that negative feedback focuses on the employee's behavior, rather than on the employee personally.

NOTES ▶

1. J. W. Marriott, Jr., and Kathi Ann Brown, *The Spirit to Serve Marriott's Way* (New York: Harper-Collins, 1997).
2. Ibid.
3. Dawn Sagario, "Pssst! Have You Heard that Gossip may be Damaging to the Workplace?" *Courier-Journal* (Louisville, KY) October 31, 2005, sec 2D.
4. William B. Werther and Keith Davis, *Human Resources and Personnel Management* (New York: McGraw-Hill, 1993).

CHAPTER 14

EMPLOYEE DISCIPLINE

I hire every employee with the optimistic sense that he or she will succeed. I don't like to give up on an employee. But if an employee is not performing up to standard, I will let them go.[1]

Charlie Trotter, chef/owner, Charlie Trotter's, Chicago

CHAPTER OBJECTIVES

After completing this chapter, you will be able to

- Identify four common instances in which discipline is necessary and explain how management can avert them.

- Understand the difference between preventive and corrective discipline.

- Explain progressive discipline and the importance of management's involvement when it is administered.

- Describe the six don'ts of discipline and their negative impact on an effective disciplinary process.

- Describe the five dos of effective discipline and explain the importance of each.

- List three critical factors that will help you know when it is time to fire a problem employee.

- Recognize the legal implications of termination and discipline.

 **HRM IN ACTION** Those who hire sometimes have to fire. It is a fundamental principle of management that individuals who are given the responsibility for meeting company goals must also be given the authority to do what it takes to accomplish those goals, which, in some cases, may lead to terminating employees who are not performing to an acceptable standard. In the hospitality industry, managers must not only meet the organization's expectations, but they are also charged with the task of working hard to meet and even exceed customer expectations. They do this by working with their employees. While no manager enjoys the negative emotional experience that normally accompanies disciplining or terminating an employee, the **discipline** process is one of high importance in a properly managed lodging or food service establishment. Of course, the unpleasantries of firing an employee can often be avoided by hiring the right person for the right job in the first place.

CAUSES FOR DISCIPLINE

The hospitality industry employs a great diversity of people who come from many different cultural backgrounds, educational backgrounds, age groups, and socioeconomic backgrounds. Toss these hard-working individuals into a hot kitchen or a busy, bustling hotel or restaurant, and it's easy to understand how conflicts may occur. **Conflict** is most evident when a manager or a supervisor has to discipline an employee. Discipline is action taken by management to encourage employees' compliance with the company's stated rules, standards, and procedures—in other words, to develop self-discipline. Discipline should *not* be equated with punishment, as we will learn later in this chapter. Why do employees engage in behavior that leads to disciplinary problems at work when they are fully aware that the disciplinary process itself is unpleasant and often disruptive? You may be surprised to learn that, in many cases, management is to blame. How can this be? Let's review some of the most common issues that foster the need for disciplinary action and consider what managers can do to avert these problems.

Cause 1: Rules and Procedures Are Vaguely Written, Misunderstood, and Ignored

Having procedures and policies that are not in writing is the same as having no policies at all. Unwritten rules, or rules that are simply "understood," are sure to be broken because people interpret things in different ways. Imagine a restaurant setting where it is understood that employees who arrive to work 5 to 10 minutes late every day will not be reprimanded by management. Management may not totally approve of this situation, but for fear of conflict, they tend to look the other way. This may not be a big problem until an employee's tardiness leaves an important station unattended, which could result in the delivery of substandard product or customer service. Suddenly, an increased number of

TALES FROM THE FIELD

I was working as the front-office manager in a medium-sized hotel that was part of a large, national chain. The hotel was too small for a human resources department, and when I arrived at work one morning after having a couple of days off, the general manager told me he had fired Tom, one of my best bellmen. He said that he had sent Tom into a banquet room to vacuum the floors after a function, and when he checked his work, he found debris left on the floor, so he fired him on the spot. I was shocked. Tom was a super nice guy, very polite, and very diligent. He always completed his work on time and up to standards. I knew that this GM had it in for Tom for some reason and was just looking for a way to get rid of him. The worst part was that Tom filed for unemployment, and the GM made *me* go to the unemployment office hearing to dispute Tom's claim. There were no write-ups, no past instances of improper behavior—nothing. I was embarrassed to even be there, since I truly felt Tom deserved to collect the unemployment check. Needless to say, Tom won his unemployment dispute with our hotel and was awarded full benefits. What a waste!

Gary, 28, West Lafayette, Indiana

customer complaints prompt a management crackdown, leaving employees bewildered and confused about the manner in which certain rules are enforced.

While larger hospitality operations and those that are unionized are more likely to have written rules and regulations, it is not difficult to imagine this scenario occurring in smaller hotels and restaurants, where rules are often established and dealt with on the fly. All hospitality operations, whether large or small, unionized or not, should have a complete set of written rules, policies, and procedures that everyone knows and understands. This information is most often contained in the employee handbook that you learned about in Chapter 7, as well as in any operations and training manuals that the company may use. Depending upon the size and scope of the business, these rules, policies, and procedures will generally include the following:

- A complete, written account of the operation's policies, regulations, rules, and procedures that managers, supervisors, and employees must follow. For legal considerations, it is important that the business's policies and procedures regarding matters that require disciplinary action be well documented. We will learn more about this later in this chapter.

- Restrictions and provisions required by federal, state, and local laws such as alcohol sales, employment of minors, minimum wage and overtime requirements, health code provisions, and fire and safety regulations.

■ General rules of the organization pertaining to breaks, time clock issues, parking restrictions, uniform requirements, hours of work, absences and tardiness, sick days, smoking, meals, drug and alcohol issues, as well as employee dealings with guests and customers.

When policies and procedures are clearly stated in writing, employees are less inclined to misunderstand or ignore them. As a result, management is likely to encounter less conflict when enforcing these rules. The most effective action that management can take to avoid the need for employee discipline is to clearly communicate the organization's established rules and regulations at all times during the day-to-day operations. However, in order to avoid the need for disciplinary action, management must create a work environment in which employees recognize that they have an obligation—not only to management but to their coworkers as well—to perform effectively.

How to Ensure Acceptance and Compliance

Clearly stating the company's policies and procedures in writing is the best way to avoid employee misunderstanding, but what can management do to ensure their employees accept and comply with company policies? During all stages of the employer/employee relationship, management must emphasize that those who fail to perform at satisfactory levels or who engage in specific acts of misconduct are breaching their obligation to the company. Following are appropriate times and venues to emphasize such policies:

■ *The job interview.* The interview provides management with an opportunity to make a potential employee aware of the basic requirements of the open position. The manager should clearly explain what would be expected of the employee if hired and ask the employee if he can conform to these expectations. If you suspect an interviewee may become a disciplinary problem in the future based on your interaction during the job interview, you are better off losing a potential employee at this stage of the relationship than later down the road.

■ *New-employee orientation.* Present all new employees with a clear set of rules and guidelines as soon as the employment relationship begins. A well-written employee handbook should be presented to all new employees on their first day of employment. The new employee's supervisor should review every page of the book with the employee, and the employee should be required to sign a form acknowledging her receipt of the employee handbook.

■ *The employee handbook.* It is essential that the employee handbook clearly states all potential disciplinary violations in writing. Because of the legal considerations that you learned about in Chapter 7, the handbook must specify that its list of violations is not all- inclusive. The handbook should further detail procedures for disciplining employees so that employees are aware of the organization's established disciplinary methods.

- *Probationary period.* New employees in many organizations are considered on **probation** during their first 60 to 90 days of employment. This generally means that if during or at the end of the probationary period management feels that the new employee is not a good fit for the organization, the employee can be legally terminated for any reason. While this may not make much sense in those states that adhere to **at**-will employment laws that you learned about in Chapter 4, it does allow for a period of time during which managers and supervisors can frequently discuss the company's expected conduct and its disciplinary policies with new employees. Keep in mind also that some organizations have gotten away from the term probationary period, preferring instead to use "training period" or "orientation period."

- *Day-to-day operations.* Managers and supervisors should continually remind employees of their obligations to the organization as well as praise employees for positive performances.

- *Staff and department meetings.* Staff meetings present a venue for effectively communicating issues of employee conduct and discipline.

- *Disciplinary meetings.* Review the rules and why they are in place.

- *Annual or semiannual performance appraisals.* Each employee's performance evaluation should include a thorough discussion and a written record of all incidents of misconduct committed by the individual employee during a given year. Any employee bonus and salary increase should be adjusted accordingly to reflect incidents of employee misconduct or poor performance.

Once employees realize that management is extremely serious about establishing and communicating ground rules for performance and conduct within the organization, employees—and even management—are less likely to misunderstand, ignore, or not enforce the policies.

Cause 2: Employees Lack Sufficient Abilities, Knowledge, Skills, or Aptitude

It is no surprise that those employees who do not have the necessary skills, abilities, and aptitude to perform their job duties properly often find themselves in troubled waters. In most cases, management is to blame because the interviewer did not match the right applicant with the right position, hired a misfit altogether, or, in some cases, hired a perfectly qualified individual but then failed to provide the proper training and supervision to ensure his success. Hospitality managers must work very hard to ensure that they are hiring the right individuals for the right positions. A good "fit" is essential and will eliminate a lot of future employee problems. Then, proper and ongoing new employee orientation and training are of the utmost importance.

Employees who do not know what they are supposed to do or how they are supposed to perform their required tasks tend to decrease productivity, lower the quality of customer service, and cause problems that require disciplinary action.

Cause 3: Employees Have Personality and Motivational Problems

Management takes a gamble each time a new employee is hired. As with any gamble in life, there are financial risks at stake. The time and money invested in the interviewing and hiring process, as well as the downtime required to train the new employee in order to make the employee productive, are expensive. Combine these factors with the possible overtime costs incurred when an operation is understaffed and the costs associated with unhappy customers due to poor service and/or product quality, and it is easy to see why replacement costs for some operations can be as high as $4,000 per employee.

Some hospitality managers try to take the easy way out by only hiring individuals who have previous hotel or restaurant experience. These managers are trying to reduce training costs, and they often feel that an experienced applicant can be up and running in no time, with little or even no training. This logic is severely flawed. Each operation is different, and while an applicant who has previous experience is not necessarily a bad thing, this should not be the overall determining factor when hiring new employees. Chef Charlie Trotter, owner of Chicago's famous restaurant, Charlie Trotter's, hires for passion, putting a premium on such qualities as enthusiasm, dedication, and commitment.[2] Trotter is always willing to consider a nontraditional candidate for a service staff opening, if he senses the person has the "right stuff." Many of Trotter's waitstaff come from nonfood or nonhospitality backgrounds such as marketing, engineering, consulting, and even the musical symphony. Trotter has not reached the astronomic levels of success that he enjoys today by making bad hiring decisions or by failing to provide extensive and ongoing training. Because of his attention to detail during the hiring and training process, it's a safe bet he does not have many disciplinary problems in his restaurant operation.

With respect to motivation, some experts suggest that you cannot motivate anyone. Rather, motivation comes from within. Even so, successful hospitality managers can hire individuals who are self-motivated, and then provide the kind of work environment in which those individuals can excel. Happy, well-trained, motivated employees are a sight to behold. Such individuals will not languish for long in a shoddy, poorly managed hospitality business. These happy, well-trained, motivated employees are easier to find than you might think; just visit the most successful restaurant or hotel in your own community and there they will be! You will learn a lot more about the importance of motivation and leadership in Chapter 15.

Cause 4: Troublesome Environmental Factors

Environmental factors can be both internal and external. **Internal environmental factors** that often cause disciplinary problems typically result from poor management and supervision. Examples of internal environmental factors are improper or lazy hiring procedures, failure to train employees, poor or inadequate supervision, missing tools and supplies, or equipment that is in disrepair. All of these internal factors can lead to morale problems, and low employee morale will almost always lead to disciplinary problems. The good news is that internal environmental factors are almost always under management's direct control and can be altered to deter the occurrence of discipline problems.

On the other hand, management does not easily influence **external environmental factors.** Such factors may include problems employees have at home with family members, marital problems, legal problems, drug or alcohol problems, financial struggles, and even problems at school; in other words, life has a way of interrupting even the best-laid plans at work. Since larger organizations can afford to staff a professional human resources department, they often have the upper hand in these matters because they can sometimes offer the kind of employee assistance that is beyond the financial reach of smaller, privately owned hospitality businesses. These types of formal programs are usually referred to as **employee assistance programs,** or **EAPs.** Such programs usually rely on a blend of in-house administration and external counselors to advise employees about personal problems. Because smaller companies are unable to employ a full-time counselor, community services are especially useful when the manager is addressing external environmental problems that affect employee performance on the job.

PREVENTIVE AND CORRECTIVE DISCIPLINE

Sometimes despite the hospitality manager's efforts to achieve a workplace that is free of misconduct, certain employee behavior is inappropriately disruptive or unacceptable. While all organizations are different, Figure 14.1 illustrates some of the behaviors that may lead to disciplinary procedures in the hospitality workplace.

Although the list presented in Figure 14.1 is by no means all-inclusive, it does represent some of the more common employee behaviors that lead to discipline within the hospitality industry. We will discuss the progressive nature of discipline—**oral warning, written warning, suspension,** and **termination**—later in the chapter. Needless to say, when such infractions do occur, discipline is needed. There are two types of discipline: preventive and corrective.

Preventive discipline is any action taken by management to encourage employees to follow standards and rules in an effort to prevent infractions. In other words, preventive discipline encourages employee self-discipline. For example,

Minor Offenses: Follow the Progressive Discipline Process

1. Absences or tardiness
2. Smoking in unauthorized locations
3. Unauthorized breaks
4. Miscellaneous rule violations
5. No call, no show
6. Excessive lateness
7. Insubordination
8. Improper use of equipment
9. Failure to report an accident or injury

Major Offenses: Immediate Termination

1. False statements made on the job application
2. Time clock violations
3. Gambling, fighting, bringing weapons to work
4. Drug or alcohol use
5. Willful destruction of company property
6. Sexual harassment or abuse

Figure 14.1

Activities that tend to lead to employee discipline.

Photo 14.1

An employee's negative behavior should be corrected immediately.

managers and supervisors should develop programs to control absences, lateness, and grievances. Management should also communicate standards to employees and encourage them to follow the established standards. In addition, management should set the proper example by adhering to the same policies and procedures to which they expect their employees to adhere. Management should also encourage employee participation in setting standards, because employees tend to better support the rules that they themselves have helped to create. Employees will react more favorably if the standards are stated positively instead of negatively, such as "Safety first!" rather than "Don't be careless!"

Corrective discipline is an action that follows the violation of a rule. The goal for management when corrective discipline occurs is to discourage further infractions and to ensure future compliance with established standards. Most hospitality operations maintain a policy of progressive discipline, which means that the severity of the disciplinary action increases in relation to the severity of the violation. Oral or verbal warnings, written warnings, suspension without pay, and, finally, termination are the usual disciplinary actions that occur when a traditional progressive discipline system is instituted within an organization. The purpose of progressive discipline is to give an employee an opportunity to take corrective action before more serious penalties are applied. Each of the stages of a traditional progressive discipline system is presented in more detail.

Oral or Verbal Warning

This is traditionally the first stage of progressive discipline, and it is primarily applied to employees who have committed minor violations. A hospitality business may or may not require written documentation when a verbal warning has been administered to an employee. Whether or not the employee is actually given written documentation of the verbal warning, it is always a good idea for the manager or the supervisor to make a notation about the warning, including the details of the violation, the date, and a general transcript documenting it.

Written Warning

As an employee's violations become more serious in nature, the disciplinary actions administered by management also becomes more serious. A written warning is just that: It details, in writing, the infraction, the date and time, what happened, and the potential consequences of future violations. It is more permanent in nature than the verbal warning, which is typically perceived as a more temporary "record" of reprimand. The written warning may stay in the employee's file for a period of time, but most organizations will then remove it if no further violations occur after a certain period of time has elapsed—12 months is a typical time period.

Suspension

The next step in the traditional progressive discipline process may be suspension without pay. This step is usually only taken if the prior two steps have not achieved the desired results. Of course, depending upon the nature of the infraction, some managers may elect to skip steps one and two and go directly to suspension. There is very little agreement about whether suspending an employee without pay is an effective method for changing behavior, because most hourly employees in the hospitality industry are likely to seek another comparable paying position at a different hotel or restaurant, rather than await the

ethical dilemma

Lou is a national sales manager for a large hotel chain, and he has just had lunch with an old college roommate who happens to work for a competitor hotel chain. They discuss business during lunch, and they realize that they are each going after the same piece of business with a mutual, potential client. Lou and his old roommate decide to split the sale, and now they will each receive a profit. The sale might have gone to either hotel chain before Lou and his friend made their deal, and now both chains will receive something out of this arrangement.

When Mrs. Adams, Lou's immediate supervisor, learns of this arrangement, she realizes immediately that both sales managers have broken antitrust laws, but she is not sure whether or not she should expose Lou and make him a public pariah or if she should allow Lou and the company to maintain their dignity. She is not even sure if Lou is aware that he broke any laws, and she also wonders whether it really matters because no one really got hurt. How should Mrs. Adams address this issue with Lou? Which of the *10 Ethical Principles for Hospitality Managers* has Lou violated, if any? If Mrs. Adams decides to let this go, will she be in violation of any of the 10 principles? Does this situation need public disclosure in order to initiate a behavior change in Lou, or is the company better off handling this internally, if at all?

completion of a long suspension without pay. Of course, this would depend upon the individual's length of service, compensation, and benefit package. Some argue that suspension may be an effective way to discipline managers and supervisors, who tend to be paid higher wages and who, presumably, would need more time to find a comparable position. Some organizations suspend without pay with the hope that the employee *will* actually find another job and not return to work, thus, effectively *firing himself!* This procedure, however, is a poor method for managing disciplinary problems.

Termination   The final and ultimate stage in the progressive discipline process is firing or dismissing the employee who refuses to change unacceptable behavior or who has committed a very serious violation. This final step may be management's only option if the employee's behavior seriously interferes with a department or the organization's business operations. Depending upon the seriousness of the infraction, the other steps in the progressive discipline process may be altogether bypassed and the employee may be terminated immediately with no warning.

These steps in the progressive discipline process are almost always initiated by the employee's immediate supervisor but typically require approval by a higher-level manager in a smaller operation and by the human resources department in larger organizations. Oversight by upper management is important to guard against any subsequent legal actions and to ensure uniform application of rules throughout the company.

SIX DISCIPLINE *DON'TS*

While some hospitality industry employees may feel that their managers seem to experience some perverse pleasure from administering discipline, the fact is that managers and supervisors most often dread it. The process is unpleasant for all who are involved and is often handled ineffectively. Part of the reason for this is that there are many psychological factors at play that seem to interfere with a constructive discipline process. In this section, we'll review some important dos and don'ts for handling discipline in the workplace, beginning with the don'ts.

Don't Regard Discipline as Punishment
Perhaps one of the biggest mistakes that hospitality managers make when administering discipline is that they consider discipline to be a form of punishment. Managers who make this error tend to apply negative sanctions, expecting that this will have some positive effect on employee behavior. Unfortunately, the use of negative sanctions alone brings about unpredictable results. In rare cases, negative sanctions may work because of the associated fear factor, but more often than not, they have a negative effect and may contribute to an increasingly poor manager-employee relationship. For example, when a housekeeping supervisor prepares a written warning for a room attendant who has failed to properly clean a guest room, the supervisor warns the employee that any further infractions will result in termination. While this is a clear example of a negative sanction, it will only succeed in changing the room attendant's behavior if the following conditions are met:

1. The room attendant values her job or fears the threat of losing her job.
2. The room attendant sees the written warning as fair and consistent with the offense.
3. The room attendant acknowledges and respects the right of the housekeeping supervisor to impose the written warning.

Unless these three elements are in place, the room attendant will respond to the written warning with either resentment or will overtly, or covertly, counterattack authority. Alternatively, the housekeeping supervisor may consider discipline in its original sense: an opportunity for the employee to learn. In this case, the discipline she administers to the room attendant should focus on what the room attendant needs to learn in order for her behavior to be consistent with the hotel's room cleanliness standards. Keep in mind that it is okay for discipline to have "teeth," but it should serve as a means to an end by fostering acceptable employee behavior.

Don't Make Discipline a *Me Against You* Confrontation

Discipline should not be seen as something done *to* an employee, rather it is something done *with* the employee. Effective discipline requires that the manager and the employee work together to solve a specific problem. The fundamental goal of discipline should be to encourage employees to work with managers to identify causes of problematic behavior and to take action to correct these problems. Discipline should be a "we" process, not an "I" process.

Don't Do Too Little Too Late

Sometimes, hospitality managers are too slow to respond to an emerging issue or problem with an employee. A manager may choose not to address a particular problem with an employee, if he feels that the problem is just a quirk or a fluke rather than a continuing issue. Another reason for a manager's delayed response may be that the manager views discipline as a source of disruption in the workplace and prefers to avoid the process altogether in order to maintain harmony. More often than not, managers dread the discipline process and tend to hold off on taking disciplinary action until the last possible moment when the behavior is the furthest from acceptable based on the company's standards. Doing too little too late is problematic because it sends a message to employees that undesirable behavior will be accepted or not even not noticed. This laissez-faire approach may also have an adverse effect on the manager down the road, especially if the problematic behavior increases in frequency and intensity to the extent that it can no longer be ignored. When a manager does not acknowledge an employee's problematic behavior, allowing it to increase in severity, the manager will often develop animosity toward the employee that makes constructive interaction difficult. Even if a manager has done nothing to stop an employee's unacceptable behavior, over time, the manager will begin to harbor angry feelings toward the employee as a result of the employee's repeated offenses. It is very important that inappropriate employee behavior or actions in the workplace be, at a minimum, noted and that the employee be reprimanded, upon the initial occurrence. There is no need for the manager and employee to have a lengthy, difficult discussion, particularly if the event is relatively minor, but the dissatisfaction should be communicated promptly so the behavior does not continue. The lengthy, unpleasant discussion typically occurs as a result of not addressing behavioral problems sooner rather than later.

Don't Create New Rules "on the Fly" If a rule does not exist to cover inappropriate employee behavior, do not apply discipline as if it did. Discuss the behavior with the employee, and then implement a new rule for later application.

Don't Take a Nonprogressive Approach Unless Unavoidable Determining how and when to apply progressive discipline to employees presents a challenge to a manager who wants to avoid doing "too little too late." Progressive discipline begins with a minimal use of power, by providing quick verbal counseling or a verbal warning. Over time, progressive discipline may require stronger actions, if the problematic situation continues. Managers who delay disciplinary action tend to wait until the situation has become so severe that it must be addressed immediately. At this point, the manager must resort to applying harsh sanctions against the employee, because the inappropriate behavior has now become more extreme. When a manager does not practice progressive discipline and reacts to an ongoing problem previously not addressed by taking extreme disciplinary action against the employee, both the employee and coworkers may perceive the manager's method of discipline as too harsh. The key here is to begin disciplining the employee with the least forceful action as early as possible, unless, of course, the offense is so severe that it requires that the manager take immediate harsh action, such as issuing a written warning or terminating the employee. This way, the employee and other coworkers will see that the manager's disciplinary actions are justified based on the employee's reaction to each of the actions taken to correct the employee's problematic and unacceptable behavior.

Don't Ignore the Root Causes Sometimes employees do not succeed at the workplace because they lack the proper skills, or they may have underlying personal or psychological problems. And, in some instances, employees are not successful because the system developed at their workplace is not set up to ensure employee success. When hospitality managers do not know the root causes underlying a performance problem, it makes it extremely difficult to work with an employee to improve performance. For this reason, in many situations, when managers provide positive rewards or negative sanctions, they have little effect on behavior because managers are unaware of the root causes of the problem.

FIVE DISCIPLINE *DOS*

When administering employee discipline, consistency is often the difference between management's failure and success. Paying attention to the don'ts mentioned previously and adhering to the dos that follow will ensure that management achieves that consistency.

Upon discovering a potential disciplinary problem, the manager must determine the following:

Who: Determine which employees were directly or indirectly involved in the incident.

What: Determine the specific details of the incident.

Where: Determine the location of the incident.

When: Determine the time that the incident occurred.

Why: Determine whether there were any underlying circumstances.

Figure 14.2   Investigate the *who? what? where? when?* and *why?* of the situation before administering employee discipline.

Do Thoroughly Investigate

When the hospitality manager has made the initial decision to discipline an employee, the manager must then conduct a thorough investigation of all the facts surrounding the incident. The manager should have two goals in mind when investigating a situation: (1) to confirm that the incident actually occurred and (2) to identify any underlying causes of the misconduct and determine whether there are any mitigating circumstances such as events that may have been out of the employee's control. It is essential for managers to conduct a thorough investigation before confronting the employee. An employee facing potential disciplinary action will likely attempt to deny the occurrence of all or part of the incident or perhaps will even fabricate circumstances surrounding the incident to avoid being disciplined. A manager's thorough investigation of the incident will demonstrate that he is fully aware of the details of the incident when disciplining the employee. Figure 14.2 details the *who, what, where, when,* and *why* factors the manager must investigate before disciplining an employee.

The *why* portion that you see in Figure 14.2 is perhaps the most important part of the investigation. Determining why the situation occurred will allow management to create a fair, reasonable disciplinary response. Also, if the reason why an employee engaged in a particular behavior is determined, similar misconduct in the future will be more easily avoided.

Do Confront the Employee

While praising an employee in public is positive, managers should never discipline or confront an employee in the presence of coworkers. The humiliation of a public reprimanding will most certainly yield a negative response from the employee, including, possibly, violence. When disciplining an employee, a manager should always speak to the employee in private. Even if the infraction is a minor one, a manager should take the employee aside—out of earshot of other employees—before reprimanding the employee. Figure 14.3 presents the steps a manager should take when making minor corrections to an employee's behavior.

Photo 14.2   Employees should never be disciplined in front of coworkers.

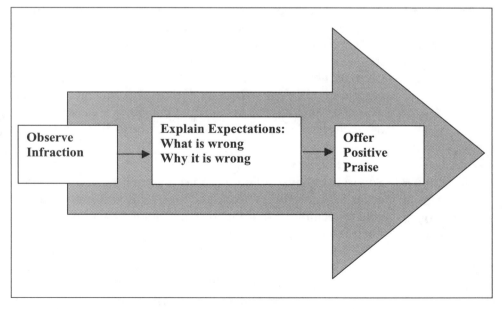

Figure 14.3   Steps management should take when making minor corrections to employee behavior.

When more serious infractions occur, the manager should take the employee to a private office area to discuss the situation. The employee should have an opportunity to tell his side of the story, and a manager's final disciplinary decisions should not be made until the employee has presented any reasons for his unacceptable behavior. The manager should maintain a calm but serious tone during this interaction and must avoid anger and other emotional reactions to the employee's account of the incident. It is also very important for the manager to remain impersonal during this interaction. Criticism should be focused on the employee's behavior, not on the employee personally.

Do Get a Commitment

While it is important for a manager to make it clear that she is there to help the employee find a solution to the problem behavior when disciplining him, it is also important to remember that the employee actually "owns" the problem. This type of conversation should not end until there is agreement between the manager and the employee about how to prevent similar misconduct in the future. The manager should encourage the employee to suggest how to avoid such behavior in the future and should help guide the employee toward a workable solution. A written record should be created of the discussion and any resulting agreements.

Do Use Progressive Discipline When Possible

If at all possible, discipline should be progressive in nature. As you learned earlier, when managers use this system, penalties become progressively stronger as employee misconduct or poor performance is repeated. Providing a quick, informal counseling session for minor infractions may be followed with an oral warning, a written warning, suspension, and, finally, termination if the infractions become more serious. It is important to follow up and provide feedback to the employee during any warning period. The manager should also praise the employee for making progress during this period. Generally, an employee receives a "clean slate" if he has performed satisfactorily for a specified period of time.

Do Follow Up on Employee Discipline

Supervisors must follow up on individual incidents of employee discipline in order for the process to be effective. This will help to achieve the underlying goal of facilitating a productive, harmonious workplace. It is important to monitor the employee who has been disciplined to determine whether the discipline has had a positive effect on behavior. During this phase, the employee should be given frequent opportunities to discuss his or her progress, and supervisors should try to determine whether the underlying problems that caused the misconduct are being satisfactorily resolved. If the employee exhibits subsequent good conduct, then the employee should be praised in order to reinforce such behavior.

WHEN TO TERMINATE AN EMPLOYEE

Sometimes an employee's conduct is so egregious in nature that it warrants immediate termination. When an employee steals, resorts to violence at work, or is in unlawful possession of controlled substances, he has no longer fulfilled his obligation to the company, to management, or to the other employees. These are examples of **gross misconduct** at the workplace. The types of gross misconduct that would lead to immediate termination will vary from organization to organization. In cases of gross misconduct by employees, the question of whether or not to fire the employee is usually fairly straightforward and termination will typically occur. However, there will be other instances of misconduct when things are not so clear-cut. This is why it is so important to have *all* of the organization's discipline policies in clear, written form.

How does management know when it is time to terminate a problem employee? Consider the following three critical factors:

■ *Has the problem employee begun to take advantage of you and the company?* In many cases, the problem employee tends to react in one of two ways to disciplinary action. He will either "fight" the disciplinary action by initiating an intimidation campaign against management in order to save his job or he will remain as a passive employee on the payroll doing little work to earn his paycheck. When it is clear that the employee is not going to make any efforts to improve his performance and behavior, then it is time to terminate.

■ *Is the employee a drain on morale in the department and is the employee negatively affecting productivity?* Problem employees have a way of poisoning a manager's relationship with everyone he comes into contact with: other employees, other managers, customers, and even suppliers. As a result, productivity and even profits may suffer, if guests and customers notice the negative morale within the organization. And management runs the risk of losing its best employees when morale is low. When these factors are evident, it is time to terminate the employee.

■ *If management delays an employee's termination, is management creating an even bigger problem for the future?* The fact is, the longer management waits to terminate a problem employee, the more difficult the termination process becomes. If management does not take immediate action, it sends the message that the problem employee's behavior is not really a "problem" at all. It is difficult for a manager to terminate an employee, and this practice provides legal ammunition for the employee in the event that he *is* eventually terminated. Often, the manager feels like a failure because the efforts he has made to rehabilitate the problem employee have failed. Managers who make good hiring decisions are rarely confronted with this problem, although as discussed previously in the text, there are never any guarantees when dealing with people.

LEGAL IMPLICATIONS WHEN TERMINATING AN EMPLOYEE

No company enjoys when a lawsuit is filed against it. When faced with a lawsuit, large hospitality organizations have attorneys at their disposal and enough cash reserves to successfully fight off most lawsuits and a lawsuit will rarely bankrupt the organization. Small operations, on the other hand, do not have this luxury, and a lawsuit could certainly cause a small hospitality operation to go out of business. Currently, an employee who feels that her termination was unjust can sue the employer claiming **wrongful discharge,** even in at-will employment states, which we discussed in Chapter 4. For this reason, it is essential that the company's disciplinary procedures be followed properly, that supervisors and managers be trained in the disciplinary process, and that all incidents of discipline be properly documented.

When the decision to terminate an employee is uncertain, management should consider the following points:

- *Is there a specific policy that supports the termination?* In other words, if the employee has violated a clearly stated policy, this fact will support the decision to terminate the employee.

- *Do management's past practices support the termination?* Discipline that is not administered consistently, especially with regard to employee termination, is difficult if not impossible to defend successfully in the event of a lawsuit. Lawyers who file claims against the company on behalf of a terminated employee will ask questions about the treatment of other employees committing similar offenses or of those who performed in a manner similar to the terminated employee. It is best for management to ask these questions first before making the decision to terminate a particular employee. When a lawyer uncovers cases in which certain individuals were treated differently from his client, the terminated employee, this is normally a **prima facie** case for discrimination, or a "slam dunk" for the terminated employee and he will most likely win the lawsuit.

Terminating an employee who shows no willingness to change disruptive behavior can be best for all parties involved. When management has a difficult time terminating a problem employee, it is often a result of management not being aware of the potential pitfalls associated with the termination process and not planning for them in advance. There is no easy way to terminate an employee, but there are simple guidelines than should be followed, and the hospitality manager who is compassionate and sensitive can often avoid nightmarish legal and operational problems that follow a bungled termination.

GUIDELINES FOR TERMINATING AN EMPLOYEE

There are no hard-and-fast rules that dictate the way in which a manager should approach an employee termination. Certainly, the prudent manager will have proper documentation to support the decision to terminate. Examples include the following:

1. A signed statement that the employee has received a copy of the employee handbook and is familiar with the organization's rules and regulations is essential.

2. Management should have documentation that backs up any written warnings, verbal warnings, and previous disciplinary issues, and that documentation should be current and relevant.

3. It is often prudent to have another manager present who may act as a witness during a termination proceeding.

4. Management should determine through state and local laws the requirements for issuing the employee's final paycheck and collecting company property such as uniforms, keys, and other such items.

5. Management should keep the details of the termination confidential on a need-to-know basis only.

Perhaps one of the most important actions that management can take when forced to terminate an employee is to leave the employee with dignity. The termination is not the end of the world for either the employee or the manager, so it is best to encourage the employee to move on and to put the incident behind him.

SUMMARY

- Administering employee discipline or even an occasional termination is an important responsibility held by hospitality managers, but it is one that is dreaded by most managers.
- Hiring the right individual in the first place will often alleviate future disciplinary problems.
- Some of the common causes of disciplinary problems in the hospitality workplace are the lack of clearly written policies and procedures for employees to follow, management has hired employees with inadequate skills and abilities, and employees sometimes have personality or motivational problems.
- Internal environmental factors, such as poor management and external environmental factors, such as an employee's personal problems at home, may also contribute to disciplinary problems in the workplace.

- Practicing preventive discipline is effective because the goal of this method is to foster a workplace that is free of misconduct. However, when this sort of disciplinary method fails, corrective discipline is used and its goal is to discourage further infractions and encourage employee compliance with standards.
- Progressive discipline normally consists of a sequence of disciplinary actions including verbal warnings, written warnings, suspension, and finally, termination. As the seriousness of the violation increases, so does the discipline that is administered.
- Discipline should not be regarded as punishment, but rather it encourages employees to change inappropriate behavior and to comply with the organization's standards of acceptable behavior. Discipline should not be administered too late, and management should take a progressive approach to employee discipline whenever possible.
- When administering discipline, management should conduct a thorough investigation, should get a commitment from the employee to find a solution to the problem, and should follow up on all instances of employee discipline to confirm that improved behavior has resulted.
- When terminating an employee, management should ensure that the organization's stated policies and procedures regarding discipline are being followed, and management should ensure that the termination is consistent with past practices of the organization.

PRACTICE QUIZ

1. Rules that are written or unwritten are sufficient when administering an employee discipline policy so long as everyone understands the rules.

   A. True   B. False

2. Managers cannot terminate employees who are in their beginning probationary period of work in at-will-employment states.

   A. True   B. False

3. Employee misconduct and disciplinary actions should be documented on the employee's performance evaluation.

   A. True   B. False

4. Improperly trained employees may become disciplinary problems in the workplace.

   A. True   B. False

5. If management observes an employee violating a minor policy, it is okay to counsel the employee in front of coworkers so long as management does not yell at the employee.

   A. True   B. False

6. All of the following are examples of internal environmental factors that may cause disciplinary problems except

A. Lack of training.

B. Improper employee supervision.

C. Financial troubles that the employee may be experiencing at home.

D. Inadequate equipment or supplies.

7. The goal of employee discipline should be to

A. Punish employees who violate rules and regulations.

B. Show employees who is the boss.

C. Document problems in the event that the employee must later be fired.

D. Change inappropriate behavior and to encourage compliance with standards.

8. Before administering discipline, management should only conduct a thorough investigation

A. If they do not believe the employee's story.

B. If they have adequate time to conduct such an investigation.

C. Management should *always* conduct a thorough investigation.

D. If there were witnesses to the violation; otherwise, no investigation is necessary.

9. An employee who commits an act of gross misconduct would likely be

A. Given a verbal warning.

B. Given a written warning.

C. Suspended with or without pay.

D. Terminated immediately.

10. Before terminating an employee, managers should ask themselves

A. If the employee understood the rules or the policies.

B. If there is an actual written policy that supports the termination.

C. If past practices are consistent with terminating this employee.

D. All of the above should be considered.

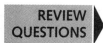
REVIEW QUESTIONS

1. Explain why managers who are given responsibility to accomplish tasks and meet goals must also be given authority to do so. Provide examples from your own experiences when this concept was both successfully and unsuccessfully applied.

2. Assume you have just given an employee a written warning for coming to work late. This is the third time this month that the employee has violated the policy. How long do you feel the written warning should remain in the employee's file? What factors do you base your decision on? If you choose to remove the written warning from the file at some point in the future, will there be any record of the incident at all? If so, where? Explain your answer in detail.

3. With respect to employees in the hospitality industry, how effective do you feel suspension, as a disciplinary procedure, would be? Why? Would there be circumstances in which suspension would be less effective? More effective? Explain your answer in detail.

4. Why do managers sometimes delay the disciplinary process, and when they do, what sort of problems may this delay create? Aside from creating problems for the manager, do problems arise for the problem employee and his coworkers as well? How exactly?

5. List and explain some of the legal ramifications that management must consider both before creating an employee discipline policy as well as when administering discipline. What steps can managers take to deter terminated employees from filing lawsuits against their organization? Explain in detail.

HANDS-ON HRM

Ron Bishop is a professional mystery shopper employed by a large East Coast company that provides "shopper-spotter reports" for hotels and restaurants throughout the United States and Canada. Ron has just gotten off the phone with the company's dispatcher, and he has agreed to complete a "bar report" at a new restaurant that recently opened near his hometown. The restaurant belongs to a fast-growing dinner chain that typically targets the mid- to upscale-steakhouse market.

Ron's visit to the restaurant must include 60 to 90 minutes at the bar, where he will order drinks and an appetizer, all the while observing the restaurant's bartenders for alcohol awareness issues, potential theft, pouring and measuring techniques, general bar maintenance, and customer service. After completing his report, Ron will e-mail it to his home office, where it will be reviewed, retyped in proper company format, and sent to the restaurant chain's regional manager via overnight express mail.

Ron takes his job seriously, and he realizes that the information contained in his reports could possibly cost an employee his or her job. On more than one occasion he has reported dishonest activity at one restaurant, which most likely resulted in a bartender's dismissal, only to discover the same bartender serving at a different restaurant a few miles away. "Doesn't anyone ever check references anymore?" he often wonders to himself.

As Ron arrives at the restaurant he's been assigned to visit, he is impressed. Beautiful creek stone; a large, sweeping deck overlooking the river; warm lighting; and each table is set with what appears to be nice china and stemware, all perfectly placed on starched, white tablecloths. The clientele is decidedly upscale, he notes, and the waitstaff and greeters are cheerily bustling around the spacious dining room, tending to seated guests as well as new arrivals. "Good evening, sir," the host says to Ron. "Table for one?" "Thank you, no," replies Ron. "I'm just going to meet a friend in the bar." "Very good," says the host, "right this way."

Ron arrives in the lounge and manages to grab the last open stool, which is positioned near the center of the bar. *Good,* he thinks to himself. *I have a great view of both sides of the bar, and the cash register is straight ahead of me; I'll be able to observe all of the action.* The bar is busy, and Ron notes that there are two bartenders working: one, a tall, blond male whose name tag reads "Luke," and the other, a stockier, dark-haired male whose name tag reads, "Josh." As Ron waits for one of the bartenders to approach him, he makes some mental notes about the overall condition of the bar: lots of dirty glasses stacked on the bar near the end; some ashtrays need to be emptied and cleaned; a few guests trying to get the bartenders' attention; and several waitstaff near the service area, apparently waiting for their drink orders to be filled. Both Josh and Luke appear to be engaged in conversation, neither of them making any concerted effort to tend to the business at hand.

Shortly, Luke approaches Ron and says, "What can I get you tonight?" Ron appears to think for a moment and says, "Oh, I think I'm in a bourbon mood. What kind of nice bourbons do you have?" "Pretty much the usual," Luke responds somewhat abruptly. "Turkey, Beam, Old Fitz, Gentleman Jack; whiskey's whiskey, I always say." "Do you have Woodford Reserve?" asks Ron. "It's $8 a shot," says Luke. "That's fine," Ron replies. "On the rocks with a side of ice water and a wedge of lime please."

Ron observes as Luke fills a rocks glass with ice, removes a bottle from underneath the bar, and with his back to Ron, pours the bourbon into the glass, and replaces the bourbon bottle underneath the bar. As he sets the glass in front of Ron, he says, "That'll be eight bucks." Ron places a $20 bill on the bar and asks Luke, "Where's the men's room?" Luke waves toward the end of the bar and says, "Right through there on your left." Ron walks toward the doorway but pauses momentarily, turns around, and observes Luke putting the $20 bill in his pocket. He then removes some bills off of a small pile he has lying next to the cash register and places them at Ron's seat. When Ron returns to his stool, Luke says, "There's your change, man. Thanks."

Throughout the rest of his visit, Ron observes Luke make 20 to 30 cocktails for various customers. Sometimes, Luke rings the sale into the register, and sometimes he quickly turns with his back to the customers, pockets the money, and makes change from the small pile lying next to the register. Ron also observes that Luke does not always use the jigger for measuring; sometimes he free pours the alcohol into the glass, and on one occasion, he observes Luke drinking a shot of what appeared to be tequila.

Ron also observes that Luke seems to be pretty chummy with an older gentleman sitting at the end of the bar, and on three occasions, he observes Luke refilling the gentleman's drink, but he neither rings up a sale nor adds the drinks to the gentleman's tab, which is lying on the bar in front of him. The customer seems to be somewhat inebriated, as he is begins to speak loudly and laugh a lot, and his face is flushed. Ron watches the guest get up and begin to stagger toward the men's room. "Whoa, easy there, Mr. Johnson," a friendly server says, and he takes the guest's arm until he steadies himself. "He'll be fine, Eric," Luke says to the server. "Ol' Johnson can hold his liquor." He's probably good for another two or three rounds, yet."

As Ron finishes his second drink, he notes the time on his watch. He has been at the bar more than 80 minutes, and he knows he has enough information to complete his report. He thanks Luke as he leaves the bar, and once outside, he sprints toward his car. "I need to turn this report around tonight," he says to himself. As he starts his car, he flips open his cell phone and calls his dispatcher at the home office. "Sheila," he says when the dispatcher answers, "I've got a 'red flag' coming to you via e-mail in about an hour; you may want to get someone in there so that you can turn this report around and ship it out tonight."

QUESTIONS ▶

1. List and discuss all of the potential problems that Ron observed during his visit to the bar. How serious are the infractions observed by Ron? Are any of the infractions serious enough to warrant immediate termination? Be specific.

2. When management receives Ron's report, what do you think the reaction will be? Why? Do you feel that management should discipline Luke? If so, how exactly should they approach him? Should the contents of Ron's report be shared with Luke? Why or why not?

3. If management decides to terminate Luke based upon the contents of the mystery shopper's report, what assurances are needed from the mystery shopper company? Why?

4. Based on Ron's behavior in this case study, does he appear to be someone who is reliable and someone whose reports are reliable? Explain. What special skills and characteristics should a successful mystery shopper possess?

Discipline Action taken by management to encourage employee compliance with company rules and procedures.

Conflict In the workplace, this occurs when one party interferes with the goal-achieving efforts of another party.

Probation A time period of 60 to 90 days during which an employee can be terminated by upper management for any reason.

Internal environmental factors Factors and situations within the organization's control that may lead to employee disciplinary problems.

External environmental factors Outside factors and situations that may lead to disciplinary problems—usually not within management's control, but within the employee's control.

Employee Assistance Programs (EAP) Formal counseling programs to which larger organizations may refer employees who are experiencing personal problems.

Suspension A period of time during which the employee is not allowed to work within the operation and receives no pay.

Termination The firing of an employee.

Preventive discipline Actions that management can take to encourage employees to follow standards and rules so that infractions are prevented before they occur.

Corrective discipline Actions administered due to a violation of the rules or standards of a particular organization.

Progressive discipline An approach to discipline that begins with sanctions that increase in severity as the violation increases in severity. The typical sequence of disciplinary actions, which consists of a verbal warning, followed by a written warning, suspension, and, finally, termination.

Verbal warning Verbally counseling or "warning" an employee when management observes a violation. Verbal warnings may or may not be documented.

Written warning A more formal warning that is provided to the employee in writing and that usually details the violation as well as what the employee could expect if such violations were to continue.

Gross misconduct Conduct that is seen as particularly egregious and that normally constitutes immediate termination.

Wrongful discharge A type of lawsuit that claims that an employee was terminated improperly.

Prima facie A Latin legal term. Literally translates to "on the face of it." It is a legal presumption that facts presented will control the outcome of the case, unless they can be proved untrue.

1. Reprinted with permission from *Lessons in Service from Charlie Trotter* by Edmund Lawler. Copyright 2001 by Edmund Lawler, Ten Speed Press, Berkley, CA, www.tenspeed.com.
2. Ibid.

CHAPTER 15

EMPLOYEE MOTIVATION THROUGH QUALITY LEADERSHIP

I don't believe in management. I have no time for it. But I am very interested in leadership.[1]

Charlie Trotter, chef/owner, Charlie Trotter's, Chicago

CHAPTER OBJECTIVES

After completing this chapter, you will be able to

- Explain the relationship between employee motivation and quality leadership.

- Define motivation and discuss early theories of motivation.

- Explain how management implements motivational strategies.

- Define leadership and identify the similarities and differences between leadership and management.

- Discuss the evolution of leadership theories and their impact on modern management.

- Explain the difference between formal and informal authority.

- Define technical skills, human relations skills, and conceptual skills, and explain their importance to the overall success of a hospitality manager or supervisor.

- Evaluate the importance of adopting your own leadership style.

311

 **HRM IN ACTION** The hospitality industry is a people industry. But, for once, let's not focus on the people who are our guests and customers but on those people who are *serving* our guests and customers. Those who work in the hospitality operation are the company's most valuable asset, more valuable than the equipment, the supplies, and even the building itself. Without the employees, there would be no need for these other "assets." When management takes care of its employees, the employees will certainly be more motivated to take care of the guests and customers. However, this sequence of events does not happen by chance.

As you have learned throughout this book, it takes a great deal of skill and effort on management's part to do things right. Proper interviewing and hiring techniques ensure management matches the right applicant with the right position, a solid orientation and training program ensures that all employees know how to do whatever it is they are supposed to do, and effective communication skills ensure that employees are kept in the loop when absolutely necessary and are provided with quality feedback from management. These are just some of the activities hospitality managers and supervisors must practice every day to ensure the overall success of the operation.

These activities and other management efforts are best accomplished through quality **leadership.** What is quality leadership? Leaders are known to get results, but they cannot do this alone; they need employees to help them achieve their goals. And the best way to get results is to motivate them to perform, rather than ordering them to do so. Yet, many managers fail in their efforts to motivate their employees because they are not completely clear about the concept of motivation and its impact on successful leadership.

RELATIONSHIP BETWEEN LEADERSHIP AND MOTIVATION

To become effective leaders, hospitality supervisors and managers must have some basic understanding of motivation. Motivation is something that comes from within. Managers cannot motivate their employees, but they can provide the kind of work environment in which their employees can self-motivate. This is why it is so important to make quality hiring decisions when seeking new staff because successful hospitality managers must ensure that the individuals they hire have a strong motivational commitment, or the ability to self-motivate. Communication is often the key. Rather than a manager *ordering* employees to get from point A to point B, a leader communicates the task in such a way that the employees *want* to get from point A to point B. No hospitality organization can succeed without a certain level of commitment and effort from its employees. For that reason, successful managers and supervisors must have some basic understanding of motivation and some of the theories behind it to ensure that they maintain a motivated staff.

MOTIVATIONAL THEORIES

Managers and management scholars have developed many theories about motivation. **Motivation** is best defined as the factors that cause and sustain behavior. In other words, motivation explains why people do the things they do. Motivational theories help to inform managers about how they should treat their staff in order to achieve the highest levels of employee motivation. Like other management theories, motivational theory has evolved from early approaches, which sought the one "correct" model for motivating employees, to more modern approaches, which realize that motivation arises from the interplay of both individual and environmental factors.

EARLY THEORIES OF MOTIVATION

The earliest theories of motivation primarily consist of three different views: (1) the Traditional Model, (2) the Human Relations Model, and (3) the Human Resources Model. Basically, the only thing these three theories have in common is that each one attempts to construct a single model of motivation that would apply to every employee in every situation. Aside from that, each one provides a very different way of viewing and explaining human behavior in the workplace.

The Traditional Model
The **Traditional Model** was the brainchild of Frederick W. Taylor (1856–1915). Taylor and other early scholars are credited with an approach to management known as the **Scientific Management Theory.** This theory arose in part due to a need to increase worker productivity in the United States at the beginning of the twentieth century, when skilled labor was in short supply. Based on Taylor's research, he believed, among other things, that more efficient workers should be paid higher wages than less efficient workers. In other words, managers should determine the most efficient way to perform repetitive, on-the-job tasks and then "motivate" workers with a system of wage incentives: the more they produce, the more they earn. The Traditional Model of motivational theory makes the following assumptions about workers:

- Most people do not like to work.
- Most people will avoid work if at all possible.
- What people do is less important than what they earn for doing it.
- Few people want or can handle work that requires creativity or self-direction.

As you might imagine, this model began to fail as productivity in the United States increased and it took less workers to get the job done. As more workers were laid off and as companies began to reduce the size of the wage incentive, workers started to demand job security over short-term, minor wage increases.

TALES FROM THE FIELD

Before turning my life around by getting an education, I worked as a maid in a large chain hotel. We had a good department and everyone got along, but one day the executive housekeeper came to us and announced that an entirely new system for cleaning rooms was about to be implemented, and anyone who was unable to completely finish a room in 23 minutes would have to be let go. The new system included a new way of making beds called the 'once-around method,' which required the maid to start at one corner of the bed and completely make the bed by working down, around the end, and up to the opposite corner. I couldn't imagine how I would be able to make a bed that quickly and had pretty much accepted that I would be fired. But management conducted plenty of training, and one of the neatest things they did was to move two king-sized beds into our beautiful hotel lobby, break us maids into teams, and stage bed-making contests in the middle of the lobby during peak guest arrival times. The training supervisors wore striped, referee shirts and had whistles and stopwatches. It was amazing how much fun we all had and how quickly we learned to make those beds using the new method. As I recall, every single one of us learned the technique and got 'certified' by our executive housekeeper.

Louise, 48, Louisville, Kentucky

The Human Relations Model

The **Human Relations Model** of employee motivation proposes that the boredom and repetitiveness of many tasks actually *reduce* employee motivation, while social contact helps to create and sustain motivation. In other words, management can motivate their employees by making them feel useful and important. This theory of motivation is attributed to Elton Mayo (1880–1949) and some other associates from Harvard, who developed theories of management that would later be known as the **Behavior School of Management**. Mayo was interested in helping managers deal with the "people side" of their organizations. The Human Relations Model of employee motivation assumes the following about workers:

- Workers want to feel important, valued, and useful.
- Workers want to belong and to be recognized as individuals.
- These social needs are more important than money in motivating people to work.

According to the Human Relations Model, workers are expected to accept management's authority because supervisors treat them with consideration and allow them to influence how tasks should be accomplished to a certain extent.

The Human Resources Model The **Human Resources Model** is attributed to Douglas McGregor and other theorists, who basically criticized both of the earlier models as being oversimplified and flawed because they focused on just one or two factors of motivation, either money or social relations. McGregor determined that managers have basically two different sets of assumptions about their employees. The traditional view, which McGregor calls **Theory X,** assumes that most people do not like to work and will avoid work whenever possible. A more optimistic view, one which McGregor called **Theory Y,** assumes that people actually do want to work and that under the right circumstances, they derive a great deal of satisfaction from work. Table 15.1 contrasts the Traditional, Human Relations, and Human Resources Models of motivational theory.

TRADITIONAL MODEL ASSUMPTIONS	HUMAN RELATIONS MODEL ASSUMPTIONS	HUMAN RESOURCES MODEL ASSUMPTIONS
1. Most people do not like work and will avoid it if possible. 2. What people do is less important than what they earn for doing it. 3. Few people want or can handle work that requires creativity.	1. People want to feel useful at work. 2. People want to belong and be recognized as individuals. 3. These social needs are more important than money in motivating people to work.	1. People like to work and want to contribute to meaningful goals that they have helped establish. 2. Most people can exercise far more creativity and self-direction than their present jobs demand.
MANAGEMENT POLICIES UNDER THIS MODEL	MANAGEMENT POLICIES UNDER THIS MODEL	MANAGEMENT POLICIES UNDER THIS MODEL
1. Employees should be closely supervised and controlled. 2. Tasks must be broken down into simple, repetitive, easily learned steps. 3. Managers must establish detailed work routines and enforce them firmly.	1. Managers should make each worker feel useful and important. 2. Managers should keep employees informed and listen to their objections to management's plans. 3. Managers should allow employees to exercise some self-direction on routine matters.	1. Managers should utilize their employees' underused abilities and talents. 2. Managers should create an environment in which all employees may contribute. 3. Managers must encourage full participation in important matters.
MANAGEMENT EXPECTATIONS UNDER THIS MODEL	MANAGEMENT EXPECTATIONS UNDER THIS MODEL	MANAGEMENT EXPECTATIONS UNDER THIS MODEL
1. Employees will only tolerate work if the pay is decent and the boss is fair. 2. If tasks are simple enough and people are closely controlled, they will produce.	1. Sharing information and involving employees will satisfy their needs to belong. 2. Satisfying these needs will improve morale and reduce resistance to authority.	1. Expanding employees' influence will lead to direct improvement in operating efficiency. 2. Worker satisfaction improves as employees are allowed to fully use their personal resources.

Table 15.1 Comparison of three historical views of motivational theory.

Before we criticize these early theorists for what may appear to be a very antiquated view of employee behavior, we need to remember that most of their research was conducted in the early years of the United States' Industrial Revolution, when management science was just in its infancy. Much of McGregor's later theories led to what is known today as **participative management,** which is currently practiced by many successful hospitality managers and supervisors. We will learn more about this management style later in this chapter.

LATER THEORIES OF MOTIVATION

Later theories of motivation include Maslow's Hierarchy of Needs and Herzberg's Motivation-Hygiene Theory. These theories focus on the worker's inner needs and how they motivate behavior.

Maslow's Hierarchy of Needs

Abraham Maslow's **Hierarchy of Needs** has no doubt received the most attention from managers than any other theory of motivation, since it classifies human needs in a logical, convenient way. His theory was published in 1943 in his book *Motivation and Personality.* His theory, simply known as Maslow's Hierarchy, has important implications for hospitality managers and supervisors. Maslow's theory viewed human motivation as a hierarchy of five needs, ranging from the most basic physiological needs such as food, water, and air to the highest needs for self-actualization, the desire that most individuals have to maximize their own potential. Maslow's Hierarchy of Needs is often arranged in a pyramid as in Figure 15.1. He believed that each *need* must be at least partially satisfied before the individual desires to satisfy a need at the next higher level.

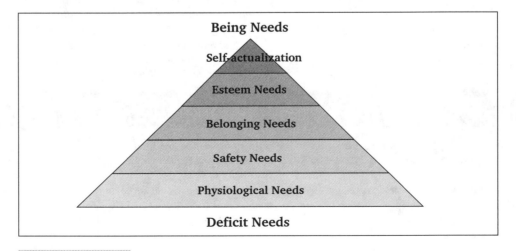

Figure 15.1   Pyramid of Maslow's Hierarchy of Needs.

As you can see, Maslow's five needs, beginning with the most basic to the highest, are arranged on a pyramid from the bottom up. The five human needs identified by Maslow are as follows:

1. *Physiological needs.* Our most basic human needs such as air, water, shelter, and food.

2. *Safety and security needs.* Our need for a safe working environment as well as wages to sufficiently feed, shelter, and protect ourselves and our families.

3. *Social or belonging needs.* Our need to feel like we are an integral part of the company in which we work, that the work we do matters.

4. *Esteem needs.* Our desire for achievement, competence, status, and recognition.

5. *Self-actualization needs.* Our desire to look for meaning and personal growth in our work, as well as our desire to seek out new responsibilities.

Maslow identified the bottom four needs as **deficit needs;** in other words, if you don't have enough of something, you have a deficit, or a need. He identified these four basic needs as survival needs. Maslow referred to the highest level as **being needs.**

Before hospitality managers attempt to offer incentives designed to provide employees with opportunities to grow esteem, or feelings of belonging, (Maslow's top three needs), employees require a sufficient living wage as well as job security, freedom from coercion or arbitrary treatment, and clearly defined rules and regulations. Maslow stresses two important beliefs: (1) that the employee will not be motivated to move to a higher level on the hierarchy until the most basic level needs are met and (2) that individual differences are greatest at the highest level. For example, some employees find self-actualization by producing work of the highest quality, while others may prefer to develop creative, useful ideas. When managers and supervisors take the time to get to know their employees and become aware of their different self-actualization needs, they can use a variety of motivational approaches to enable employees to achieve personal as well as company goals.

HERZBERG'S MOTIVATION-HYGIENE THEORY

Frederick Herzberg conducted a study in the late 1950s in which he determined that employee job satisfaction and job dissatisfaction is a result of two separate sets of factors. This theory was called the **Two-factor Theory,** and today is widely known as the **Motivation-Hygiene Theory.**[2] Job *dissatisfiers* were termed **Hygiene factors,** which included such things as salary, working conditions, company policy, and the employees' relationships with their supervisors.

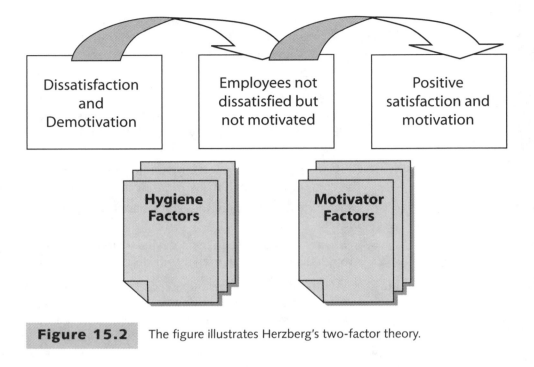

Figure 15.2   The figure illustrates Herzberg's two-factor theory.

Job *satisfiers* were called **motivating factors,** which included achievement, recognition, responsibility, opportunities for advancement, and the work itself. Figure 15.2 illustrates Herzberg's two-factor theory.

Herzberg's work has been criticized because it does not take individual differences into account. In other words, a job-related factor that causes dissatisfaction in one person may bring satisfaction to another. Nevertheless, today, Herzberg's theory is still regarded as relevant because it influences the way that managers think about how job characteristics themselves affect overall employee satisfaction, motivation, and work performance.

MODERN APPROACHES TO MOTIVATION

While each of the previously mentioned theories is important and is still well regarded, the focus is mostly on employee *needs* and how those needs will motivate behavior. More contemporary approaches to motivational theory consider not only employee needs but also such factors as the employees' *abilities* as well as how employees *perceive* their roles in the workplace. The final two theories that we will consider are sometimes called **process theories of motivation** because they consider the *thought process* that helps employees decide how to act. Two key process theories are the expectancy approach and the equity approach.

The Expectancy Approach

This approach to motivational theory has received considerable support from research, and it is easily applied in business settings, including businesses in the hospitality industry. Unlike earlier theories that tend to assume that all employees are alike, the **expectancy approach** focuses on the differences among employees and situations. This theory suggests that employee motivation will depend upon three components or relationships:

1. **Performance-outcome expectancy:** *"If I do this, what will be the outcome?"* Employee expectations will determine employee decisions about their behavior. For example, a hotel room attendant who is thinking about exceeding his daily room-cleaning quota might expect praise, a bonus, no reaction, or even hostility from the other room attendants.

2. **Valence** *(the power to motivate):* *"Is the outcome worth the effort to me?"* The outcome of a particular behavior has the power to motivate, or valence. For example, to an assistant restaurant manager who values money and achievement, a promotion and a transfer to a higher-paying position in another city may have high valence; to someone who values her home-based colleagues and friends, such a promotion would have low valence.

3. **Effort-performance expectancy:** *"What are my chances of achieving an outcome that will be worthwhile for me?"* An employee's expectations about how difficult it will be to perform successfully will affect his decision about behavior. Given a choice, employees tend to select the level of performance that seems to have the best chance of achieving an outcome they value.

Implications for Hospitality Managers

These three components or relationships associated with the expectancy approach should help managers to best determine how to provide a motivating work environment for their employees. Managers should be able to answer each of the following questions in the affirmative:

Do the rewards we are giving actually have any value to the employees who receive them? Rewards are not motivators if they are not suitable for the individual who receives them. An award should be tailored to the individual as much as possible. Rather than rewarding a hotel employee with the customary but uninspired gift certificate for dinner for two in the hotel dining room, consider some other creative choices:

- For the housekeeping employee who is a single parent and finds it difficult to get a night out with friends: A bonded babysitter and a rented limousine for an evening out on the town.
- For the hipster bellhop: A six-month subscription to Napster, iTunes, or some other music download Web site.
- For the struggling college student bartender: Three days off with pay during final exam week.

ethical dilemma

Marion accepted a general manager's position at a posh, Midwestern resort, and she and her family made a permanent move to the area. Her eldest son, Steve, soon landed a good job in restaurant point-of-sale systems with the Quacker POS company nearby. As the resort's general manager, Marion soon saw the need for a new POS system that would support the resort's busy food and beverage operations. Although the resort had a bidding policy, Marion purchased a Quacker system, even though some other systems sold for less and had more suitable features. Steve handled the sale and received a healthy commission. Had the purchase gone through the normal bidding process, the Quacker model would not have been selected. However, because Marion was the GM and had final decision authority, she did not feel that it was wrong to bypass the system by skipping the bidding routine. Was Marion's decision to bypass the bidding process an ethical choice, or did she violate one of the *10 Ethical Principles for Hospitality Managers?* If so, which one? How will her decision affect her relationship with the owners of the resort, the resort's other managers, and employees?

Have we determined the performance standards that we desire so that we can tell our employees what they must do to be rewarded? Without proper training and an effective performance evaluation system in place, many employees do not know what to do, how to do it, and how well—or to what extent—they need to do it.

Are our performance goals attainable? If performance goals are too difficult or impossible for employees to achieve, their motivation will be low. For a lot of employees, no matter how hard they try, they are not likely to be high performers. This situation may be the result of inadequate training or a flawed performance appraisal system that judges personality traits as opposed to objective, observable behaviors. If employees feel that they are likely to receive a lukewarm evaluation no matter how hard they try, they are not likely to find the self-motivation to excel.

Are our rewards actually linked to performance? When employees see the relationship between performance and rewards as weak, they are rarely motivated to achieve high levels of performance. This situation occurs when employees are evaluated and rewarded in areas such as seniority, having a "good attitude," and other subjective performance criteria. The truth is that hospitality organizations usually get what they reward, not what they want. So it is important that management carefully consider a reward system that is actually designed to motivate the employee behaviors that are desired.

Making the Reward System Cost-Effective

Believe it or not, employee motivation is not all about money, gifts, nights out on the town, and days off with full pay and benefits. While money is important, it is often not the key motivator, assuming the hospitality business provides competitive wages and salaries. The actual jobs themselves can be rewarding if they are designed with employees' higher needs in mind. When independence, creativity, and **employee empowerment**—the authority managers bestow upon front-line workers to address customers' problems without the need for management intervention—are built into the job design itself, they can be intrinsically motivating to many employees. While the current trend toward empowering employees has removed many of the traditional control mechanisms used to monitor employees, this has not always been the case. Rosabeth Moss Kanter's book *The Change Masters*[3] was one of the earliest books to focus on employee empowerment. Kanter studied corporations that were successful in their efforts related to change and innovation and companies that were not so successful. Kanter said that it was almost as if management within the unsuccessful companies had a set of "Rules for Stifling Innovation" hanging on their office walls. Figure 15.3 lists Kanter's rules, which are still an effective road map today for how *not* to do things in business.

1. Regard any new idea from below with suspicion—because it's new and because it's from below.

2. Insist that people who need your approval to act first go through several other levels of management to get their signatures.

3. Ask departments or individuals to challenge and criticize each other's proposals (that saves you the job of deciding; you just pick the survivor).

4. Express your criticisms freely and withhold your praise (that keeps people on their toes). Let them know they can be fired at any time.

5. Treat identification of problems as signs of failure, to discourage people from letting you know when something in their area isn't working.

6. Control everything carefully. Make sure people count anything that can be counted, frequently.

7. Make decisions to reorganize or change policies in secret and spring them on people unexpectedly (that also keeps people on their toes).

8. Make sure that requests for information are fully justified, and make sure that it is not given out to managers freely. (You don't want data to fall into the wrong hands.)

9. Assign lower-level managers, in the name of delegation and participation, responsibility for figuring out how to cut back, lay off, move people around, or otherwise implement threatening decisions you have made. And get them to do it quickly.

10. And, above all, never forget that you, the higher-ups, already know everything important about this business.

Figure 15.3   Ten Rules for Stifling Innovation (*Source: Reprinted with permission from Simon & Schuster Adult Publishing Group from* The Change Masters *by Rosabeth Moss Kanter. Copyright ©1983 by Rosabeth Moss Kanter.*)

The Equity Theory   This final model of employee motivation ties into the rewards system discussed earlier because this theory emphasizes the employee's perception of equity or fairness with respect to the award received. **Equity theory** states that an employee's motivation, job performance, and overall job satisfaction will be dependent upon how the employee perceives the fairness of not only the reward the employee receives but also the rewards given to other employees. Employees make comparisons between their own job efforts and the rewards they are given with the job efforts and the rewards given to other employees within the organization. Imagine how you would feel if you were asked to train a new employee within your department only to discover that your company is paying the trainee a higher wage or salary than you. This inequity does not motivate you to high levels of performance. When employees feel that the reward system is unfair, they are more likely to put less effort into their work, call in sick more often, or even seek employment elsewhere.

PUTTING MOTIVATIONAL PRACTICES TO WORK

If you are starting to feel that motivation practice and theory are difficult subjects that touch on different disciplines, you're right. In spite of enormous amounts of research, and we have only scratched the surface here, the subject of motivation is still not clearly understood because to understand it thoroughly, one must understand human nature itself and therein lies the problem. But if you think about your own workplace experiences, you will probably agree that most employees—no matter what their official rank in the organization—have the same basic desires:

- Employees want to engage in enjoyable activities.
- Employees want to feel good about themselves as individuals.
- Employees want to feel good about their work and their accomplishments.
- Employees want to feel good about their futures or where they are headed.
- Employees want to earn fair pay for their efforts, especially their extra efforts.

In short, most employees seek praise, convenience, fun, money, importance, success, and advancement. We'll refer to these seven conditions as *motivators,* and review some management strategies that will encourage these conditions.

Employees Seek Praise   Employees are more likely to be motivated when they receive sincere praise from their managers and supervisors and recognition and honest appreciation for a job well done. Hospitality managers can utilize a variety of techniques to accomplish this type of motivation, and the important thing to remember is that there are usually little to no financial costs involved. Recognition of employees at staff and department meetings and more formal activities such as providing monthly employee luncheons, employee of the month programs, and even company newsletters are effective ways for managers to let employees know that their hard work is appreciated.

Employees Seek Convenience

The work process needs to be hassle-free, and hospitality managers need to remove as many roadblocks as possible that may prevent employees from effectively accomplishing their required tasks and duties. One hotel housekeeper thought she was "saving on supplies" by holding so many wash cloths in emergency storage that room attendants were forced to make up rooms and then had to come back to those rooms hours later with clean washcloths, once laundry had finished washing, drying, and folding them. Needless to say, many room attendants simply waited on the clock for the laundry to catch up, and many guests did not receive clean washcloths in their rooms. Not much of a motivator! It is critical that management identify such needless aggravations and inconveniences and eliminate them.

Employees Seek Fun

Employees are most productive when they enjoy the work that they are doing. If you think that nobody really enjoys washing dishes in a restaurant kitchen or cleaning guest rooms in a hotel, you are wrong. Humans differ in their affinity for performing various types of activities: What one person loves, another person hates. When there is a choice of two or more tasks to be done, management should *ask* the employee which one she would prefer to do. Another way of finding out what employees like is through observation. When an employee is pursuing an activity with tireless effort and a smile, it usually means the employee enjoys what he is doing. If the employee is having trouble mustering energy and a smile, it usually means he finds the task nonenjoyable. It is also important during the application and interviewing process to match job applicants with the kinds of tasks and activities that they enjoy.

Employees Seek Money

Everyone wants to be fairly compensated for a day's work, and hospitality industry employees are no exception. Management must first ensure that the organization is paying competitive wages and salaries that are in line with what competing hospitality businesses pay their employees. Surprisingly, most employees will not rank wages or salaries as their number one motivational factor, so it is not necessary to attempt to meet a competitor's wages dollar for dollar. An employee who receives routine praise and respect and who is offered opportunities to grow, both professionally and personally, simply will *not* leave a well-run operation to work for the competition because it pays 50 cents more per hour. Employees who go above and beyond what is expected of them or who occasionally do extra work for management should be given a comparable, one-time bonus.

Employee-of-the-month awards are an effective way to recognize employee achievement and foster a positive work environment.

Employees Seek Importance

Not everyone wants to be a manager or a supervisor, so this is not the type of importance referred to here. But all employees want to feel that the work they do is important to the overall success of the operation, so it is up to management to let them know how important they and their accomplishments are. An employee who does important things is important; an employee who does unimportant things is unimportant.

Employees Seek Success

Success means winning, so employees need to be engaged in winning situations. How does management accomplish this? Management encourages winning situations by helping employees to set realistic goals that benefit both the employee and the company and then celebrating every employee's success in meeting these goals, as if a favorite horse has just won the Kentucky Derby. This also requires that management be willing to share information with their employees so that significant "wins" can be communicated. For instance, "Congratulations team! We increased hotel occupancy last month by 14 percent!"

Employees Seek Advancement Employees who consistently perform above and beyond what is expected of them should be offered career advancement opportunities that are directly tied to their good work. Larger hospitality organizations have more flexibility in this respect because there are often more opportunities to promote employees to higher levels of responsibility. But even smaller operations can be successful if they think creatively. Often employees simply want to be given more challenging work, so management must think of ways to continually challenge the employee so that, she is always learning new things. Teach a front-desk agent how to handle group reservations, train the dishwasher in end-of-month inventory reporting, allow the restaurant cashier to assist with the weekly schedule, train a line cook on how to place weekly orders with the restaurant's purveyors, encourage bar staff to audition live entertainment. The list is endless, but the tasks should be approached in such a way that management is not simply piling on extra duties, but rather helping to develop employees so that they can step up to the next level when and if they desire to do so.

WHAT IS LEADERSHIP?

What is leadership and how is it different from management? There are probably as many different definitions for leadership as there are people who have attempted to define the concept. And since thousands of scholars have studied leadership, the definitions seem endless. One definition that has gained wide acceptance is this: *Leadership is the process of directing and influencing the task-related activities of the organization's employees.*[4] In other words, successful leaders are able to encourage people to perform their duties voluntarily, willingly, and to the best of their abilities. Leadership involves other people—employees. By their willingness to accept directions from the leader, employees help make the leadership process possible; without them, the leadership qualities of a manager would be irrelevant and ineffective.

EARLY LEADERSHIP THEORIES

Are leaders born or do they possess traits than can be learned? Some of the earliest efforts made by researchers in their attempt to understand leadership were to identify the personal characteristics of leaders. This **trait approach to leadership** compared the traits of effective leaders with those of ineffective leaders. These studies also compared the traits of those in organizations who emerged as leaders with those who did not. As a group, leaders were found to be brighter, more extroverted, and more self-confident than nonleaders, but the theory ultimately failed because it did not determine whether these traits were the *causes* of leadership ability or actually the *results* of the kind of characteristics people exhibit once they have reached leadership positions.

The **behavioral approach to leadership** attempted to isolate the *behaviors* that effective leaders exhibited. In other words, instead of focusing on who effective leaders were, this approach focused on what effective leaders *did*. Researchers using both the trait and behavioral approaches primarily learned that effective leadership depended upon many variables, such as organizational culture, the nature of the tasks, and even the nature of the employees themselves. No one trait or style was common to all effective leaders or effective in all situations.

A new theory of leadership began to evolve when researchers determined that an individual's personality as well as certain situational factors could impact overall leadership effectiveness. The **contingency approach to leadership** concentrated on such factors as the leader's personality, past experiences, and expectations; the expectations of the higher-level managers; the nature of the job tasks that employees needed to perform; the characteristics, expectations, and behaviors of the employees themselves; the expectations and behavior of peers or other equal-level managers; and, finally, the culture of the organization and its policies. So, based on these approaches to leadership, what personal traits or behavioral characteristics must an individual possess to give him the ability to lead others? Management scholars have been debating this question for years, and there is still no real consensus. A decidedly unscientific answer might be this: "We can't really define leadership, but we know it when we see it." Figure 15.4 contrasts some management and leadership behaviors.

1. *Managers* drive people and instill fear and uncertainty.

2. *Managers* say, "Go and do it!"

3. *Managers* make work a grind and wear people down.

4. *Managers* are all about "me, me, me."

5. *Managers* seek front and center for themselves.

6. *Managers* often seek credit for themselves.

1. *Leaders* guide people and inspire enthusiasm.

2. *Leaders* say, "Let's go!"

3. *Leaders* make work interesting.

4. *Leaders* are all about "we."

5. *Leaders* quietly give guidance from the sidelines.

6. *Leaders* believe in giving credit where credit is due.

Figure 15.4   Managers versus leaders.

MODERN VIEWS AND CHARASMATIC LEADERSHIP

One area of growing interest is **charismatic leadership,** in which the focus is on individuals who have exceptional impact on their organizations. A good example of a charismatic leader from the hospitality industry is Norman Brinker, who has either started or has been instrumental in the development and growth of several well-known casual dining chains including Steak and Ale, Bennigan's, Chili's, On the Border, Romano's Macaroni Grill, and Rockfish Grill.[5] One thing that almost everyone agrees on is that charismatic leaders tend to be **change masters,** or individuals who are not content with doing things according to the status quo. The primary characteristics associated with charismatic leadership are as follows:[6]

- Possesses a compelling vision or sense of purpose.
- Has an ability to communicate that vision in clear terms that followers can understand.
- Demonstrates consistency and focus in his or her leadership efforts.
- Understands his or her own strengths.

FORMAL AND INFORMAL AUTHORITY

While it is true that all managers are not leaders, there may also be leaders in the organization who have no actual managerial duties. Managers have been given **formal authority** to supervise others in accomplishing the tasks necessary to meet the organization's goals and objectives. Employees are expected to follow and adhere to the wishes of management, or suffer the consequences. Sometimes employees who do not have managerial duties and who lack formal authority emerge as leaders in organizations because they possess **informal authority.** This means that these individuals have certain traits or characteristics that compel others to follow them, despite the fact that they are not officially in charge. To function as both a manager and a leader, an individual needs both formal and informal authority. When hospitality managers promote a line employee to the position of supervisor and, thus, grant the new supervisor formal authority, problems often occur when the supervisor's employees reject that formal authority. Situations such as this may occur for a number of reasons, but the primary one is that managers often promote the wrong person.

DECIDING WHOM TO PROMOTE

Perhaps one of the hospitality manager's most important tasks is promoting an hourly employee to the position of supervisor. Decisions such as this should be given very careful consideration, but all too often, some managers take the easy way out by promoting the individual with the most seniority or the individual with the greatest amount of technical skills, such as the fastest line cook or the most efficient server. The result of such poor decisions can be disastrous. The skills required to be an effective supervisor or manager are different than those of a good line cook or server, so past success in a nonsupervisory role has limited value in predicting how well an employee might perform as a supervisor. This is simply because managerial work is different from nonmanagerial work.

Becoming a successful manager requires that you develop three broad categories of skills: **technical skills, human relations skills,** and **conceptual skills.** Robert Katz first identified these three categories of skills and determined that an employee's place in the organization determines their relative importance.[7]

Technical Skills

Technical skills are probably the ones that new supervisors are most familiar with. A recently promoted front-desk shift supervisor would likely have a closer working knowledge of the technology and skills of those who report to her. The supervisor's job would be to assist the desk clerks in either acquiring these skills or utilizing them to achieve the hotel's desired financial results. As the supervisor moves up the organizational chain, a direct, hands-on knowledge of technical skills becomes less necessary.

Human Relations Skills

Human relations skills are the supervisor's interpersonal skills and are, frankly, the glue that holds everything else together. The new supervisor must be able to get along well with others, communicate effectively, be a good coach, deliver constructive feedback, guide performance, and sometimes even make difficult choices about whether a particular individual should continue on the team. These are perhaps the most important skills of all for employees who manage and supervise others, yet they are frequently the skills that are most lacking.

Conceptual Skills

Conceptual skills refer to the supervisor's ability to see the big picture. In other words, managers need to be able to see how each action and task fits into the overall scheme of the entire organization. Managers with excellent conceptual skills are able to develop ideas and solve problems creatively.

While most entry-level employees will eventually develop effective technical skills, managers and supervisors are expected to place more emphasis on human behavior and have a more highly developed set of interpersonal skills. For the supervisor, skills such as listening, providing constructive feedback on employee performance, competently dealing with difficult people, and sometimes orchestrating complicated team dynamics are more important than being the fastest cook on the line or the most efficient server in the dining room. All this takes place while the supervisor continues to meet her own personal work goals, guiding the people she manages towards theirs. Most supervisors do not fail due to a lack of technical skills; they fail because they lack human relations skills.

Because effective supervisors are linked directly to the overall success of the operation, managers must make wise and informed choices when determining whom to promote. Supervisors must not only manage the task, but they must also manage the work lives of the employees who accomplish the task. Effective supervisors know how to do both at the same time.

What's Your Style?   New supervisors and managers need time, training, and development before they can be expected to find their own voice when it comes to managing others. From the classical approaches to motivation and leadership, which tend to be more autocratic and dictatorial—think, my way or the highway!—to modern-day theories, which focus on democratic, or participative styles of leadership, which style should you adopt in order to be an effective hospitality manager and leader? Frankly, there is no one perfect style of leadership that is effective in all situations. As the executive chef of a restaurant who is brainstorming a new menu, you might choose a more participative style, in which employee input is actively sought and encouraged. If the building is on fire, you would need to be decidedly more autocratic. Figure 15.5 provides an overview of different **leadership styles.**

Today's hospitality industry employees are likely to favor a more creative, participative style of leadership, as opposed to the old-fashioned notions characterized by command-and-obey styles. A more **people-centered approach** to management is one in which leaders focus on the interpersonal relationships they have with employees, exhibiting true caring and concern for employee welfare.

Which Style Is Best?   The truth is that different styles are needed for different situations, and each manager and supervisor needs to know when to exhibit a particular approach. The four leadership styles provided in Figure 15.5 are autocratic leadership, bureaucratic leadership, democratic leadership, and laissez-faire leadership. There are clearly situations and circumstances in which one style may be more

LEADERSHIP STYLE	DESCRIPTION	WHEN EFFECTIVE	WHEN INEFFECTIVE
Autocratic leadership	A classical approach to leadership sometimes called the carrot-and-stick approach. It is characterized by reward and punishment. The manager retains the power and the decision-making authority.	May work when supervising new or untrained employees, with employees who need detailed orders and tasks, when there is limited time in which to make a decision.	Ineffective when employees expect to have their opinions heard; with more educated, creative employees; or when morale is low and turnover and absenteeism are high.
Bureaucratic leadership	Management is "by the book," everything is done according to procedure and policy. Manager is more a police officer than a leader.	May work with employees who perform routine, repetitive tasks; when employees are working with equipment that require set procedures to operate.	Ineffective when work habits form that are hard to break or when employees have lost interest in their jobs, or when employees only do what is expected of them and no more.
Democratic leadership	A participative style of leadership that encourages employees to be a part of the decision-making process. The leadership style is more coach or facilitator.	Style is effective when used with skilled and experienced employees or when changes must be made that affect employees.	Ineffective when there is no time to seek employee input or when manager is threatened by this style of management.
Laissez-faire leadership	A "hands-off" or "free-reign" style in which manager gives employees the freedom and authority to set goals, make decisions, and resolve problems.	Effective when employees are highly skilled, experienced, and educated or when employees are trustworthy and take pride in their work.	Ineffective when it makes employees feel insecure about lack of management or when manager cannot provide regular feedback to let employees know how they are doing.

Figure 15.5   Overview of leadership styles.

or less effective than another, so it is safe to say that the most effective style of leadership depends upon the situation. Following are some other factors that may also determine which style of leadership a manager should use:

1. *The manager's personal background, including such things as personality, experience, values, ethics, and knowledge.* These factors tend to influence the manager's thinking in terms of what she thinks may or may not work.

2. *The employees being supervised.* Because employees are individuals with different personalities and backgrounds, the style a manager uses will vary depending upon the employee and to what he will best respond.

3. *The hospitality business itself.* This will influence the manager's leadership style because of company values, beliefs, policies, and philosophies.

When choosing a leadership style, successful hospitality managers and supervisors must remain adaptable and not get themselves locked into only one way of doing things. When managers have a vision and demonstrate effective leadership qualities, committed employees will follow them anywhere. Consider the following example from nature:

"LESSONS FROM THE GEESE" [8]

Do you have as much sense as a goose? When geese fly in the "V" formation, the whole flock adds considerably more to its flying range than if each bird flew alone. Whenever a goose falls out of formation, it suddenly feels the drag and resistance of trying to fly alone and quickly gets back into formation to take advantage of the power of the formation. When the lead goose gets tired, it rotates back in the wing, and another goose flies point. The back geese honk from behind to encourage those up front to keep up their speed. Finally, when a goose gets sick and falls out, two geese fall out of formation with it until it is either able to fly or it is dead. They then launch on their own, or with another formation, to catch up with the group.

Good leaders are made, not born. If you have the desire and willpower, you can become an effective leader. Good leaders evolve from a never-ending process of self-study, education, training, and experience.

SUMMARY

- Effective management efforts are best accomplished through quality leadership and motivation.
- Managers cannot motivate their employees, but they can provide the kind of work environment in which employees can self-motivate. This is why only individuals who have a strong motivational commitment should be selected during the hiring process.
- Motivation consists of the factors that cause and sustain behavior, and scholars have been studying motivational theories since the early twentieth century.
- Modern scholars realize that there is no one correct theory of motivation, that motivation arises from the interplay of both individual and environmental factors.

- Early theories of motivation associated with the scientific school of management are the Traditional Model, the Human Relations Model, and the Human Resources Model.
- Later theories of motivation included Maslow's Hierarchy of Needs and Herzberg's Motivation-Hygiene Theory.
- More modern approaches to motivational theory include the expectancy approach and the equity approach.
- Employees are motivated by a number of job and manager-related factors, including praise, convenience, fun, money, importance, success, and advancement, so managers must practice motivational strategies that encourage these conditions.
- Leadership is the process of encouraging employees to perform their duties voluntarily, willingly, and to the best of their abilities, but leadership is not the same as management because employees willingly follow leaders.
- Early approaches to leadership theory include the trait approach and the behavioral approach. Newer models include the contingency approach and charismatic leadership.
- All managers have formal authority but may lack informal authority; leaders not only have formal authority but will also possess informal authority.
- There are various styles of leadership, including autocratic, bureaucratic, democratic, and laissez-faire, but the best approach is one that takes into account specific conditions, situations, and circumstances.

PRACTICE QUIZ

1. Managers cannot motivate employees; only employees can motivate themselves.

    A. True   B. False

2. Early motivational theories focused on charismatic leaders to determine which traits would best define motivational leadership.

    A. True   B. False

3. Theory Y model of leadership suggests that people actually like to work and that they derive satisfaction from their jobs under the proper conditions.

    A. True   B. False

4. McGregor's later theories of motivation led to participative management.

    A. True   B. False

5. The style of leadership that works best in today's hospitality industry is the laissez-faire style.

    A. True   B. False

6. This theory of motivation states that employee motivation and job performance is dependent upon how the employee perceives the fairness of the reward.

   A. The employee empowerment theory

   B. The motivation-hygiene theory

   C. Maslow's pyramid theory

   D. The equity theory

7. Which style of leadership would be best when training inexperienced kitchen employees on the proper method for operating a deep fryer?

   A. Autocratic style

   B. Bureaucratic style

   C. Democratic style

   D. Laissez-faire style

8. Which of Maslow's five needs defines the employee's need to feel like he is an integral part of the company?

   A. Physiological needs

   B. Safety and security needs

   C. Social or belonging needs

   D. Esteem needs

9. According to Herzberg, job dissatisfiers are referred to as

   A. Deficit needs

   B. Process factors

   C. Higher-level needs

   D. Hygiene factors

10. The Human Relations Model of employee motivation focuses primarily on

   A. Employee wages

   B. Employee social relations

   C. Leadership personality traits

   D. Leadership behavioral traits

REVIEW QUESTIONS

1. Explain which leadership style—autocratic, bureaucratic, democratic, or laissez-faire—would be most effective when dealing with a hotel sales manager who you recently hired to boost corporate group bookings. Which management style would be least effective? Why? What other factors would you want to consider before determining the best leadership style to use in this situation?

2. Apply Maslow's Hierarchy to a typical hotel or restaurant kitchen where employee morale and motivation is low. What specific conditions would you want to investigate to ensure that employee needs are fulfilled in all five of Maslow's categories?

3. Describe two or three situations that may occur in either a hotel or a restaurant when management decides that the autocratic style is the best leadership style to use. Explain why you chose the situations you did. Describe a situation where this leadership style might be least effective. Why?

4. Compare and contrast the traits and behaviors of an effective manager with whom you have worked with those of an ineffective manager. How did their personality traits and behaviors differ? Were there any similarities? Explain your answer.

5. Explain employee empowerment in your own words and write a short policy in which you *empower* the waitstaff in your full-service restaurant. Be sure to include the reasons that you are empowering the employees as well as any limitations you may impose in your policy. As written, what is the logic behind your new empowerment policy? Could it be changed in any way to make it more effective? Explain.

HANDS-ON HRM ▶

The Delmar Hotel is a turn-of-the-century property that is located in the heart of a mid-sized, northeastern city. The hotel has been meticulously restored, and its upscale restaurant, The Mahogany Room, was recently awarded five-diamond status by the prestigious AAA organization, making it the only five-diamond restaurant in the state. Joel Mersch has been a waiter at The Mahogany Room for more than three years, and he has observed closely as Adam, the hotel's food and beverage director, has turned the restaurant around. First, the hotel hired a new chef who had an excellent reputation in fine dining. Then, Adam went to work on the service aspect, training all of the waitstaff in the finer points of fine-dining service. Thousands and thousands of dollars were invested into improving the depth and breadth of the restaurant's wine list, and, now, rumor has it that The Mahogany Room is being considered for a prestigious award to be given by the magazine *Wine Spectator*. To top it off, the restaurant's chef has been invited to prepare a special meal at New York's famed James Beard House. *We've really hit the big time,* thought Joel. *Business will be booming for months with all this great publicity.*

One afternoon as Joel is arriving to work, Adam calls him into his office. "Joel," Adam begins, "You're one of the best waiters I've ever seen. Your tips are consistently among the highest of all of the wait staff, and your ability to manage and organize your work station is impressive." Adam goes on to praise Joel's knowledge of the menu as well as the quick manner in which he memorized the new wine menu. After a few more minutes of heaping praise on Joel, Adam says, "I'd like to offer you a promotion. We are creating a new position of head waiter, and I think you would be perfect for the job."

At first, Joel is shocked; he is one of the youngest and least experienced of the entire waitstaff. While he is pleased that Adam is impressed with his abilities, he is not sure that he would be the best choice for the position. "What exactly would this position entail, Adam?" asks Joel. Adam explains that Joel would be responsible for training all new hires, developing the weekly work schedule, and handling some routine paperwork that he would have to complete at the end of each evening's shift. Adam adds, "This is something that corporate wants to happen. I won't be able to spend a lot of time training you, but I will get you started on the right foot, and then, of course, make myself available to you as the need arises." Adam tells Joel to think about the offer over the weekend and to come in Monday to let him know what decision he has made.

QUESTIONS ▶

1. Should Joel accept this promotion? Why or why not? What additional questions might Joel want to ask Adam before deciding to accept or decline Adam's offer?

2. What skills does Joel possess that would assist him should he decide to accept the promotion? What skills would he need to further develop and why?

3. If Joel does accept the promotion, what challenges is he likely to face considering that he is among the youngest and least experienced of the current wait staff? How could Adam better prepare Joel to face those challenges?

4. Does Joel risk his future with this organization should he decide not to accept Adam's offer? Why or why not? How might Joel present his reasoning to Adam should he decide to decline the offer?

KEY TERMS ▶

Leadership The process of directing and influencing the task-related activities of employees.

Motivation The factors that cause and sustain an employee's behavior.

Traditional Model An early model of motivational theory that assumes that managers understand the work better than the employees and that employees are essentially lazy and can only be motivated by money.

Scientific Management Theory An early approach to management that sought to scientifically determine the best methods for performing work tasks and training and motivating employees.

Human Relations Model A model of motivational theory that assumes that managers can motivate employees by making them feel useful and important.

Behavioral School of Management An approach to management in which scholars trained in sociology, psychology, and other fields see to understand how to effectively manage people in organizations.

Human Resources Model A model of motivational theory that assumed that employees want to work and that under the proper conditions, employees could derive a great deal of satisfaction from work.

Theory X According to Douglas McGregor, a traditional view of motivation that assumes that employees dislike work and can only be motivated by money and coercion.

Theory Y According to Douglas McGregor, a view of motivation that assumes that employees actually enjoy work and derive a great deal of satisfaction from work when the proper conditions are met.

Participative management A democratic style of management in which employees participate in the decision-making process.

Hierarchy of Needs A theory of motivation that states workers are motivated to meet five types of needs that can be ranked within a hierarchy.

Deficit needs Basic, lower-level needs associated with Maslow's Hierarchy.

Being needs Higher-order needs associated with Maslow's Hierarchy.

Two-factor Theory Frederick Herzberg's theory that job satisfaction and dissatisfaction arise from two different sets of factors: motivating and hygiene.

Motivation-Hygiene Theory See *Two-factor Theory*.

Hygiene factors According to Herzberg, dissatisfying workplace factors such as low pay, and poor working conditions and company policies.

Motivating factors According to Herzberg, satisfying workplace factors such as achievement, recognition, and responsibility.

Process theories of motivation Motivational theories that study the thought processes by which people decide to behave in certain ways.

Expectancy approach A motivational theory that specifies that an employee's effort to achieve high performance is determined by the employee's perception of whether high performance *can* be achieved, whether it will be appropriately rewarded, and whether the reward will be worth the effort.

Equity theory A motivational theory that emphasizes the employee's perception of whether or not rewards and punishment are equitable and fair as a determiner of self-motivation.

Performance-Outcome Expectancy Employee expectations will determine employee decisions about their behavior. For example, if I do this, what will be the outcome?

Valence The motivating power of a specific outcome of behavior.

Effort-Performance Expectancy An employee's expectations about how difficult it will be to perform successfully will affect his decision about behavior. For example, what are my chances of achieving an outcome that will be worthwhile for me?

Employee empowerment Giving employees the authority to make decisions and solve problems without the need for management approval.

Trait approach to leadership Leadership theory that compares the traits of effective and ineffective leaders in order to determine which personal traits are necessary for effective leadership.

Behavioral approach to leadership Leadership theory that compares the behaviors of effective and ineffective leaders in order to determine which behaviors are necessary for effective leadership.

Contingency approach to leadership Leadership theory that assumes that the best management technique will depend upon different types of situations and circumstances.

Charismatic leadership Leaders who, through their personal vision and energy, inspire followers and have a major impact on their organizations.

Change masters An individual who is successful in guiding the process of change in organizations. Charismatic leaders are typically referred to as change masters.

Formal authority Authority given to a manager by virtue of his or her position in the organization.

Informal authority A type of authority that comes from having certain traits or characteristics that inspire followers, whether the "leader" has formal management authority or not.

Technical Skills These include basic techniques or processes that employees must be able to perform in order to accomplish specific tasks.

Human Relations Skills These skills include the individual's ability to communicate effectively with employees and to interact in a positive way with others.

Conceptual Skills The ability to conceptualize or to see the big picture. Examples include the ability to think creatively and to solve problems.

Leadership Styles The four leadership styles are autocratic leadership, bureaucratic leadership, democratic leadership, and laissez-faire leadership. The circumstances of a particular situation will help to best determine the type of leadership style necessary.

People-centered approach A style of management that focuses on interpersonal relationships with employees and exhibits caring and concern for employee welfare.

NOTES ▶

1. Reprinted with permission from *Lessons in Service from Charlie Trotter* by Edmund Lawler. Copyright 2001 by Edmund Lawler, Ten Speed Press, Berkeley, CA, www.tenspeed.com

2. Frederick Herzberg, *The Motivation to Work* (New York: Wiley, 1959).

3. Reprinted with permission from Simon & Schuster Adult Publishing Group from *The Change Masters* by Rosabeth Moss Kanter. Copyright ©1983 by Rosabeth Moss Kanter.

4. James Stoner and R. Edward Freeman, *Management,* 5th ed. (Englewood Cliffs, NJ: Prentice-Hall, 1992).

5. Clayton W. Barrows, "A Profile of Norman Brinker," *Journal of Hospitality and Tourism Education* 17: 3 (2005), 7–11.

6. W. Bennis, "The Four Competencies of Leadership," *Training and Development Journal* (August 1984).

7. Robert Katz, "Skills of an Effective Administrator," *Harvard Business Review* (September-October 1974), 90–101.

8. Dr. Robert McNeish. "Lessons from the Geese", (Unpublished work, used with permission, 1972).

INDEX